T0320956

Evolve

Leaders work hard to develop strong leadership capabilities in today's modern organizations, for the benefit of their teams and for their own careers. But, sometimes conventional leadership theory fails to explain why our efforts fail to make an impact, and arguably are becoming less and less successful. Why would this be?

The answer lies in our evolutionary history. Leadership is integral to our success and evolution as a species, as larger better functioning groups out-survived fragmented groups that did not benefit from strong leadership. Leader-follower relationships are, therefore, deeply ingrained in our brains, our instincts and our behaviour. But, our modern world, with its technology, connectedness and complexity, has evolved much faster than our brains—and our leader-follower behaviour has not caught up.

Evolve charts the fascinating development of our evolutionary history to provide a profound understanding of human behaviour around leadership. It also establishes a framework for the modes of leadership that shape the world today. Through case studies and real-world examples, you will gain powerful insights into the nature of leadership now. More importantly, these insights inform the actions you can take in your own life to enable you to become a more aware, mindful, impactful, and successful leader.

Graeme Findlay is an Associate Fellow at the University of Oxford Saïd Business School on the faculty of their Executive Education programs. He consults to industry as an executive coach and change management advisor. Prior to specialising in leadership development, Graeme held executive management roles and was accountable for delivering operational transformations and performance turnarounds on world-scale mega-projects. His passion for high performance teams led to academic research at Oxford University and HEC Paris. Graeme holds a Masters degree in Consulting and Coaching for Change.

Evolve

*How Exceptional Leaders Leverage
the Inner Voice of Human Evolution*

Graeme Findlay

Routledge
Taylor & Francis Group

LONDON AND NEW YORK

First published 2019
by Routledge
2 Park Square, Milton Park, Abingdon, Oxon OX14 4RN

and by Routledge
711 Third Avenue, New York, NY 10017

Routledge is an imprint of the Taylor & Francis Group, an informa business

British Library Cataloguing-in-Publication Data
A catalogue record for this book is available from the British Library

Library of Congress Cataloging-in-Publication Data
A catalog record has been requested for this book

ISBN: 978-1-138-59100-4 (hbk)
ISBN: 978-0-429-49073-6 (ebk)

Typeset in Optima
by Apex CoVantage, LLC

MIX
Paper from
responsible sources
FSC
www.fsc.org   FSC™ C013985

Printed in the United Kingdom
by Henry Ling Limited

For Alison

Contents

Contents

Contents

Acknowledgements

My heartfelt thanks goes out to a number of people, without whom this project would not have come to fruition;

Sue Dopson, associate dean of faculty at Oxford University Saïd Business School for her guidance with my research;

Beth Findlay, my daughter and research assistant, not only for her research but for her ideas and direction;

Nick Van Buuren for his editorial assistance;

Soon-Joo Gog, Nicole Hoenig, Mauro Locarnini, Renaud Prodel, Lone Ronberg, Martine Lepert, Corinne Lemercier, Tara Phillips, Megan Rock, Frédéric Beziers, Aude Boucomont, and Vincent Cheney, all members of my Consulting and Coaching for Change cohort at Oxford University Saïd Business School and HEC Paris, who donated their time to participate in a pilot program and provided expert feedback on the meta-model. I thank them for gifting me their knowledge and experience, but most of all for their love and encouragement;

Christine Dawood, Apoorva Mathur, Diego Ornique, Peter Collins, Francis Tsakonas, Davina Erasmus, Kike Kasim, Nankhonde Van Den Broek, Prashant Radhakrishnan, Yuri Nakasato, Hamza Al-Kuwari, the other members of the cohort who provided their love and support;

Tim Wall, one of the finest leaders who I have worked with, for backing my approach. Without his support, my adventure would have ended very quickly.

Preface

"Leadership – All you need to know"
"Five easy steps to being an exceptional leader"
"Your leadership make-over – it's easy"

Put this book back down if you are looking for easy answers to leadership. Leadership is, at the very least, complicated. And at the extreme, it's so complex that it defies human endeavour. If leadership were easy, then we would have solved the big problems of the world, all of which we have the technical solutions to. If you are looking for easy answers, the books you want will be just down the shelf. You can tell them by the way they claim to have the answer, the way they espouse theories with no academic backup, and the way they promise to transform your life. You might even get some deep and meaningful statements to fill your Facebook feed with. These books are also distinguished by their complete lack of impact on your leadership.

I approached the study of leadership not only from an academic background but from a career as a practitioner. I held senior leadership positions in large enterprises. I was accountable for real outcomes, often in difficult and complex circumstances. I observed the leaders that I worked for and with. Some were terrible, most were average, a small number were brilliant. I observed my own leadership as dispassionately as I could. I was a good leader; better than most, but not as good as some. I always tried to understand why. For me, part of being a leader was constantly trying to develop the leadership capabilities of my team through coaching and education. Sometimes I wasted their time and mine. Sometimes, however, the people that I coached and mentored exceeded my wildest expectations. When this happened, I found it extremely rewarding. This was my calling.

To fulfil this calling, I knew that I needed to supplement my practical experience as a leader with the theoretical understanding of leadership. I searched for the best education program in the world and found it at the Oxford University Saïd Business School and HEC Paris, a *Mastère Spécialisé* (MSc equivalent) in consulting and coaching for change. I launched into my studies in search of the final pieces of a jigsaw that I had largely completed. Instead, I found more questions. The more I studied, the more my ignorance seemed to multiply. In this massive and complex field, where was I to focus my research? The choices seemed infinite, each with infinite potential threads to follow, with a very real potential that I would get lost in academic detail and forget my purpose. It was at this juncture that I was gifted with an extraordinary piece of luck.

My studies necessarily required frequent long-haul flights between Australia and Europe, and I soon tired of reading heavy academic journals while coping with crowded flights and time changes. To break the monotony, I selected a book that promised an easier reading style. The book was *Sapiens* by Yuval Noah Harari, and it consumed me. It was not my first introduction to the cognitive revolution nor to social constructionist thinking, but it wound them together in a most compelling way. I finished the book and filed away the experience, ready to be accessed for an interesting dinner party discussion some time. I returned to my heavy research. As I continued to refine my research direction over the next few months, I found myself continually returning to the book and reflecting on the significance of the cognitive revolution when it comes to leadership. I came to believe that we have missed or at least underplayed its significance in leadership theories.

The cognitive revolution is a series of expansionary steps in the ability of humans to cooperate in larger and larger groups. And where there is cooperation amongst humans, there is always leadership. If we want to learn more about leadership, then the study of human evolution through the cognitive revolution should be central to theory development.

This became the central tenant of my research and subsequently this book. However, the primary purpose is not to create a new line of leadership research – the purpose is to give real leaders facing real leadership challenges a research-based approach to improving their leadership capabilities. By understanding the interplay of brain development and social developments of our ancestors through the cognitive revolution, we can understand the strong drivers that exist in us today.

This may make leadership sound even more complicated and complex. The purpose of this book is to cut through this and bring order in a way that accelerates our learning. The approach to this is meta-modelling. Please don't be put off by the fancy term – the underlying premise is simple. A meta-model arranges knowledge into a structure that brings order. It tames the ever-expanding knowledge base and ties the loose ends of existing theories to a solid frame. With the help of meta-models, we can draw together data from multiple sources to form powerful new insights – insights that can transform your impact as a leader.

Introduction

Let's start at the end so we know where we are headed. See Figure 0.1, the proposed meta-model in diagrammatic form. I have named it the differential voice.

The differential voice is based on four major "modes" of leadership – heartfelt voice, command voice, prosocial voice, and futurizing voice. These are "outer voices". Outer voice is literally what a leader says and how she says it, but it is also a metaphor for everything that followers witness and experience when interacting with the leader. It is what a leader does.

The reason that effective leadership actions group into these particular modes has to do with human evolution. Through a period known as the cognitive revolution, humans started to cooperate in larger and larger groups, outcompeting smaller groups. The traits leading to greater cooperation became a competitive advantage, prevailing in subsequent generations. Where there is cooperation, there is always leadership. By focussing on the mechanism of cooperation for key transition periods, we will come to understand the four distinct outer voices of leadership that still prevail today. The significance of the size of the cooperative group is represented by the "Leadership Reach" arrow. As the size of the group increases, or as complexity of the operating context increases, so does the requirement for a higher differential voice.

It is tempting to think that this is all we need to know. If we understand what to do as a leader when exercising each outer voice, then, surely, we can improve our leadership. Unfortunately, this is simply not the case. There is overwhelming evidence in both academic research and practical application that leadership development is possible only with the development of self-awareness in the leader and through exploration of the psychology of the leader-follower interaction. The differential voice explores this through

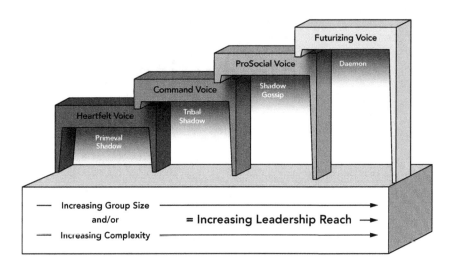

Figure 0.1 Differential voice meta-model

the concept of "inner voice". Again, this is both literal and metaphoric. Most people experience the phenomenon of silently talking to themselves, and we will see how the nature of this inner voice is significant. Inner voice will also be used as a metaphor for all nonobservable and unconscious impacts on our leadership. The inner voices – primeval shadow, tribal shadow, shadow gossip, and daemon – all line up with an associated outer voice. This may seem a little too convenient, too "neat". I aim to show that it is entirely logical that they line up. The same evolutionary influences that shaped the outer voices to be successful left their imprint on our subconscious.

The diagram is not just a pretty way to list some concepts. There is meaning in the construction depicted. Notice how three of the "blocks" depicting the outer voices rely on other blocks to stand up. These "higher differential" voices rely on the "lower differential" voices being established. For example, a command voice works only if built on a foundation of a heartfelt voice. At the extreme, a futurizing voice requires that all the lower differentials are established. The use of the terms *higher* and *lower* does not confer that higher differentials are better – it is purely to verbally represent the dependency of the higher differentials on the lower differentials.

I aim to make an entire unifying theory of leadership accessible to all motivated readers of this book. At first glance the diagram might strike you as overly complex or complicated. Let me assure you that I will make it very easy to understand. Contrary to initial impressions, it will help to simplify our journey by continually grounding and connecting what would otherwise be disparate concepts. Whether we are talking evolution, anthropology, social science, brain development, complexity, or leadership action, all will connect via this diagram. It will become our demystification tool.

Let me start our journey by first demystifying what I mean by meta-model.

A meta-model is a model of models. A meta-model does not to seek to create new knowledge. It seeks to organise existing knowledge in a way that leads to new insights. This is important to us in our journey. You will not find anything in this book that has not been thought of previously. It would be quite a task anyway given that a Google Scholar search on "leadership" yields 3.5 million results. In our case, we will stick to approaches that have been tested via academically rigorous methods and avoid the mountain of questionable material generated by the self-help industry.

We can think of the differential voice meta-model, as represented by the diagram, as a framework from which to build our knowledge. As new concepts are introduced, we will place them within the framework. This will allow us to look at wildly different concepts – say, psychological safety and creating a vision for the future – and slot them into the framework. We can characterise and organise them in a logical way. The real power in meta-modelling though, is to then use this framing to understand them better. By understanding how they "fit", we come to understand the concepts themselves better by being able to talk to them with a common language. I promise that powerful new insights will emerge that have the potential to transform your leadership.

The book is divided into four parts representing four different intents. Part one is devoted to understanding the theory. Part two brings the theory to application in today's world. Part three looks at the traps and pitfalls. Finally, part four is devoted to case studies.

Part one – theory

We will commence our journey in chapter one with an overview of the four major outer voices – heartfelt, command, prosocial, and futurizing. These are the four major modes of leadership. By observing leaders in action and analysing what they do (as opposed to what or how they are thinking), we can categorise most actions into these four categories. This, in itself, is not particularly noteworthy. Volumes of material exist based on categorising leadership actions to understand them better. The differential voice is unique in assigning a hierarchy to the outer voices. Higher differential voices can be truly effective only when the lower differential voices have been established. This concept is explored in more detail in the companion book to this one – *Evolved Organizations: Understanding the ancient to drive the modern* (referred to as *Evolved Organizations* from now on) – where the hierarchy of outer voices is evidenced through multiple case studies. However, it is not necessary to read *Evolved Organizations* before you read this book. Rather, it is recommended as further reading if you want to get additional insight on how the outer voices function in practice and get a deeper understanding of the basis for outer voice hierarchy.

In this book, we introduce the outer voice hierarchy with a case study of a leader trying to create a grand vision who fails in spectacular fashion. Futurizing does not work in isolation. It is successful only when founded upon the establishment of the other voices. This sets up an exploration into "why?". We are drawn to a piece of circumstantial evidence in chapter two. Our brains are layered, with the various layers representing different periods of our evolution. Could it be that the layered nature of our brains is connected to a layered "need" for the different leadership voices?

A major tenet of this book is that our psychology has an evolutionary basis, as does leadership. We have been amazingly successful as a species since learning to cooperate in larger and larger groups. Evolution has rewarded the traits that have us cooperate better, and where there is cooperation, there is leadership. Starting at chapter three, I will therefore use our evolutionary journey as the basis for building the differential voice.

Do not be misled, however, into believing that this book will dwell in "reptilian brains" or how our behaviours today are the same as those of our prehistoric ancestors living in bands on the African savannah. I will spend comparatively little time on this. The period of most interest and relevance to leadership in todays' world is the cognitive revolution – the period where the capability of *Homo sapiens* exploded due to leadership based on new social skills. Stepping through this period in chapters four, five, and six will build the basis of the differential voice, whereas chapter seven will show how this basis still shows up in the world that you inhabit today.

My focus in this book is on your leadership development, not arguing academic detail on evolution. Chapter eight starts to bridge the gap between the evolutionary basis for leadership and the psychology of leaders and followers. In particular, we are looking for a mechanism that you can use to understand the things that you do unconsciously as a leader that disempower you. It is in this context that I will introduce "inner voice". Examining your inner voice and evaluating the impact on your outer voice leadership style will become your constant endeavour for the rest of the book (and hopefully for the rest of your life).

Part two – application

Chapters nine and ten concentrate on the inner and outer voice combinations given to us by the period before the cognitive revolution, whereas chapter eleven focusses on the leadership that utilised the dramatic increases in our language abilities that occurred during the cognitive revolution. These explorations, however, do not dwell in prehistory. This is an examination of how to lead in today's world using these outer voices, which still resonate strongly with followers today.

As a leader, you want to make a big impact on the future of the world, a world that is thoroughly modern and complex. Chapter twelve is devoted to this capability, called the futurizing voice.

We finalise the differential voice meta-model in chapter thirteen by connecting the outer voices to the complexity of the leadership situations that we face.

Part three – traps and pitfalls

Leadership is not simple, and there will never be a formula for it. The nuances are important, and so it is for the leadership differential. Chapter fourteen will explore what happens when a leader violates the central tenet of the leadership differential and uses a higher differential in the absence of the lower differentials. Chapter fifteen goes one step further. This chapter explores the dark side – when effective leadership is used irresponsibly or even for evil.

To fulfil its intention as a meta-model, it is essential that the differential voice encompasses leadership within complex social systems, a major stream of academic study of organisations. An associated pitfall, however, is that situations are mistaken for being complex when they are not. This is not just ineffective, it is counterproductive. Chapter sixteen explores this important subtlety.

Part four – the ultimate case study

Calling the differential voice a meta-model is a bit arrogant – can it really cover all leadership approaches? If so, it would explain the most powerful leadership phenomenon in history as well as the most significant leadership events of modern times. To put it to the test I selected the ultimate case study.

The most powerful leadership phenomenon in history has been religion. Can the leadership differential explain how religion functions as a leadership approach? You can be the judge as you read my analysis in chapter sixteen. Chapter seventeen is devoted to one of the most significant leadership events in modern history; the American Civil Rights movement.

Takeaways and leadership development actions

The purpose of this book is to give you knowledge that you can take away and put into action in your workplace. This is not a one-off process. As a leader, you must constantly change your leadership to adapt to your ever-changing context. You will naturally select the concepts from the book that are most useful now, whereas other concepts may be needed later.

To allow for quick access to the key concepts when you pick the book up in the future, and to consolidate the learnings, I have finished key chapters with "Takeaways" and "Leadership Development Actions". The Takeaways summarise the content of the chapter, whereas Leadership Development Actions are just that – potential actions that you could take to enhance your leadership based on the content of the chapter.

PART 1

Theory – the human evolutionary basis of leadership

Crushed by a million tons of flipcharts

It would be a rarity for someone in your position not have been in 'one of those team vision workshops'. Perhaps you had an inner voice conversation similar to this one that I had once. . . .

I wonder how many other people have had the life slowly crushed out of them sitting in this room. This room. This room. I'm so sick of this room. With its beige walls and its beige ceilings with my beige team-mates and oh-so beige Julie. Hang on. Is that beige? Off white perhaps. Yes, off-white. Julie's beige, but the walls are definitely off-white. Dotted with blue-tack stains and sticky tape remnants. And over there where someone used a permanent marker and it bled through. Just how many flip-charts have been on these walls? A million. No, hang on. Two hundred business days a year, twenty flip charts per day, ten years . . . yeah, a million. That's a ton of paper. No, a million tons of paper. A million tons of flipcharts crushing the spirits of people in this room. Some of them sitting on this chair in fact. I think I can see the stain. Eeaw – I'm sitting in it! That's someone's life-force – inexorably crushed out them by the force of a million tons of flipcharts. And now it's on me. I can feel it. I'm being crushed. Crushed! Let me out of this . . . uh oh. . . . She's looking at me. . . . DAMN. . . . She's asked me a question. . . . DAMN. . . . What were we talking about . . . what was it . . . vision . . . have a stab at it . . . think idiot, think . . . go big . . . go obtuse . . . yeah . . . obtuse. . .

"Julie, I've been reflecting on the deeper question here. We're all one-hundred and ten percent committed to the "World Class" part of the vision. But the fact is that we don't know what "world class"

actually is. We're so internally fixated. That's why I am so focussed on benchmarking. When we say 'the industry benchmark', they're not just words. If we're to be world class, we have to benchmark ourselves against the world. Sorry to derail the conversation, but I think that's the bigger question we should be answering."

. . . waiting, . . . waiting . . . she bought it! Wow. Not only did I cover up, I sounded great. I sounded big picture. Woah. Go hard son. And now Imran has picked it up. Woah. You are hitting home runs, lad. Now Joe is on it. Fantastic.

Perhaps the greatest disservice ever done to the field of leadership development is to tell leaders that they need to create a vision for their team. Not only are acres of flip chart paper wasted but also countless hours of organisational effort. The resultant slogans end up in dusty photo frames and chipped coffee mugs in the kitchenette. The underground network is soon mischievously misquoting the output or playing jargon bingo. The vision statement designed to inspire quickly becomes a rallying point for cynicism.

The vast majority of vision-making activities are not only ineffective, they are counterproductive. And yet visioning, and other mechanisms of futurizing, are essential to long-term viability in our modern world. Visions can be incredibly powerful, and yet for most leaders creating visions is counterproductive. How can this be?

The answer is that simplistic approaches to visioning ignore basic human behaviour. These behaviours have been honed over millions of years of evolution. We humans are unique on this earth in that we have disconnected our development from our genes. All other animals can develop their species only through long-term evolutionary change. They have multigenerational evolution. We have multievolutionary generations! But we don't show up as a perfectly designed instrument. We bring with us the baggage of the past. It is critically important that you understand this if you want to become an exceptional leader.

As you learn about these ingrained behaviours and practice spotting them (mainly in yourself, as it turns out), you will be astounded at how straightforward they are and baffled that you didn't see them before. But it makes sense. You are ever-present in your life; you cannot escape yourself. How can you look at yourself objectively if you can't get away from yourself?

I will return to our problem of failed visioning later in this book. It serves as just one example of the futility of looking at leadership in a systematic way. I will lead you through an exploration of leadership in a *systemic* way. This difference between systematic and *systemic* is crucial. A systematic approach tries to understand things by breaking them down into their component parts and seeing how the individual parts work. A systematic approach to visioning would teach you better skills at visioning: how to seed the conversation, how to think laterally, how to speak in a way that will inspire the audience, how to step through expansive then contractive thinking. A systematic approach identifies what's not working (visions not working), identifies why (vision-building skills lacking), and applies solutions (teach vision-building skills). It is the diligent application of logic to cause-and-effect scenarios based on observable data.

The irony of the systematic approach is that if you ask even the most ardent supporter, they would tell you that there seems to be a bunch of stuff influencing the outcome that you can't observe. A *systemic* approach looks for what can't be (easily) observed. Instead of breaking things into smaller and smaller parts to understand the components, *systemic* thinking focusses on building a bigger picture of the whole. It focusses on what is unsaid, as much as on what is said, on what is unconscious as much as what is conscious. It will look to origins of emotions as well as to the logic of actions.

My *systemic* view will be enabled via the differential voice meta-model. Let's look at our visioning for an example of meta-modelling. A significant body of academically rigorous research supports the idea that the teaching of visioning skills improves outcomes. Our meta-model approach, therefore, gives the tick to skills training. But it doesn't accept this in isolation. It looks for approaches that unearth the less visible. And, as we will find out, this uncovers that a number of prerequisites must be met for people to truly engage in visioning.

The meta-model that I am proposing is called the Differential Voice®, which focusses on the different "operating modes" of leadership. The differential voice clusters these operating modes according to their predominant characteristics. As a leader, these are your outer voices. There are four outer voices: heartfelt voice, command voice, prosocial voice, and futurizing voice.

These outer voices have a hierarchy. We will explore the origin of this dependency in detail as we progress through the book. The lower differentials act as building blocks for the higher differential voices. A command voice demands that heartfelt voice is established; a prosocial voice can be built only on the foundation of a command voice and a heartfelt voice, as

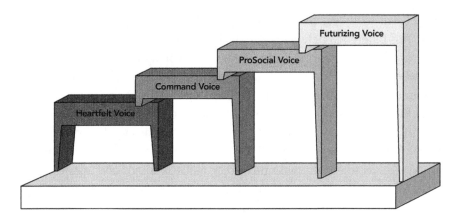

Figure 1.1 Outer voice hierarchy

shown in the diagram. Remove a lower differential, and all layers above it collapse.

This is represented in the next diagram. Note that I have used a simplified version of the diagram shown in the introduction. The intention is that we will progressively build the diagram, block by block, as we progress through the book. This puts the onus on me to provide evidence for every single piece of the meta-model as I progressively build the diagram to its final form.

Let us start with a high-level description of the outer voices.

Heartfelt voice

A leader's capability to create an inner circle of trusted allies. To create an environment where people feel safe; an environment where it is OK to say what you think, to discuss difficult issues and stand for each other's success; where there are deep relationships and shared purpose.

Command voice

A leader's capability to get things done. To deliver reliably. To ask for things once and get the required outcome. To speak and get action. To get people's commitment to delivery. To turn ambiguity into action. To plan and to deliver to plan.

Prosocial voice

A leader's capability to create a positive social environment and sense of community behind the business objectives. An environment where formal and informal communication channels transmit positive messages; where successes are celebrated and shared; where teams interact positively with other teams.

Futurizing voice

A leader's capability to create the case for change that causes a community to take coordinated action in service of big goals.

As we explore the layered nature of the differential voices, we will begin to understand why visioning fails. Visioning is an activity within the operating mode of futurizing voice. It fails far more often through the lack of prerequisite voices (i.e., lacking one or more of heartfelt, command, or prosocial) than it does through poor skills of futurizing.

In a 1987 reelection speech, the then prime minister of Australia, Bob Hawke, powerfully declared to the nation that "By the year 1990, no child in Australia will live in poverty". These twelve words were to haunt Hawke for the rest of his political career and beyond.

I like to imagine the inner voice conversation of one of Hawke's ministers as he made the proclamation. . . .

*This is going well. The old goat might be a massive grandstander, but you've got to give it to him – he knows how to play an audience. Every word he says swings a few more votes my way. This'll make 'em take a bit more notice of me. I might have only snuck in last election but I'm ridin' the wave here. Ooh . . . love that line on employment. Upskilling. That's the word. I'm gonna hammer that in my speech at trades hall next week. Upskilling . . . yeah. Wonder if I could get the tech college director onside. That'd get regional airplay. This is going well. Righto, Bob, time for welfare. This will resonate with my voters. Do it. A nail to the heart of those conservatives. Here goes. . . . **noooooo** . . . did he say that . . . noooo, Bob. What have you done? You did not say "no child **will live** in poverty". That's not what we agreed. You did not just promise the entire country that we would*

eliminate child poverty in three years, did you? You did not say. . . .
Careful . . . the press have noticed our reactions, straight face, straight
face, just look like you are listening intently to every word that com-
plete moron is saying. I knew this would happen. That trumped up
idiot can't help himself. Thinks he's bloody Martin Luther King. He
gets to play grand statesman changing the world by sacrificing my
seat. Idiot. Idiot. Idiot. How do I recover from this? I'll be answering
questions on this forever. Won't get a word in on anything else. And
what do I say! Oh God. I'm screwed.

No one was more surprised at Hawke's statement than his inner circle of ministers and campaign specialists. The script they had agreed on was "By the year 1990, no child in Australia will *need to* live in poverty".[1] Far from the declaration being a rallying point for them, they were shocked by their leader making an outlandish election promise on their behalf. One can imagine the strength of their inner voice. Their reelection prospects had just been compromised; their very survival had been threatened! Rather than being a rallying cry, the twelve words had negatively impacted Hawke's relationship with his inner circle and thus his heartfelt voice as a leader.

What the twelve words did create, in quite dramatic fashion, was frenzied activity in the media and the opposition party playing to the nation's cynicism. With no prosocial voice at work to counteract this, the cause was lost. The statement went on to haunt Hawke for the rest of his tenure as prime minister, frequently dominating press conferences and parliamentary question time. He subsequently described it as his biggest regret.[2] The levels of child poverty increased during the period,[3] and arguably, the long-term goal of eliminating child poverty was sidelined.

To get a firsthand account of the episode from the perspective of a member of Hawke's inner circle, I sought out Brian Howe for an interview. Howe served in a variety of cabinet positions under Hawke, including the role of deputy prime minister. At the time of the child poverty announcement, Howe was the minister for social security. In terms of accountability, he was the biggest stakeholder within Hawke's inner circle, having personally driven the creation of the family welfare package, which was the policy that sat under the election promise. His taskforce working on the policy had, for the first time, used analytical means to determine the quantum of welfare payments. Prior to this, the quantum of welfare payments was largely arbitrary. Howe and his team drew on the work of Professor Ronald Henderson, who had carried out the first systematic estimates of the extent of poverty in Australia. The policy was based on an escalating regime of welfare payments to low-income families that would, over time, lift their income "above the Henderson poverty line". This was the origin of the reference in Hawke's reelection speech.

I asked Howe what went through his mind at the moment that Hawke made the statement in his speech. "It's unprintable", he replied. He goes on to say that "I've had to wear that for over thirty years".

It is important to put Howe's response in context. His overall assessment of Hawke as a leader is extremely positive. He considers, as do many independent observers, that the cabinet of the time was of the highest quality and that Hawke got the best out of it. "He was assiduous in his preparation and on top of the detail right across the government. He ran a very good cabinet. Everything was debated. There were no factional elements. He was a good leader in a government managing a massive shift in Australia".

We can get a sense, therefore, of the sense of betrayal that members of the inner circle must have felt when Hawke decides to ramp up his rhetoric in the spur of the moment. Hawke realises his mistake and is embarrassed. He hopes (in vain) that it will go away. "He never spoke to me about it afterwards", says Howe.

The irony is that the public discourse on the failure to eliminate child poverty has masked the importance of the family welfare assistance that was introduced. The increase in social welfare payments in Australia was one of the highest in the OECD during the period.[4] Generations of Australian children benefitted from this. However, child poverty is much more than a family welfare payment. The level of unemployment is a huge influence. Other welfare payments, such as unemployment benefits, are important as are subsidised healthcare, public housing, early childhood education, and so on. So, although the policy would indeed lift family income above the Henderson poverty line, it was in no way a comprehensive action plan to attack the overall problem of child poverty. Hawke's command voice was half-baked.

With a damaged heartfelt voice, a half-baked command voice, and with no prosocial voice to combat the media storm, Hawke was doomed to fail.

Hypothesising that the outcomes would have been better if Hawke had the benefit of an approach centred on differential voice is presumptuous. Child poverty continues to defeat our collective efforts as a society. We can certainly say, however, that more could have been achieved. Howe certainly thinks so and says that "It was a lost opportunity. He just says it. He hasn't thought about it much. I don't think personally that he was all that committed to it. It was politically important for him at the time to demonstrate to the electorate that we are not just about austerity. So in a sense he just backs away from it because he thinks it was stupid thing to say and gets heavily criticised as a result. Tony Blair on the other hand, borrows all our concepts, makes a commitment on child poverty in Britain and makes a pretty good job of dealing with it".

Let us therefore examine what an idealised Hawke would have done if he were indeed committed to the outcome and had the benefit of an understanding of the differential voice.

Idealised Hawke already had the benefit of a highly competent and committed inner circle. He would have leveraged this to build a shared purpose of eliminating child poverty. Rather than unilaterally making the decision to include the family welfare package as a political instrument, he would have built collaboration around this higher purpose. A united inner circle would have considered the welfare package in the context of everything else that needed to change and all the other critical objectives.

His command voice also had a significant start. A well-researched and thorough plan existed for the family welfare package. Healthcare was also very much on the table at this time through the reintroduction of a healthcare system called Medicare (which incidentally Hawke was very passionate about). By integrating these two major planks with other areas such as public housing and early childhood education, a comprehensive plan would have been developed. Structure and governance would have been established to track implementation. This plan would give substance to the initiative and provide the potential for creating the early wins so critical for success in big initiatives.

The flourishing of gossip after the initiative was announced was entirely predictable. A strong prosocial voice would not only help to counteract this but also provide the mechanism to start building coalitions with like-minded individuals across all walks of life, including not only social welfare advocates but also the opposition political party and the media. Hawke was a master of driving diverse stakeholders to collaborative agreements, and this would have been his opportunity to shine.

We now picture Hawke making his reelection speech. His words are exactly the same, "By the year 1990, no child in Australia will live in poverty". The reaction of 99.99 percent of observers is exactly the same but not for his critical inner circle or the other stakeholders who had been engaged through the planning and through his prosocial voice. Hawke is then able to elaborate on his vision in a much more substantial way. He goes on to talk about the suite of policies that underpin the vision, how they work in concert to address the multiple dimensions of the problem. He able to genuinely reflect the deep sense of commitment that he and his ministry feel for this issue. He is able to talk about how the program will be run, who will be responsible, and how progress will be tracked. With this expression of all the foundational differential voices backing up a cause that everyone connects to our idealised Hawke start to bring about transformational change to an entire society.

The premature rolling out of grandiose visions is perhaps one of the greatest collective failings of leadership. Spurred by stories such as President Kennedy's "man on the moon" speech or Martin Luther King Jr.'s "I have a dream", countless leaders have mistakenly believed that their bold declarations are enough to drive transformational change. Many have fallen victim to an industry that would have you believe that if you work on your oratory skills you have the ability to speak a new exciting future into existence. This is the "Hollywoodisation" of leadership development, which has served the industry so poorly. Some even use Hollywood movies as training material. *"Just watch Al Pacino in* Any Given Sunday *or Mel Gibson in* Braveheart, *and you'll learn to be an exceptional leader"*. This is just fantasy feeding fantasy.

The travesty of the situation is that good people working hard on trying to improve themselves succumb to the allure of the approach and try their own grandiose vision. When they fail, it hurts! Embarrassed at ever being so presumptuous as to think that they have the right stuff, they consign themselves to a life of unfulfilled potential.

Every person is capable of being a better leader. Most people are capable of being a far bigger leader than they think is possible. You are capable of being an exceptional leader. But to reach your potential, you need to put the effort in to understand yourself. No shortcuts. You should not be daunted, however. Every concept in this book is remarkably simple. You will not fail for a lack of ability to grasp the concepts. And if you are prepared to put the work in, the differential voice provides the scaffolding you need to achieve your best.

Takeaways

We have introduced ourselves to "outer voice" as a metaphor for our leadership capabilities. This is a compendium of all the tangible behaviours, skills, and attributes that can be observed when we act as leaders. These are grouped into the major "operating modes" of leadership – heartfelt voice, command voice, prosocial voice, and futurizing voice. These operating modes do not act independently. They have a hierarchy and rely on each other. Higher differentials require lower differentials to be successful.

Heartfelt voice is the building of deep relationships to create an inner circle of trusted allies.

Command voice is the capability to get delivery performance from followers – a leader's capability to get things done. Command voice is truly effective only when built on the foundation of the heartfelt voice.

Prosocial voice is a leader's capability to create a positive social environment around the business objectives – an environment where informal communications build a positive sense of community. The prosocial voice is only fully effective when built on the foundation of heartfelt voice and command voice.

Futurizing voice is a leader's capability to drive large-scale positive change. As demonstrated by the case study of Bob Hawke, it fails when not founded on the heartfelt voice, the command voice, and the prosocial voice.

Footnote: The existence of the hierarchy of differential voice in modern leadership practice is central to the development of the differential voice framework. It will be carried forward throughout the rest of this book. If you are looking for more evidence beyond the single example of Bob Hawke, it can be found in *Evolved Organizations*.

Notes

1 Masanauskas and Philip, "Bob Hawke's Biggest Regret".

2 Masanauskas and Philip.

3 Whiteford, Redmond, and Adamson, "Middle Class Welfare in Australia".

4 Gough et al., "Social Assistance in OECD Countries".

2 Our flawed and magnificent brain

In observing through the case study in the previous chapter that there might be a layered nature to the outer voices of leadership, we are drawn to the question of why this might be. This question is central to our exploration through the rest of this book. What is it in the makeup of followers that might cause them to look for multiple layers of leadership? What are they thinking? How are their brains working when they respond to leadership? We can immediately zero in on a piece of evidence that could either be circumstantial or prove to be significant. Brains are made up of multiple layers. Could the undisputed evidence of a layered brain have anything to do with followers looking for multiple layers of leadership? Let us examine first the nature of the brain's "design".

Our brains were not "designed" for the world that we have now built. We are unique amongst earth's creatures in having outstripped our genetic limitations. Other animals change their behaviour over time, but this behaviour change is directly tied to the evolution of their DNA. We, on the other hand, change our behaviour every time we create a significant new technology or as a result of social or political influence. In the blink of an eye (in evolutionary terms), the agricultural revolution turned us from hunter-gatherers to farmers; the Industrial Revolution created factory workers; and the post-Industrial Revolution delivered us into the complex world we now inhabit.

Because of this speed, our brains have been left behind. Leadership is one of the most advanced functions that a human can undertake, and our most important tool is flawed. But, before we despair, it is important to put this into context. It is not as simple as having a brain designed for the ancient world and trying to use it in the modern world. Even our ancient ancestors did not have perfectly designed brains for their challenges. Operating in the prehistoric world, our brains were "flawed" just as all animals are. Evolution does not work towards an optimum design. It has no higher purpose. We need to dive into this if we are to understand how humans come to function the way they do; expanding such understanding expands our ability to then lead them.

When Darwin adopted the term "survival of the fittest", he perhaps did a disservice to his theories. "Survival" of an individual is obviously of vital importance for a species to progress, but it does not stand alone. How would we have evolved to give birth to such helpless offspring if survival of the individual was the primary driver? If it were the case, our babies would be able to run and fend for themselves within a few hours of birth, as is the case for many other animals. The term "fittest" can also be misinterpreted as evolution promoting the strongest individuals who outcompete weaker individuals. This is only a small part of the story. Evolution promotes "reproductive fitness": a compendium of multiple factors that result in maximising the passing on of genes to successive generations. This process is best imagined using Dawkins's metaphor of the selfish gene.[1] Genes obviously can't actually be selfish, but it helps to envisage a gene trying every trick in the book to maximise its place in the world through successive generations, which enhances the chances of a species thriving as a whole. When viewed in this way we begin to understand why it is that we are wired for traits such as altruism and empathy. These traits are often detrimental to the individual and would be eliminated under a purely competitive interpretation of "survival of the fittest". But these same traits are beneficial to the collective, resulting in a higher overall level of reproduction into the next generation.

Our "flawed" brain then is a result of selfish genes at work. But remember that it is a metaphor. Genes don't actually have intelligence. They have no will. They have no agenda. They have no agency. And the sole mechanism for progress is reactive. It is a random mutation that creates the environment for the genes' progress. Evolution keeps mutations that increase reproductive fitness and eliminates mutations that detract from it. We need to place double emphasis on the word *random*. Evolution does not have a higher purpose. It does not have a design in mind. It is able to work only with minute, stepwise, random changes and has only a blunt tool of stop-here/keep-going. It cannot, therefore, optimise the design for the current circumstances; it always carries the baggage of the past.

Our brains are the result of millions upon millions of tiny changes implemented on the brains of very ancient forebears. By definition, evolution can travel only in these tiny steps. It cannot "rub out" an old bit to replace it with new. As a result, our brains carry our evolutionary journey in their very construction. The incredibly powerful outer layers of our brains are built upon more basic layers underneath. Importantly, though, the layering of the brain is not discreet. All areas of the brain are "wired" to all other areas – a logical outcome of evolution. A random mutation in the genes of one of our ancestors increased the ability to grow a beneficial new layer of the neocortex (the most recently developed part of the brain – *neo* means new). However, the increase in this individual was minute – so small that we wouldn't be able to see it. It would be thousands of generations before the physical change was significant. For the tiny change in the neocortex to be beneficial it had to improve the capability of the brain. Clearly, then, this small "new" bit had to work seamlessly with the "old" brain. This carried on through the generations with each new incremental piece of neocortex being integrally wired to the previous piece and back to the "old" brain.

Each piece of new brain brought new capability, but only capability that enhanced reproductive fitness was carried forward. This leads to an interesting allocation of functions within our brains. One might imagine, for example, that the neocortex might grow new capabilities for the detection of threats. Surely as civilisation progressed, more sophisticated mechanisms for dealing with threats would emerge. This is not the case. Threats are managed by our amygdala. The amygdala is dedicated to very specific memories of threats and extending these into generalised scenarios. It monitors the information coming from our senses and is constantly matching the information against threat scenarios.[2] The amygdala is located in the old brain. As we will see as we go through this book, this location is often unhelpful in the modern world. As leaders responsible for driving change we will frequently confront resistance as a result of seemingly illogical amygdala-driven reactions. We can be left wishing that the neocortex had taken over the function of threat surveillance and consigned the amygdala to the scrapheap. That way, people would respond more logically and rationally. We don't get that choice. We are stuck with the amygdala doing the job.

We can surmise that at many points in time during human evolution, a random mutation occurred in an individual that started to move threat surveillance to the neocortex. This fractional change did not offer any advantage to reproductive fitness over amygdala-driven threat response. Therefore, this potential line of evolutionary change was snuffed out. It is irrelevant that neocortex-driven threat response would be better in the modern world.

Evolution moves only in miniscule sequential changes. Wishing for step changes is fruitless.

Layers

The brain is very complex. An examination of its morphology in any detail does not serve the purpose of this book. It is useful, however, to examine the three main layers of the brain, which represent three major evolutionary developments.

The innermost and evolutionary most ancient part of the brain is the peri-aqueductal grey (PAG) matter sitting at the base of the skull where the spinal column enters. Some commentators call this the "reptilian brain". I discourage the use of this term because it infers such basic functionality as to appear irrelevant to us. Although it does indeed mange the most basic functions that you would find in a reptile, it is far more sophisticated in us. As we have just discussed, in humans the PAG is wired to the outer layers of the brain, and this means that it plays a key role in our emotional motivations. Azmatullah[3] summarises these into the following five fundamental motivations:

the care and nurturing system
the grief and distress system
the fear, anxiety and anger system
the sexual desire system
the seeking pleasure and play system

Calling these "motivational systems" is a bit misleading. These are prime-val urges. For example, the fear and anger system is the "fight or flight" response, which hits us like a freight train, and we all know how debilitating the grief and distress system can be. So, although this part of the brain is very old in an evolutionary sense, it still plays a major part in shaping our behaviour.

Sitting like a fist over the top of the PAG and underneath the cerebral cortex (which includes the neocortex) is the "middle' layer of the brain called the limbic system. At a point in evolution that predates *Homo sapiens*, it was it was the outer brain layer. We can think about its function in our modern brain by thinking about the Latin origin of the word *limbic* – *limbus*, which means border or edge, leading to the phrase "being in limbo". The limbic system is "in limbo" between the five primeval urges of the PAG and the higher-thinking functions of the cerebral cortex. It moderates our behaviour based on finding a balance between two.

It is evident then, that the higher-level thinking capability of the cerebral cortex does not get to run the show for us as much as we might like it to. It is simply impossible for us to fire up our advanced brain without the signals in some way interacting with our ancient brains. We might like a brain hierarchy that favours our modern brain, but in fact, we can say that the opposite is true. As situations get increasingly stressful, our outer brain layers start shutting down to favour the ancient brain that has been honed for our physical survival.

Here, then, is some circumstantial evidence for the concept of differential voices. A leader has the skills to engage with people's brains in a way that has them become followers. It is a reasonable hypothesis that if brains are layered, then a leader's effectiveness would correlate to the ability to engage all of those layers. Furthermore, because the functioning of each layer relates to a particular evolutionary period, different skills would be required for each layer. Hence the hypothesis for differential voices. It is only a potential theory at this stage. Just because brains are layered does not automatically mean that leadership is layered, but we have an intriguing possibility to follow.

At this point we do need to remind ourselves just how magnificent our flawed brains are. In many ways, it is the flaws that shine a light on the magnificence because of their unparalleled adaptability. We have the ability to rewrite our brains. For every flaw we have literally millions of opportunities to self-correct and adapt. The extent to which this brain plasticity can be put to use continues to astound the experts.

And it is this adaptability that has underwritten our unparalleled progress from a marginal creature on the verge of extinction to one that dominates the world and starts to look beyond.

Takeaways

The structure and functioning of our brain is the result of our evolution.

Physically, the brain has distinct layers. Each of the layers corresponds to period of our evolutionary past, with the most ancient being at the core and the most recent being the outermost. All layers of the brain are connected to all other layers, and they work together.

Evolution resulted in a brain that maximised reproductive fitness in a pre-historic world. It was not "designed" for our modern world.

We can begin to postulate that the behaviours we exhibit in the modern world are related to the evolutionary layers of our brain. This would suggest a basis for the different outer voices and a reason why higher differentials rely on the lower differentials.

Notes

1 Dawkins, *The Selfish Gene*.
2 Morrens and Sabbe, "L. Cozolino: The neuroscience of human relationships".
3 Azmatullah, *The Coach's Mind Manual*.

3 | **Evolution**

What is your inner voice saying to you right now about this book? Maybe it is less polite than you would be if you were talking to me in person. . . .

Evolution. Did he say evolution? Can I groan out loud? It's supposed to be a book on leadership, not monkeys and cavemen. Cavemen – maybe he can help me with Arthur. He's so close to a caveman that it doesn't matter. Hang on. Stop goofin' off. Pay attention – you paid good money for this book.

From London Zoo to Africa

Dawkins[1] runs an intriguing thought experiment, which I will adapt and expand to focus on leadership. Put yourself in the London Zoo with your left hand touching the chimpanzee enclosure. We are going to start a people chain to the chimpanzee's native sub-Saharan Africa. Your right hand holds the hand of your mother. She in turn holds hands with her mother (your grandmother) who holds hands with her mother (your great-grandmother) and so on (at some point you will obviously need to time travel to keep the thought experiment going). As the chain continues across the city of London and across the English countryside, we are stepping back the generations, one person at a time. This is the other reason we have headed towards Africa. With every person in the chain we are getting closer to our ancestors in Africa. Look to the right to see your line of forebears. The line of *Homo sapiens* (I'll use "sapiens")[2] heads off to the east towards St Pancras

International Train Station, a 20-minute walk away. We are going to St Pancras because we are going to use the Eurostar train line. That way we can go through the Channel Tunnel to Paris, and no one drowns in the English Channel. Because it is a thought experiment we can suspend the trains for a while.

As we travel down the sapiens' line, what do we notice? Initially not much. Putting aside individual characteristics, everyone in the line looks very much the same. Apart from the fact that you are considerably healthier and better nourished, you could fit into the line anywhere and not look out of place. Equally well, if you struck up conversations along the way using a universal language, you are impressed by their intelligence. They may not be educated and their circumstances might be very different, but they are just as smart and talented as you are. What if you took the one as a baby and raised her in today's world? What if she ended up in your team at work? The answer is that nothing special would occur to you. She would just be another team member responding to your leadership. As we continue along the line of sapiens standing on the train tracks we wonder how long this situation will last.

Back at the zoo, you look across into the chimpanzee enclosure. To your bemusement, the chimpanzees have copied you. A chimpanzee stands facing you with her mother, grandmother, great-grandmother, and so on. The line stretches away out the gate. Every one of your ancestors faces an ancestor of the London Zoo chimpanzee. You look closely at your chimpanzee. It is a very different creature from you with a set of behaviours that seem completely unrelated. Your chimpanzee functions within her troop, which has a defined social structure built around a set of leadership behaviours. So, what would happen if she were to turn up in your team at work? Clearly the situation is nonsense. A few, very dedicated scientist have managed to establish a leadership relationship with chimpanzees but only after years of devoted interaction and only for the most basic of tasks. Our line of enquiry at this point looks tenuous, but let's persist.

We track the parallel lines of sapiens and chimpanzees towards St Pancras station. But before we get there, something strange appears. Behind our sapiens line is a new creature facing our backs. Her right hand holds her mother's, and a line of ancestors extends into the distance. But her left hand is empty. She is the end of the line of Neanderthals (*Homo neanderthalensis*), the last of a unique species that inhabited the earth for hundreds of thousands of years. The chimpanzee in front of us is still unrecognisable as any sort of relation. The Neanderthal behind us however is unmistakably a cousin. Bigger and thicker set, with a sloped forehead, jutting jaw and much more hair, but unmistakeably related. She is human! All creatures of the genus *Homo* are human – we have just gotten used to being the only one around. The genetic test confirm that your sapiens forbear and this Neanderthal share more than 99 percent of their DNA. That's a lot of similarity. Maybe you could raise this lady in the modern world and coopt her into your team at work. Alas, you have barely any more success than with the chimpanzee. She is more intelligent and can do more complex tasks. She can do rudimentary planning and communicate in a way that the chimpanzee cannot. But there is something missing. A big something. Despite this, she also continually surprises you with the depth of her personality and the complexity of her emotions. And you are often startled at the similarities despite her different appearance. You start to conclude that there is common ground there somewhere.

Neanderthals are not the only parallel line to the sapiens and chimpanzees. *Homo soloensis, Homo floresiensis,* and *Homo denisova* make their own dead-end appearances. It is interesting to imagine what it might be like today if we sapiens had not been so ruthlessly efficient at eliminating them. The multiple lines of humans will progress for a long time before they progressively consolidate with our line at *Homo erectus.* But we still have a way to travel to get there. We haven't even reached St Pancras yet!

Thinking about your experience with coopting the Neanderthal into your team, you hit upon a superb recruitment strategy. Your many-times-great-grandmothers look like great potential team members. You can personally vouch for their DNA! With the ability to time travel, you can transport them back to being babies, then forward into the modern world, then fast-forward through their upbringing. They arrived fresh faced at your desk ready for their career. You have a seemingly endless supply of intelligent, talented, and creative people. Your success blossoms.

You are only a couple of miles along the Eurostar tracks out of St Pancras when you get a feeling that things aren't going as well as they have been. Your new recruits just don't seem to be quite as on the ball as they used to be. And this realisation has snuck up on you. It is not as if one recruit has seemed any worse than the previous one. In fact, you can't even notice the difference with the candidate one hundred people back up the line. And yet when you view it at a macro scale, you know that something has changed. The thing is that they still look exactly the same. Give or take individual variances, this one looks just like your mother. But your new recruits are not as "with it". Not as creative. Lacking in imagination. Lacking the fine nuances of language necessary in your business.

You are starting to go backwards through the cognitive revolution. Sometime around 70,000 years ago, sapiens developed the ability to think in unprecedented ways. It is not that their brains got bigger. Anatomically, there is no difference between a 200,000-year-old sapiens and a modern one. And yet cognitively, there is a huge difference. Why? The truth is that we don't know exactly. The most likely explanation is that it was an accident – an entirely random mutation of the brain gave the recipient the tiniest bit of extra reproductive fitness. We got it; the Neanderthals didn't. Supporting this theory is the fact that Neanderthals were otherwise better equipped than sapiens. They were bigger and stronger. They actually had slightly larger brains. And importantly – at a time when the earth was entering an ice age – they had more hair for warmth.

Although we don't know the cause of the change in mental abilities, we do know the impact. The art of the time shows that abstract imagination was kick-started, and evidence of rituals indicated that we had developed newfound communication skills. This is of profound interest to our study of leadership.

Going forward, I will name your recruits from before the cognitive revolution "pre-cogs". Those in the midst of the change will be "intra-cogs", and those with mental abilities similar to yours "post-cogs". That makes all of us post-cogs. However, when I use the term "post-cog", I will generally be talking about people who lived in ancient times, prior to the agricultural revolution.

You will have noticed something else as you pause on your trip along the Eurostar tracks. When you observe the societies that each person lived in, there has been a major change in the leadership dynamic. Specifically, leaders now have smaller groups of followers. Back at the zoo, leaders had very large groups of followers. The British prime minister has power over millions of people. The CEO of your company is a leader of ten thousand people. You are also a follower of Manchester United, just one of an estimated 350 million fans worldwide. You have gotten used to humans cooperating on a grand scale, but it was not always the case. You think that perhaps this is just reflective of modern communications and literacy levels. But then you remember that several of your many-times-great-grandmothers lived during the Roman Empire. The emperor ruled over 100 million people with no advanced communications and with literacy rates at a fraction of a percent. Something else is going on.

But this has now changed as you walk back in time through the transition from post-cogs to intra-cogs. This is the time when your many-times-great-grandmothers are leaving Africa in bands. As they go about eradicating the Neanderthals (either literally or by outcompeting them for resources), you notice that leaders are limited to creating multiple hunter-gatherer groups. These communities of around 150 people provide a significant advantage over Neanderthals who seemed unable to cooperate in groups larger than forty or fifty. You conclude that this is no coincidence. There is a connection between the dwindling cognitive ability of the intra-cogs and the size of groups that a leader can have power over.

Let's return to your recruitment problem. You are sitting with your intra-cogs noticing a worrying decline in the mental abilities of your recruits. Unfortunately, your organisation has become accustomed to the endless supply of new recruits and is now not sympathetic at all to your whining about not having the right talent anymore. Because you have no control over the abilities of the recruits, you decide to change the only thing that you can – your leadership style.

The intra-cogs still have a lot going for them. They are ambitious and task oriented. They are skilled with their hands. They are empathetic and show emotion. They connect with others and love a good chat. They want to be liked and have good social skills. But when you talk about the future they switch off. It's okay if it's a discussion about planning what tools are required for tomorrow's task or how they will deal with a staff member who is upset. But as soon as you start talking about the company's values and vision, it is like a brick wall is constructed between you. Worse than that, they don't even seem to understand "the company". Sometimes, when you mention the company, they ask you politely to show it to them. "It's all around us", you say. "You and I are the company, the shareholders are the company, we are all the company". As you get more and more exasperated, they get more and more puzzled.

Time to change tack. Time to play to their strengths. Time to eliminate the futurizing voice – it simply does not connect. Forget trying to generate shared vision or exciting possibilities. And yet they are far more than just slaves to be driven. In fact, treating them like that would be a huge mistake. They are so good at networking that they would undo you in an instant. Office gossip would go wild, and before you know it you would be in front of HR with a dozen harassment claims. It is the opposite that is required. You recognise the prosocial voice as your leverage. Your intra-cogs still need to be treated with respect and made to feel safe (heartfelt voice) and be given clear direction and expectations (command voice), but it is the prosocial voice that will extract the best from them. You resolve to ramp up the positive and inclusive communications. You work hard at having personal connections with a wide variety of people, knowing everyone's name and encouraging a sense of fun with everyone involved. The strategy works – you should be proud of yourself. And yet, it is with deep regret that you say goodbye to your futurizing voice. You might have a happy crew of productive workers, but you have lost the ability to make a major impact. You've pretty much lost the ability to change anything substantial. And you can't grow. You notice that as soon as your team of intra-cogs nudge past the 150 mark, cracks appear. Factions start forming, and animosities emerge over trivial matters. So you keep the team at a manageable level and carry on.

Though you are not kicking the goals that you used to, the company is in a stable period, and your bosses value the dependability and productivity that your team are delivering. You continue down the Eurostar recruitment track, but in no time at all you find yourself adapting again. You have ventured back to a time before the cognitive revolution. These pre-cogs are very different from you, even though they still look the same.

Harari[3] describes the pre-cogs as an "animal of no particular significance", sitting somewhere in the middle of the food chain. Apart from long-distance running ability, they had no outstanding physical abilities. They were relatively easy prey, a situation made worse by the fact that their young were weak and helpless.

We tend to overplay the advantages of a large brain in this environment. Large brains are not the huge advantage you might think. Our brains consume as much as 20 percent of our energy,[4] and in ancient Africa this would have been a significant disadvantage. In the natural world, brains evolve to be just the right size for the animal to fill their ecological niche. If that weren't the case, then all animals would be constantly evolving bigger brains. Brains evolve to be big enough to contribute to survival but small enough not to consume precious resources. In the Australian koala, for example, evolution resulted in a reduction in brain size as the country turned more arid and resources became scarce.

Pre-cogs at least had the advantage of being able to cook their food, a skill acquired by their predecessors *Homo erectus* 2 million years prior. This allowed for a much higher uptake of energy from food and kept harmful bugs at bay. Even so, they were barely in the game and, for a time, sat on the very brink of extinction. Scientists discovered this by undertaking genetic detective work. Tiny anomalies in DNA structure get passed down through generations. This creates a unique marker that can be traced back thousands of generations. The level of genetic diversity in a species is the indicator of the size of the population at various times. Our genetic diversity is extremely low. There is more genetic diversity in a single troop of chimpanzees than in the entire human race.[5] The chimpanzees, with their smaller brains and tree-dwelling habits, were doing far better than we were in the ancient world. The lack of diversity in our DNA indicates that at one point, *Homo sapiens* were incredibly close to extinction, down to just a few thousand individuals.[6]

The stories of sapiens from this time is the script of a Hollywood blockbuster. A weak and marginal creature sitting in the middle of the food chain has been beaten to the edge of extinction. A very few remaining bands eke out a living in the badlands of Africa. The future looks grim. But the creature is smart and wily and resilient. And, at its lowest point, it gets a gift. The gift of imagination and language. It strikes out across hostile lands, through the Middle East and into Eurasia. Successive generation move a few more kilometres. As they do so, they encounter savages. These savages are stronger and more powerful than our sapiens. Battles break out over food. Our sapiens may be weak, but they are smart. They plot and plan and prevail. They rocket to the top of the food chain and set about winning the world!

Winning the world looks far-fetched for you at the moment as you struggle with your team of pre-cogs. Forewarned by your first experience of deteriorating talent, you have been progressively modifying your leadership style. Again, the talent degradation has not been sudden; you cannot spot the difference between successive individuals. But without a doubt, and within a surprisingly short distance down the Eurostar tracks, you are depressed by what you have become as a leader.

Your prosocial voice that was so successful with your intra-cogs is now entirely useless. These sapiens (you can't call them people anymore even though they still look like you) just don't have any advanced social skills. They communicate, but only in very direct ways. They can't hold a conversation about a third person or take what you tell them and cascade it down the line. As a result, you have given up on having a large team. It just got more and more dysfunctional before completely disintegrating. Now, you have a team of thirty. As you observe the society of the time you notice that this is consistent. Sapiens group sizes seem to operate best at around thirty and never bigger than fifty. And it is no wonder. As a leader, it is so exhausting. It seems like you must talk to every individual every day.

You use your command voice a lot. They need to be told very directly what to do. And if only it were that easy. Seems like every second one of them wants your job! You are constantly being challenged by some upstart who you need to put back in his place. Things have become a lot more confrontational. You remember the moment when you realised that you weren't the biggest or strongest in the group. Gulp! However, you quickly remembered that you were the smartest. Sure, you have to be bossy and direct and not back down, but that is not your real power base. Despite how dumb they are, these sapiens can still be sweet and caring. They sit for hours just focussing on each other, building deep personal relationships. They build incredible trust with selected individuals. These relationships underpin tight coalitions of six or seven. By using your heartfelt voice, you can build these coalitions with carefully selected individuals. They then support you and your leadership. This is the power base that has you continue to lead despite not being biggest, strongest, or loudest.

As you pause in front of your latest pre-cog recruit, contemplating who you have become as a leader, a movement behind her catches your eye. It's the corresponding Neanderthal. Realisation floods through you. Just a few hundred metres back up the Eurostar track you experimented with a having a Neanderthal in your team. You concluded that it would never work. But having progressively adapted your leadership style, you now see something completely different. You now have the skills to lead a Neanderthal team! In fact, when you think about it, you always did. You just had to peel away the layers of your leadership to get to the basics.

Another jolt of realisation spins you around. The chimpanzees are still there, looking the same and unchanged in their behaviour. Only now, instead of their behaviour appearing totally unrelated to you, it all makes sense. The relevance of their leadership style makes total sense to you. There might be a lot more biting and scratching, but it is just a more physical version of what you are currently doing with your pre-cogs.

You set out with the chimpanzees from the London Zoo on a generational journey to Africa to find your common ancestor in the hope of bring some insight to your leadership. Here you stand on the Eurostar tracks with the picture starting to form. And you haven't even got to Victoria Park! If you were to continue your journey, you would find it shorter than you thought. No need to go to Africa. Neanderthals and sapiens would converge halfway to the English Coast, and we would find our chimpanzee-human last common ancestor before reaching Paris.

But standing here in the heart of London, we realise that this is far as we need to go to take an evolutionary perspective on differential leadership. You look back to your new recruit. Evolution has wired her to be responsive to your heartfelt voice and your command voice. You turn back up the line and start walking towards London Zoo. Each individual you pass is ostensibly the same as the previous one. But now you understand that within every individual you pass, there is an imperceptible change to brain functioning. Each individual is fractionally more wired than the previous to respond to your prosocial voice. Until . . . there it is. A breakthrough in social cohesion marks the transition to intra-cogs and gives you the ability to lead large teams of people. But as you look forward to the coming emergence of futurizing voice, you are struck by something else. Nothing got left behind! The change can develop only one imperceptible step at a time. Therefore, each change is layered on top of what already exists and must be integrally wired to it. Our current recruits that respond to the prosocial voice still need heartfelt and command voices at times to avoid falling into poor discipline and heartless gossip. They are the sum of all that came before, as well as what emerged, layer built upon layer.

Down the Eurostar tracks and back

The story of how sapiens came from humble beginnings in Africa to dominate the earth is not just a story of human development. It is a story of leadership. Leadership is central to every development in history and, by extension, in prehistory. At the time of the cognitive revolution we started to think in unprecedented ways. We didn't just use this gift to gather more food and build better shelters – we used it to cooperate. This ability to cooperate and adapt on a larger and larger scale had world-scale ramifications. And, wherever there is cooperation, there is leadership.

By marching back the generations on our Eurostar tracks thought experiment, we have stripped back the obscuring nature of leadership in our modern world. We have pulled away the outermost layers of leadership to expose our primal core. We have connected our innermost layers of heartfelt voice and command voice to the leadership behaviour of our forebears.

Reversing our trip back along the tracks, we observed the incremental nature of the change in cognitive ability. We conclude that higher-functioning attributes of the brain can develop only progressively. This means that outer levels of functioning remain integrally connected to inner levels. From a leadership perspective, this correlates to our observation that higher-level differential voices seem to depend on the establishment of the lower differentials.

We have our hypothesis for why differential leadership exists. Now let us dig deeper.

Takeaways

When examining the influence of human evolution on leadership today, the critical period to examine is the cognitive revolution. The term *cognitive revolution* refers to a period around 50,000 ago when sapiens underwent rapid changes in capability. This was caused by the ability to think in different ways and the ability to communicate via much more sophisticated language.

Although the evolutionary changes in the brain were incremental and continuous, the societal structure underwent step changes. Each change was enabled by a new leadership capability.

Pre-cogs lived before the cognitive revolution in tribes of thirty to fifty individuals. Pre-cog leadership was via the heartfelt voice and command voice.

Intra-cog refers to the period during the cognitive revolution when societal groups grew from a maximum of fifty to around 150. The leadership that facilitated this was the prosocial voice.

Post-cogs lived after the cognitive revolution, progressively building larger and larger societal groups. The new leadership capability that enabled this was the futurizing voice.

Notes

1   Dawkins, "Gaps in the Mind".

2   Harari, *Sapiens*.

3   Harari.

4   Raichle and Gusnard, "Appraising the Brain's Energy Budget".

5   Bowden et al., "Genomic Tools for Evolution and Conservation in the Chimpanzee".

6   Hawks et al., "Population Bottlenecks and Pleistocene Human Evolution".

4 Leadership and pre-cogs

One of the things we noticed on our trip back to the London Zoo along our line of many-times-great-grandmothers is that as our ancestors got smarter, they were able to cooperate in larger and larger groups. Where there is cooperation, there is always leadership. What we were witnessing was a fundamental shift in leadership power.

Interestingly, though, the change is not continuous. Although the increase in cognitive ability progresses in imperceptible, tiny progressions, leadership power has a very few major step changes. Let's think about it in terms of leadership reach – the number of people that a leader has power over. At a point in time before Neanderthal extinction, leadership reach changes from 30 individuals to 150 individuals. This is a catastrophic development for the Neanderthal. They might be bigger and stronger, but they can't overcome a five-to-one ratio.

Why the sudden step? Logic would have us think that if increasing intelligence leads to leadership influence, then gradual change in the former would equate to gradual change in the latter. But it doesn't. We notice that the pre-cog leaders with a reach of thirty adults have gotten more sophisticated as we walk back along the tracks. The leadership used to involve a large dose of physicality. There were a lot of beatings and a lot of stroking and grooming. Increasingly, though, leadership has become verbal and gestural. Lashings are doled out in scowls and insults whereas grooming is via compliments and facial expressions. But still the pre-cogs' leadership reach is stuck at thirty. We notice that when groups do grow to fifty and beyond, factions start appearing. They grow stronger, and soon the group splinters.

We can observe the physical version of leading a group of thirty individuals by the observation of chimpanzees. Remember that their behaviour didn't look so foreign when viewed from your pre-cog leadership style. Chimpanzees function in a fission-fusion society. Such a society has a relatively stable parent group, but the group will splinter (fission) for various social or environmental reasons. They will then recombine at a later time (fusion). Our chimpanzee cousins are social animals and form close "friendships", which dominate fission group dynamics. For example, a group of close males will split from the parent group and go hunting together before rejoining at night – perhaps the chimpanzee equivalent of a mate's fishing trip. The size of the fission group varies around a mean size of four.[1]

In the fusion state, the parent group in chimpanzees consists of between twenty and fifty individuals.[2] As the size of the troop increases, the social cohesion begins to break down, factions form, and rivalries escalate. If the group continues to increase in size, then inevitably the troop will split in two. Splintered troops are irreconcilable. The best you can hope for with two troops of chimpanzees sharing the same geography is that they ignore each other. Often hostility will break out between troops. There is even documented evidence of sustained war and genocide between troops.[3]

What is it that prevents the troop from growing beyond a certain size or cooperating with its neighbouring troop? To understand, we must look to the foundations of the social system that holds the troop together in the first place. Chimpanzees are very social animals, and a web of sophisticated social relationships drives the group dynamics. Relationships are based on close physical contact. Chimps spend endless hours hugging, stroking, and grooming each other. Each act of grooming is a social exchange, building deep bonds between participants. There is an expectation of reciprocity: you groom me, I groom you. The frequency of grooming between individuals is a strong predictor of how much individuals look out for each other. When a fight breaks out, grooming partners will stand together. And when a fission group heads off on its own, it will be made up of individuals who groom each other the most.

The leadership model is hierarchical, with the alpha male at the top. Contrary to popular belief, the alpha male is not established purely on physical strength or fighting ability. It is rare that he is the most dominant physical individual. It is here that chimpanzees distinguish themselves from other apes such as gorillas. Predominantly, gorilla troops consist of the alpha male and his females. Other males are generally driven away, and males never socialise or cooperate. The population is made up of individual males with small groups of females. The male must spend time guarding his females, but he also needs to eat. Spend too much time fighting and guarding, and he will lose strength, which gives usurping males the advantage. Therefore, he can sustain only a small troop. Gorillas are too far removed from our evolution line for relevance (although you may be tempted to think otherwise if you are in the habit of frequenting a nightclub area at three o'clock in the morning) but provide a good demonstration of the limits of physical power in leadership.

How then does a chimpanzee alpha male rule? The answer is that he rules by establishing extensive coalitions of supporters, both male and female.[4] These coalitions are maintained by mutual grooming and contact. The alpha male rules by having a stable coalition of sufficiently powerful individuals. This inner circle works as a team to enforce discipline on the troop. The individuals within the inner circle then have their own coalitions and the relationships fan out through the troop. A hierarchy results, with status conferred by the number of relationship steps removed from the alpha male. Some of the troop seem happy to maintain lowly positions in the hierarchy, whereas others are ambitious, constantly seeking to improve their status. This can be done by ingratiation to an individual with higher status, by building a coalition with peers, or by exerting physical dominance.

The model is self-reinforcing. By the very fact that he is the leader, an alpha male's attention is sought out by others. The stronger an alpha male's position, the longer the queue of individuals seeking favour. This, in turn, gives him more power.

Males with leadership aspirations are the most troublesome in the troop. They are constantly disrupting the harmony. They will pick fights to demonstrate their credentials and seek relationships with key individuals to bolster their own coalition. This includes trying to disrupt the power base of the alpha male by "stealing" relationships with his coalition. The alpha male must not just focus on the relationships with his inner circle but also must monitor relationships across the whole troop. Only in this way can he be alert to the growing strength of a rival's coalition. Spotting this allows him to intervene. This can be through physical power, but the use of physical power has consequences on relationships, and this can be counterproductive in the long term. An alternative is to strike up new relationships that undermine the rival's coalition.

You might wonder why an alpha male doesn't just drive away his rival. To explain, we return to the concept of the selfish gene. The chimpanzees' selfish gene is seeking to maximise its advantage in the long term. This means reinforcing behaviours that maximise the robustness of the troop as a whole. On the surface this might lead to the conclusion that rivals should be excommunicated. However, the competing males bring physical prowess to the entire troop. They are the best hunters and the most powerful warriors in battles with other troops or predators. The troop is more likely to flourish in the long term if the competitors are tolerated.

So the alpha male has a big job. He must enforce his authority across the whole troop, metering out discipline. He must be physically strong, but as we have discovered, physical strength is insufficient. The troop is held together by the social structure and hierarchy as much as by physical strength. The alpha male must build an inner-circle coalition to back him up and leverage his leadership. Grooming is the foundation of these relationships, and he must devote time to each of his inner circle. Importantly, he must monitor all the relationships in the troop and intervene to keep the hierarchy stable and to subvert his rivals' attempts to usurp him. And he must find time to hunt, graze, and sleep to maintain his physical attributes. A big job!

It is here that we start to understand the limits of an alpha male's leadership reach. Enforcing discipline and maintaining one-to-one relationships are time-consuming activities. Because chimpanzees need to spend the majority of their day hunting and grazing, there is a limit to how many relationships can be maintained. Order can be maintained only in groups small enough to allow a critical number of one-to-one relationships.[5]

Add to this is the need to monitor all the other relationships in the troop. As the troop grows, the number of relationships explodes. In a group of thirty there are 435 one-to-one relationships to monitor. In a troop of fifty, there are 1,225, resulting in countless complex social combinations.

As the troop approaches fifty, the number of relationships becomes untenable for the alpha male. He simply doesn't have the hours in the day to do everything that needs to be done to hold the troop together. Given the ever-present ambitions of other males in the troop, it becomes inevitable that one of them will create a sufficiently strong coalition of his own, and the troop will splinter.[6]

What can we learn from chimpanzees? Well, nothing – they're chimpanzees, for goodness sake!

What can we learn from the observation of chimpanzees with a thoughtful connection to our own evolutionary history? Quite a lot.

We have followed the journey closely enough to understand that our brains have developed layers on top of the primitive brains of our pre-cog ancestors. In the brain, everything is connected to everything else. It is logical that elements of pre-cog behaviour would still be at play, if heavily disguised by the advanced functions of our contemporary brain. We lack the ability to directly observe pre-cog leadership at work. But the anthropological evidence that we have gathered supports the contention that pre-cog society was similar in many ways to the chimpanzee society we can observe today. This should not be so surprising given our genetic similarity to chimpanzees.

Chimpanzees display their own version of our command voice, maintaining discipline and authority across their troop. But their ability to lead a troop of thirty is not built on this alone. The foundation of their leadership is their equivalent of our heartfelt voice, the ability to connect deeply with their inner-circle coalition.

It is here that we get a picture of the society and thus the leadership style of our pre-cog ancestors. With their larger brains and greater language skills, we can presume that their interactions were more sophisticated. Language-based interactions would have taken over some of the functions of the physical. Instead of chimpanzee-style grooming, verbal communication would play a role in building relationships. But, we surmise that the basics of leadership were the same: leadership by command voice across a command circle built on the foundation layer of heartfelt voice across an inner circle.

I have represented this relationship in the following diagram. The block structure can be built only in a stepwise manner – inner circle block, heartfelt voice block, command circle block, then command voice block. If you try to start the structure with the command voice block, it will collapse. Equally well, a completed structure will collapse if you remove the heartfelt voice block. This is a metaphor for pre-cog leadership. Leadership is built stepwise by choosing close allies for an inner circle and then building it using the heartfelt voice. This provides the support to exercise a command voice across the tribe – a leader's command circle of thirty individuals. Even when fully established, command voice effectiveness is reliant on heartfelt voice. If a pre-cog leader failed to maintain an inner circle, then he would quickly be usurped by someone who had built a competing alliance.

Takeaways

Pre-cog refers to individuals who lived before the cognitive revolution.

Pre-cogs were anatomically identical to modern humans but did not yet have the same cognitive abilities. They lived in bands of thirty to fifty individuals, which we will refer to as a "tribe".

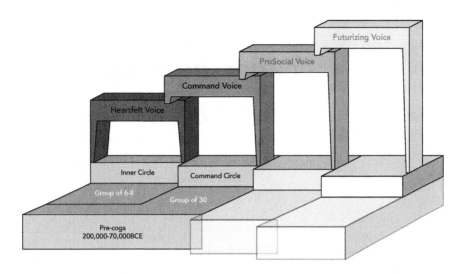

Figure 4.1 Leadership before the cognitive revolution

Leadership of pre-cogs was through the heartfelt voice and command voice. The leader built a tight coalition of six to eight individuals using the heartfelt voice, which was the sapiens equivalent of chimpanzee grooming. This was the leader's power base to control the rest of the tribe through command voice.

The command voice of the pre-cog leader enforced discipline on the band through one-to-one interactions with the individual members. Pre-cog bands were limited in size to a maximum of fifty by the number of the direct relationships that the leader could manage.

Notes

1 Chapman and Chapman, "Determinants of Group Size in Primates".

2 Chapman and Chapman.

3 Goodall, *Through a Window*.

4 Waal, *Chimpanzee Politics*.

5 Waal.

6 Harari, *Sapiens*.

Leadership and intra-cogs

We return to your journey, walking westward along the tracks back toward the London Zoo. We are walking through the transition from pre-cog to intra-cog, observing the change in society and leadership style. The change in leadership reach occurs rapidly. You first notice tribes start to interact whereas before there had only been either ambivalence or hostility. Then, within only a few generations, the tribes of thirty have disappeared to be replaced by groups of around 150 individuals. I will call this size of group a "commune".

The number of 150 appears to be quite special. It has been extensively verified by anthropological studies, not only ancient civilisations but also in more modern times. For example, 150 is the average size of a band or village in modern hunter-gatherer societies.[1] This leads us to ask why. We know that it is uniquely human to be able to cooperate in such large groups, so we immediately suspect that it has to do with our large brains. We can start to test whether there is a direct correlation between brain size and natural group size with different species of primates. We will quickly discover that it doesn't work.

However, if we change our measurement technique, we can get a very good correlation. The crucial brain measurement is the ratio of the outermost layer of the brain (called the neocortex) to the rest of the brain. Measure this ratio in any of the many different species of primates and you can accurately predict how big the natural group size will be. If we then use the same correlation for the human brain, we arrive at the magic number of 150 that we have already observed in ancient and modern hunter-gatherer societies.[2]

The neocortex is the most recently evolved part of the brain – the "top layer". It contains the most advanced functions of the brain. As we walked along the Eurostar tracks towards Paris, it was this part of the brain that was getting fractionally smaller as we transition from post-cogs to intra-cogs to pre-cogs. Again, we cannot measure the difference between adjacent individuals or even those a few hundred metres apart, but over many kilometres the decreasing size of the neocortex becomes measurable. What we are interested in is the ratio of the neocortex size to the rest of the brain, rather than simply brain size. This is highest in post-cogs and progressively decreases as we tramp out of London and across the English countryside. Observing the chimpanzees across from us, we don't see the same trend. Their ratio is lower again than our ancient ancestors, but it is stable. Their evolutionary niche was filled without the need to develop a bigger brain. This might seem strange until you remember that for the vast majority of the journey along the tracks, chimpanzees were a far more successful species than sapiens.

Just as the neocortex ratio for sapiens shrinks as we march towards the point where our common ancestor merges with the chimpanzees, it will also continue to reduce thereafter. As we continue past Paris towards Africa, the reduction trend continues. We find branches of other primates that survive today. They also found their ecological niche that did not encourage larger neocortices and have an even lower neocortex ratio than chimpanzees.

This is not all that surprising to us. We are students of evolutionary science, and our observations align with theory. What is surprising is that the way that this ratio of neocortex size to the rest of the brain is an extraordinary predictor of the natural group sizes for primates. You cut up a dead primate, dissect the brain, calculate the ratio of neocortex to the rest of the brain, and give me the number. The only information I get is this number. But that is all I need to tell you the natural group size for that primate in its natural environment.

It is when we apply the same correlation to the ratio of our brains we get our commune of 150. This is a natural group size for intra-cog humans and is still evident in our society today (more on that later). As a result, we have a correlation that works for primates at one end of the scale and for intra-cogs at the other end. This gives us a continuum that allows us to confidently assert the leadership reach of our pre-cogs and intra-cogs.

Having determined that it is the development of the neocortex that gave our intra-cogs the capability to cooperate in larger groups, we want to understand the mechanism because it will be the mechanism of intra-cog leadership. As we walk back westwards along the Eurostar tracks, past our pre-cogs with their groups of thirty to our intra-cogs in their groups of 150, we search for the answer. Clearly there has been a tipping point. What is it? We suspect very strongly that it is related to language. Language is a very recent development of the brain and is run from the neocortex, so it is an obvious candidate, and we have witnessed that pre-cogs make rotten conversation partners. So you are expecting change in language capability. But why a step change? You look at your intra-cog many-times-great-grandmother for a clue. What is that she is doing that her forebears just a few metres to the east were not? When you identify it, you can scarcely believe it could be connected. You shake your head in disbelief. Your many-times-great-grandmother has started to gossip.

The mention of gossip in a serious book about leadership might have triggered an inner voice for you . . .

> Nice shot! Haven't lost those old basketball skills. Flicked that book across the room, and it landed smack in the middle of the rubbish bin. Way to go. Gossip! For goodness sake. Hang on. Damn, maybe I shouldn't have chucked it. It's damaged now. Bookstore might have given me a swap.

This might sound like a joke. However, the concept that gossip functions to hold together large social networks has been extensively researched. Oxford University professor Robyn Dunbar has been one of the leaders in the field. Building on his involvement in the neocortex ratio theory that we have covered earlier, he has researched the theory that gossip is the language skill that is the mechanism of holding together communes of 150 people.[3] The contention is that gossip is a sophisticated language skill and is much more efficient in allowing us to maintain relationships than being confined to one-to-one communication, physical contact, or grooming. We can groom with our words. We can even groom at a distance. The development of gossip gave our intra-cogs the capability to hold large, stable coalitions. Gossip is much maligned, but the argument for its role is compelling. Our pre-cogs had language, but their interactions were still limited to the here and now. Even chimpanzees have rudimentary language. Although it has been shown that a chimpanzee can envisage the future based on past experience and plan ahead as a result, she cannot communicate the envisaged future to another. Though she can shout a warning to her friend about the approach of Bobo, a hostile individual from another faction, she cannot have a conversation with her friend about how Bobo has been acting aggressively lately and that it is best to avoid him. This is exactly what gossip allowed intra-cogs to do.

Even with a cursory examination of contemporary life, one can observe the huge capacity that we have for gossip. In the past, media empires have been founded on it. The internet has served to provide another step change. It is not unreasonable then to hypothesise about the utility of this seemingly innate capability.

Try to imagine the dynamics of a relatively isolated commune of 150 intra-cogs living without the rule of modern law. The chief of this tribe is not the most physically intimidating but rather a man of experience, leadership presence, and guile. He is recognised by the commune as a leader (often called a "big man"), but he takes care not to appear too dominant. It is a very egalitarian power structure that he presides over. Displays of hierarchy would quickly erode his authority, and he goes out of his way to display humility. He has his band of close associates, and each of them has their own informal power base. Collectively they provide leadership over a critical mass of the commune. The leader's wife has status and also manages a circle of trusted friends. Because of the status of the chief, many in the tribe aspire to join the inner circle to bolster their self-esteem and standing in the community. This "who is in favour and who is not" is a key source of gossip. Power is wielded through these conversations, and their intensity continually bolsters the hierarchy. Gossip also abounds about the individuals within the tribe that are against the established hierarchy – who is plotting, who is trustworthy, who is in which faction. The monitoring of this gossip is key to the chief maintaining his power and controlling the village. He may choose to respond to growing discontent by holding a feast or a sacrifice to the gods. Or he may choose to have an emerging rival executed.

This is a very distributed form of leadership as befits the informal nature of the interactions. It is based on a lot of talking, more talking than we can relate to. The esteemed anthropologist Jared Diamond spent a lot of his early professional career in the highlands of New Guinea interacting with tribes who were largely untouched by the outside world and still lived the way their ancestors had for thousands of years. He commented that he was "impressed by how much more time New Guineans spend talking with each other than do we Americans and Europeans. They keep up a running commentary on what is happening now, what happened this morning and yesterday, who ate what and when, who urinated when and where, and minute details of who said what about whom or did what to whom. . . . Other Westerners have similarly commented on the talkativeness of the !Kung, of African Pygmies, and of many other traditional peoples".[4]

(It is important to clarify that the people that Diamond was observing were post-cogs, not intra-cogs. However, their tribal structures were largely aligned with our definition of communes. The point about talkativeness is relevant to the distributed power structures of a commune. If you are curious about why it is that New Guinean post-cogs never came to use their post-cog abilities to develop large-scale communities, then I highly recommend Diamond's book *Guns, Germs and Steel*.[5] The ability to sustain large-scale communities required access to critical resources as well as post-cog cognitive ability, and these were simply not available in New Guinea.)

The ability of intra-cogs to utilise more sophisticated language was at the heart of maintaining cohesiveness in a much larger group than the pre-cogs could. This included the ability to gather and relay information, to assign character traits, and to postulate on scenarios. But we also know that gossip can be a destructive social force as well. As a leader, we want to be selective about the application of these skills and distinguish the good from the bad. Going forward, I will therefore diverge from characterisation of these language skills as gossip and instead use the term *prosocial voice*. I will also revert to the more generally accepted understanding of gossiping as an idle or negative activity. Going forward this will allow us to distinguish the positive application of social language towards a leader's goal (prosocial voice) from malicious small talk (gossip).

Though not in common use, the term *prosocial* is not new. It was created by social scientists as an antonym for antisocial. This makes it a useful term for leaders. As a leader, you understand the need to create a positive social "buzz" around your team, just as your ancient ancestors did with their commune. There is a reason that organisations budget for town halls, social clubs, and staff Christmas parties. It is not altruism; it is the understanding that creating a positive social community will lead to better productivity.

It is logical that the mechanism will "top out" in terms of the size of groups that can be maintained by this mechanism. If pre-cog leadership reach is limited by the extent to which direct relationships can be maintained and monitored, then intra-cog groups held together by a leader's prosocial voice will be limited by the number of indirect relationships that can be maintained. It is this limit on the number of indirect relationships that results in the maximum commune population of around 150 individuals.

The prosocial voice breaks the limitations of one-to-one relationships. As we explored in the previous chapter, there is a cost to maintaining relationships. At some point in time the marginal benefit of an extra relationship is outweighed by the cost in time. We often complain that time is precious, but to an intra-cog, it is life and death. These creatures are barely viable in the extreme conditions of the time. So, the time to devote to relationships is limited, and this would otherwise limit the size of a group.

A prosocial voice breaks this limitation. For a start, the progressive move from grooming to verbal communication now allows relationship building with more than one individual at a time. It may not be as intimate, but it is certainly more efficient. Verbal communication can also be carried out while doing other tasks, like foraging. Whereas previously an individual would have to make a choice between relationship building and gathering food, now both can be done simultaneously. We can already see the advantages over grooming and how this might lead to the foundation of large communes.

The biggest leverage of the prosocial voice, by far, is the ability to communicate at a distance. We can send messages! "Run over to the thicket and tell your uncle that I will meet him at crooked tree by the waterhole" may seem inane. But think about how sophisticated it is as a mechanism to hold large communes together. It is leadership gold. The ability to influence someone out of earshot has a dramatic impact on leadership reach.

This is evident by comparing our intra-cogs to their chimpanzee cousins on the other Eurostar track. Chimpanzees do have rudimentary language. They can shout a warning about an approaching predator. They have utterances of pleasure and displeasure. And yet the difference in their capabilities compared to your inter-cog team is startling. Your inter-cogs can do miraculous things with their language. As well as sending messages to absent parties, they can talk about what happened yesterday and postulate as to what will happen tomorrow. They can plan together and allocate tasks. And they can teach each other, even without having to physically demonstrate. All these things are important contributors to leadership reach, and we can postulate that with these attributes alone, intra-cog leadership reach would have broken the fifty limit.

To build a commune though, you need something more. The extra ingredient is a rich network of information channels. This amplifies the leader's prosocial voice. It is the step beyond sending a message to an absent party. As an intra-cog leader, you know that you only have to create the right message, and it will send itself to everyone in the commune almost instantaneously. Your intra-cogs, like you, have developed an obsessive love of information. They are drawn to it. They are drawn to the power of it. There is nothing better for them than to be in possession of information that others do not have. Intra-cogs have secrets. And secrets are power. Even the lowest intra-cog in the hierarchy can taste power through information.

What a boon for leadership! The command voice for pre-cog leadership was all push. You had to constantly be pushing the communications onto people. Your intra-cogs have created a huge pull. They are hungry for information. They want to know what you are thinking; "when we are going to move camp", "how are you going to allocate the newly initiated men to the hunting parties", "who have you got your eye on for your next mate", and above all "what are your plans to meet the challenge of Zacreb, who is becoming an increasingly powerful rival to your leadership?" As soon as you release information, zoom . . . straight to the furthest corner of the commune within minutes.

Having moved on from your pre-cog team, you are revelling in your new intra-cog paradigm. But you also quickly realise that the prosocial voice has its downsides. For a start, your intra-cogs are so hungry for information that if you withhold it or are just a bit slow, they start to make things up. It starts as speculation but then quickly spreads as the truth. You swim in a hotbed of rumours and gossip. There is no way around it – you have to deal with it. Besides, sometimes it's useful. As long as you're selective, rumours are a good source of information about the health and status of social cohesion in the commune. And spreading a rumour yourself can sometimes work in your favour. The key is to be tapped into the rumour mill. You cultivate key alliances with a broad range of individuals that you can trust with the sole purpose of understanding the gossip.

The other thing you quickly realise is that your prosocial voice does not work on its own. You shouldn't be surprised. Your intra-cog's newfound abilities haven't happened by a magical transformation of their brains. Their brain is the result of evolution. Their capabilities are the result of imperceptibly small changes in the neocortex. Each of these increments is integrally wired to the "old" part of the brain. It's clear to you that there is a pre-cog just below the surface of your intra-cog that needs to be recognised.

The reason that this is clear to you is that you see it in their response to your leadership. Dwell too long in the prosocial voice, and your intra-cogs seem to lose respect for you. You find yourself drawn into being their social leader instead of their boss. Things start to degrade quickly when this happens. Across the commune, discipline starts to break down. Tasks go unfinished or are done sloppily. Intra-cogs start gathering in groups to gossip rather than do their work. And with this idleness, the gossip starts to turn nasty and destructive. Your response to this is swift and decisive. Time for a good dose of command voice. Get everyone clear on what their job is and what your expectations are. Mete out some high-profile discipline, and get things back on track. Only after order is reestablished can you reengage your prosocial voice. You determine that you will never again let things get out of hand. You will regularly and consistently establish command voice alongside your prosocial voice.

This is looking a lot like differential voice leadership, so you go looking for heartfelt voice. You realise that you never lost it. The commune as a whole might be held together by your prosocial voice, but your individual intra-cogs are held together by heartfelt voice. Everyone wants to feel safe and respected within their inner circle. The knowledge that they are cared for by others is central to your intra-cogs' well-being. Despite the power that you can now exert, you realise that it is built upon the stability of your inner circle, all of whom you have a deep one-to-one relationship with. They are your strongest allies, and in a hundred ways every day, they shore up your leadership.

These insights allow us to continue to build our meta-model. The diagram now includes a prosocial voice operating across a commune of around 150 intra-cogs. However, the prosocial voice does not work in isolation. It relies heavily on the heartfelt and command voices. In the diagram, if you remove the heartfelt or the command block, the prosocial block will fall. Similarly, if a leader fails to exercise either their heartfelt voice or their command voice with their intra-cogs, their leadership fails. They may still be popular and well regarded, but their leadership can never reach its full potential.

You have come a long way in a relatively short trip along the Eurostar rails. You are witnessing the most significant development steps in human history, ones that will have ramifications on the entire world.

But as you pause amongst your group of intra-cogs and reflect on the relationships you have built with your inner circle, you are reminded that you are very different from them. So different, in fact, that they could never be your friends. You have cultivated them to be your closest allies at work. But they are still weird. Your futurizing voice beckons!

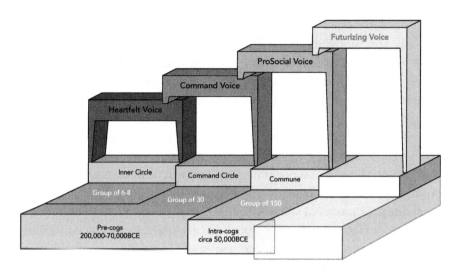

Figure 5.1 Leadership during the cognitive revolution

Takeaways

Intra-cog refers to individuals who lived during the period around 50,000 years ago during the period known as the cognitive revolution.

Intra-cog societal groups were larger than for pre-cogs. They grew to a commune of around 150.

The larger group size was enabled by a new language capability – the ability to communicate indirectly as well as directly.

Gossip appeared for the first time, and its function of assigning character traits and spreading news enabled leaders to hold together larger communes.

The prosocial voice is defined as the positive version of gossip – the leadership based on social engagement.

The prosocial voice became the dominant leadership approach during this period. The larger communes enabled by the prosocial voice outcompeted smaller bands.

Intra-cog communes were egalitarian in nature. The prosocial voice of a pre-cog leader was a distributed form of leadership.

The prosocial voice did not work in isolation. Intra-cogs were only incrementally different to pre-cogs and carried their traits. For communes to thrive, the prosocial voice was built on the heartfelt and command voices.

Notes

1 Dunbar, *Grooming, Gossip, and the Evolution of Language*; Dunbar, "Coevolution of Neocortical Size, Group Size and Language in Humans"; Hill and Dunbar, "Social Network Size in Humans".

2 Dunbar, "Coevolution of Neocortical Size, Group Size and Language in Humans".

3 Dunbar, *Grooming, Gossip, and the Evolution of Language*.

4 Diamond, *The World Until Yesterday*.

5 Diamond, *Guns, Germs, and Steel*.

Leadership and post-cogs

6

You are anxious to continue your journey back. You can't wait to have some normal team members who will respond to your futurizing voice. You know that the futurizing voice works, but you are still puzzled. How does it underpin our ability to cooperate on a massive scale? The nation of China, the Roman Catholic Church, the Red Cross, the historic car racing club – we can form cohesive groups of enormous sizes around almost any endeavour. And perhaps what is most remarkable is that we have transcended the boundaries of direct relationships. Two Jews from separate nations who have never met before will risk their lives for each other in a war because something binds them together. There is clearly another mechanism in play associated with this step change in leadership reach. We must explore to fill out the capabilities of our leader operating in this domain. I have named this large group size a "community". The diagram of the differential voice can now expand to incorporate this.

Let us recap our Eurostar journey. Starting at the London Zoo, we were firmly operating with post-cogs – it is impossible for us to envisage pre-cogs or intra-cogs even vaguely contemplating something as bizarre as a zoo. We travelled east along the tracks, going back in time and observing our ancestors as we went. With your time-machine-powered recruitment strategy you progressively observed the effectiveness of your leadership style through the ages. Your futurizing voice was the first to go as you transitioned out of post-cogs. Then your prosocial voice that was so effective with intra-cogs started to crash. You were left running your team of thirty pre-cogs with your trusty command and heartfelt voice. At this point we had journeyed far enough; our insights were sufficient. We had no need to trace our linage back to our common ancestors with either Neanderthals or chimpanzees. After dwelling

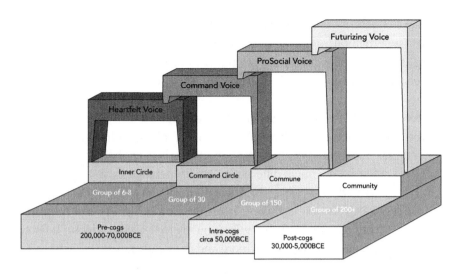

Figure 6.1 Leadership after the cognitive revolution

a while with the pre-cogs to understand the basis of the heartfelt and command voices, we did a u-turn and started to walk west towards the modern era. We were looking for clues as to why the prosocial voice emerged as the leadership capability best suited to the much larger groups of intra-cogs. Observing the emergence of gossip triggered our examination of the power of indirect communication, which underpins the prosocial voice. As we continue to walk west along our line of ancestors we are trying to repeat the process. This time we are looking for clues as to how our ancestors transcended the limits of indirect communication and began to cooperate in the thousands rather than the hundreds.

We are primed to expect that this new capability will be associated with the ability to envisage the future. Intra-cogs could plan forward based on their experience, but they could not extrapolate this into the long term. They could not envisage a long-term goal and then work that back into a plan. So, we are expecting this capability of envisaging a future to show up but we can't see how it is the whole picture. Getting a lot of people to share a vision is sure to be part of the answer, but this capability alone doesn't really stack up as the only thing that can bind thousands of strangers together.

Indeed, we do witness increasing capability in long-term planning, then envisaging goals. What's more interesting, though, is the use that this new-found capability is put to. Post-cogs are different from intra-cogs in their ability not just to envisage things in the real world but to envisage things beyond the laws of nature – literally a belief in the supernatural. Here I am using the word "supernatural" in its literal sense and will continue to do so. If something is supernatural, then it is "attributed to some force beyond scientific understanding or the laws of nature".[1] This captures a lot of things beyond ghosts and superheroes. For example, the concept of fate is supernatural – I can't touch it in the natural world, and I can't scientifically explain it.

The anthropological evidence of the emergence of "belief in the supernatural" as a critical element of post-cog society is overwhelming. Artefacts from this era take on a much different nature from that of intra-cogs and pre-cogs. Objects start to be created that have no apparent functional purpose. Where previously the artefacts were tools designed for a functional purpose, art now appeared. The art was sometimes purely for its own purpose, reflecting the growth in imagination. But more and more, art came to be intimately connected to power.

Harari[2] cites the example of the Stadel lion figure dated to 32,000 years ago. The body of the figure is human, but the head is leonine. It is an indisputable example of art, but more importantly for us, it is strong evidence of the emergence of religion. It marks the transition from "here is a depiction of a lion, an animal that we observe" to "here is the lion spirit, protector of our tribe". There is power in the joint recognition of the supernatural. It is a relatively small step to "the lion-spirit will punish disbelievers in the afterlife" and then to "the lion-spirit has anointed me as the divine ruler over all peoples. Obey me or you will be punished in the afterlife".

We know that religion serves a function or else it wouldn't have survived, but where does it come from? We may never know for sure, but a likely explanation is that it started as a logical progression for a powerful brain that was driven to understand agency, cause, and effect. Evolution doesn't work to a design, but in the long term it rewards genetic accidents that enhance a species reproductive fitness. The newfound ability of post-cogs to look forward in time, anticipate outcomes, plan a course of action, and then take that action to influence the outcome was a massive advantage. Post-cogs started to become masters of aspects of their environment rather than victims. To do this, they became masters of understanding the impact of the actions they took – their agency. Like no other animal before, post-cogs studied how one thing caused another and how they could deliberately cause things to happen. This equipped them to take action to benefit their survival. Evolution ensured that these capabilities were continually improved in subsequent generations.

Post-cogs became extremely attuned to their natural environment and built up a body of knowledge about the world, which helped them thrive. With their sophisticated language abilities, this body of knowledge could be transferred to others and passed down for subsequent generations to use, refine, and improve. A post-cog was not just the product of what she had learned, she was a product of everything that the tribe learned and selected knowledge from her forebears as well.

Post-cog parents might teach their children as they had been taught by their parents – "when there is a king tide, large fish will swim into this inlet where they normally can't go. By setting our nets across the sandbank, we can catch a huge haul as the tide goes out". This encapsulates agency, cause, and effect. By understanding that the king tide will cause the big fish to swim into the inlet, the tribe can take action (agency), which will cause the fish to be caught on the outgoing tide.

A subsequent generation might then get curious about the flow patterns of the estuary – the shape of the shore influencing the flow of water. They experiment with modifying the shore using rocks and channels. Their agency in placing the rocks and digging the channels causes the tide to flow differently, meaning that the inlet is filled on a normal high tide as well as on a king tide. The food supply increases, and the tribe prospers. Evolution ensures that curiosity and the capability to analyse agency, cause, and effect and then transfer this knowledge to their children is passed on and increased in subsequent generations.

It is a natural progression that at some point a supercurious post-cog starts to think about the cause of the tide. We might think that they would have asked themselves the question, "What causes the tides?" but that is because we have been raised in the era of scientific explanation. With their finely honed understanding of agency, a post-cog of twenty thousand years ago was much more likely to ask the question, "Who causes the tides?" They knew that they could, in a small way, influence the tides with their own agency by building rock walls and digging channels, so it would have been a natural progression of thought to create a supernatural being that caused the tides to ebb and flow.

The adoption of such a belief had no negative consequences that affected reproductive fitness. Holding (what we would currently describe as) false beliefs didn't negatively affect the fish catch or cause people to have less babies. Belief-in-the-supernatural became a neutral side effect of an extremely advantageous trait of insatiable curiosity.

In an oft-repeated pattern in evolution, this side effect accidently proved to be useful in another sphere. Evolution is full of examples of where parts of an organism prove useful in a new environment and develop to perform an entirely different function. For example, the evidence is that bird feathers initially evolved to provide warmth but their function was later "hijacked" to provide flight as well. This "hijacking" of purpose is called *exaptation*, and it applies to traits as well as physical features. In post-cogs, exaptation of the "agency, cause, and effect" trait led to the "belief-in-the-supernatural' trait. It developed over time to become a powerful force in human evolution. Along with other aspects of religion, it became the glue that held together large communities that were better able to exploit the resources and thus outcompete small communes and tribes. Far from being a neutral trait, belief-in-the-supernatural became an important enhancement to reproductive fitness.

As you talk to the first post-cogs to appear on your westward journey along the Eurostar track, you see the light go on inside them. These are the earliest humans, as you have traditionally thought of humans. You know that the line of intra-cogs and pre-cogs to the east are your ancestors, but to you they are some sort of animal/human hybrid. The creature in front of you now is a person, capable of all the functions that you are capable of. And you see this person cooperating with others in ways that are unthinkable to the intra-cogs you left behind. You observe that this newfound ability to cooperate with strangers emerges simultaneously with the emergence of the belief-in-the-supernatural trait. You see the emergence of communities where once there were only communes and tribes. But how are the two connected? What is the mechanism by which belief-in-the-supernatural is allowing leaders to establish cooperation on a much larger scale, to cause strangers to cooperate? It is time to meet the storyteller.

The storytelling leader

You continue to walk westward along the Eurostar tracks leaving the intra-cogs far behind you at Victoria Park. The people you pass are thoroughly modern, but their societies are not. These people are still hunter-gatherers. You have miles to go before the agricultural revolution will emerge at St Pancras station: 10,000 BC. You continue to witness cooperation at a community level (mainly in the form of alliances between communes to go to war with another alliance of communes), but these are sporadic and temporary in nature. The ability to cooperate in large numbers is there, but the resources to sustain a larger community are not. You see a leader emerge and pull together a large conglomeration of communes and triumph in a battle, but the following day the communes and tribes disperse to their hunting grounds to feed themselves. Without agricultural production to provide an excess of food in a centralised location, the ability to sustain a cohesive community is lost. Even the leader himself takes his place in the hunting party the following day.

With the predominance of the commune as highest level of cooperation, you observe that the prosocial voice predominates, with only brief excursions into futurizing voice. But in these excursions, you start to pick up the essence of the futurizing voice. You are starting to see the connection between leadership and belief-in-the-supernatural. The ability that these sporadic leaders tap into is based on a belief-in-the-supernatural. But critically, it is the ability of post-cogs to create a *shared* belief-in-the-supernatural that underpins the futurizing voice. The successful futurizing post-cog leader weaves together this shared belief-in-the-supernatural through imaginative storytelling.

You also have noticed a progressive change in the way that post-cogs relate to their belief-in-the-supernatural. What started out an *ability* has become a deeply held *need*. These post-cogs do not merely have the capability to believe in the supernatural, they are driven to believe. Furthermore, it is insufficient to just hold a personal belief-in-the-supernatural. They are driven to discuss, debate, and agree on a *shared* belief-in-the-supernatural.

It is this deeply held need that the occasional excursion into the futurizing voice taps into. All communes develop their own shared belief-in-the-supernatural. The leader who successfully unites the communes does so by weaving together the different communal beliefs. If one commune has a shared belief in lion spirit as protector and another commune believes that the rustling of the forest trees at night is their ancestors speaking to them, then the successful futurizing voice will create the master story that combines the two. The story might be that when the Sun disappears at night, it does so to meet with the lion spirit and the ancestors to decide on the fate of the mortals. Leadership is increasingly defined by storytelling.

As you continue your westward trek along your post-cog ancestors, you are looking for a pivotal event that could really prove this connection. It seems incredible that the modern world in which you live could have

developed through storytelling; through fiction! You need to see more con-
crete evidence. In particular, you want some evidence to point to when you
return to family and friends that demonstrates that post-cogs had this ability
before the agricultural revolution. You find it as you approach St Pancras.

As luck would have it, your ancestors inhabited an area near the Fertile
Crescent. The Fertile Crescent is an area in Western Asia and the Middle East
known as the cradle of civilisation due to the rapid development that took
place in the region through the agricultural revolution. However, you are
not there yet on your westward trek – it is on the other side of St Pancras.
As you approach St Pancras, the society that you observe is at Göbekli Tepe.
In modern-day terms, it is located in southeastern Turkey. There, on a high
mountain ridge, you find hundreds of people constructing a very large temple built of stone and mortar.

What you see is not some crude earth mounds or stone edifices. It is a
complex arrangement of enclosures that will ultimately stretch for hundreds
of metres each way. You see people hard at work, building new enclosures
and erecting T-shaped stone pillars up to 6 meters high and weighing 20
tons. You marvel at the workmanship, achieved with the crudest of stone
tools (the Iron Age is ten thousand years down the tracks), and prior to the
invention of the wheel. All of this is happening 7,000 years prior to Stone-
henge and 6,000 years prior to the Egyptian pyramids. Most significantly, the
work predates the agricultural revolution.[3] Why are these workers cooperating, and how are they being fed?

Something incredibly powerful is at work here. There are no living
quarters and no water source. The workers are trekking in from their communes. For every worker on the site, you see ten people out in the forests,
hunting and gathering more food then they and their families need to
support the effort. To keep this level of activity going, dozens of communes cooperate across hundreds of square kilometres. Because of your
observations of the futurizing voice, you know what to look for. Of course
there are no living quarters here; this is a sacred place for worship. You go
looking for gods.

The T-shaped pillars being erected are more than pillars. They are intri-
cately carved abstract humanoid figures. Their abstraction is not for lack of
skills by the artisans at work – other carvings at the site are extremely intri-
cate. They are abstract because they represent the supernatural. Here is the
evidence that you were looking for. You are witnessing cooperation across
a community of thousands and thousands of post-cogs driven by a shared

belief-in-the-supernatural. The futurizing voice that establishes this shared belief is the work of a master storyteller.

Takeaways

Post-cogs were the product of the cognitive revolution. They had the same cognitive abilities as we do today.

Post-cogs had the ability to cooperate in far larger numbers than the intra-cog communes of around 150 individuals. Communities grew larger and larger, ultimately to millions of individuals after enabled by the rise of agriculture.

The simultaneous rise of abstract art for religious purpose is no coincidence. The futurizing voice of the post-cog leader was based on the belief-in-the-supernatural.

The futurizing voice used storytelling to create a shared belief-in-the-supernatural and utilised this to exert leadership power. Religion and leadership power were inextricably linked during this period.

The emergence of the futurizing voice occurred before the agricultural revolution. It was used to form alliances between communes of hunter-gatherers. The futurizing voice was the most powerful leadership capability, but it was still built upon the lower differentials, which held together communes.

Notes

1   Stevenson, *Oxford Dictionary of English*.

2   Harari, *Sapiens*.

3   Aslan, *God*.

A primate, a gossip, and a dreamer walk into a bar

How is that inner voice of yours going? Maybe you are sceptical?

> *Too right, I'm sceptical. The world I inhabit as a leader is light years away from the world inhabited by the cogs. Society has moved on. We have moved on. And besides, I'm pretty sure that there are no pre-cogs inside my head.*

The previous chapters laid out the evidence for the discrete ways that society functioned before, during, and after the cognitive revolution. Because of the different mechanisms that held the increasingly large group sizes together, we have come to understand the different leadership styles that predominated: heartfelt and command voice for pre-cogs, prosocial voice for intra-cogs, and futurizing voice for post-cogs. We have also seen how the later leadership voices did not obliterate the previous ones.

This leads us think about society today. If the thesis holds that we, as modern post-cogs, still respond to the discrete differential voices, then we might suspect that we can still find traces of the matching discrete group sizes in today's society. Let's take a look.

Down the pub

It's time to take a break and head down to your favourite pub. You think about staying in (you're tired from all the railway track walking), but this multi-cog thing is doing your head in. Time to forget it for a while and catch up with some friends.

You walk in the door, and there are Ismir and Jane. These are dear friends, and you start a nice chat about Jane's pregnancy and all the preparations underway. You share that story about the cranky midwife with your first. You are joined by Trevor and Simon who have just walked over to you. Ismir and Jane don't know Simon and Trevor, so you make the introductions. The circle expands, and you wind them into the conversation you were having. All five of you continue to talk. The conversation continues comfortably but has lost a little of its intimacy. You start to observe the dynamics. When Jane's friend Laura slips in beside her, there is a noticeable shift. What had been less intimate with five has suddenly started to feel a little awkward with six. Thank goodness the conversation had already turned to house hunting. Would have been really awkward if you were still on pregnancies.

People are conscious of their responsibility to keep the conversation flowing but are more reticent. You can see people in the group subtly scanning the room. There it is. In a perfectly executed manoeuvre, Jane spots Tran from her book club, simultaneously grabs Laura's arm and wheels around to say hello. They have a group of three. You have a group of four. That's better!

You have just observed the powerful social forces that drive an inner circle group size. If you hadn't just been down the Eurostar tracks and back, you would be puzzled. Why would you change the nature of your conversation depending on how many people were in the group? Why would three be intimate, four or five comfortable, six a bit awkward, and seven demand that the group split in two?

And what about work? You have just had that mind-numbingly expensive management consulting firm McKinskey come through to run the reorganisation. Millions of dollars of fees, and what do they come up with? Seven. I don't care what business you are in or where you operate in the world, the answer is seven. CEOs will have seven general managers as direct reports. General managers will have seven group managers as direct reports. Group managers will have seven managers. Managers will have seven team leaders. And team leaders will have, you guessed it, seven direct reports. What if we were an IT company? Seven. A transport company or the parish council? Seven.

The inner circle grouping of around five and certainly less than ten people is alive and well in today's society. Which sets you to thinking. If the tens of thousands of intervening generations have not eliminated the tendency to clump in our little pre-cog fission groups, is the heartfelt voice you used with your pre-cog team relevant in today's world? Of course it is. The conversation you were having with Ismir and Jane was building an intimate connection, mutual good will, and care in an environment where everyone felt safe. Everyone could share unreservedly. That was the heartfelt voice. As the group expanded, it was no longer safe, and heartfelt voice lost its place.

Better check back into the conversation; you are starting to look a little weird.

Trevor is in the military, just back from active service. He is a quiet sort of a guy but is starting to open up a bit about his experiences. You join in on the conversation with no particular intention at first but that damn book reemerges.

"So Trevor. Tell me about leadership in the army. How does it really work? You see I have been reading this book on leadership".

"You can place your book in an uncomfortable place", says Trevor (or words to that effect). "We get a constant stream of officers coming down from officer school full of the latest crap about leadership. But let me tell you what really counts when your life is on the line. What really matters is your platoon. Give us a lieutenant from officer school, and we will tell him what's important. One, keep out of our way. Two, keep the brass off our backs. Leave the rest to us. Don't give us orders, just give us the objective. We'll get the job done. But we'll do it for each other, not for you".

"But that doesn't just happen. There must be some formal leadership?"

"It's the sergeant. The sergeant is the leader. And yes, it is formal, but it is different. The brass can order me about as much as they like. I'll do enough to stay out of a court-martial. But I'll charge a machine-gun post for my sergeant. You see, my sergeant can give orders and hand out discipline with the best of them. But he also knows how to get the platoon to connect. With him and with each other. He won't tolerate any crap. But when we are out there camped overnight, he won't touch his meal until he is sure that we are all looked after. Under his direction and with total trust in each other we are an unstoppable team".

"Wow". "How many men in a platoon?"

"Three sections of eight men, plus our radio, our mortar, and the sergeant. Twenty-seven men".

A platoonlike base unit has shown up a remarkable number of times throughout thousands of years of military history around the world. But perhaps after the journey we have been on, it's not so remarkable. A strong platoon has little need for formal discipline and complex procedures. The sergeant can maintain order not only on the basis of his formal authority but also through building personal relationships between himself and his inner circle, by encouraging and managing relationships between the men (building morale), and by keeping in check the individuals who seek to build other power coalitions within the group. This allows the sergeant to get reliable delivery out of his men. When the situation calls for it, he can issue orders effectively and efficiently and with no ambiguity about the outcome required. He doesn't need to bully or shout, because he has already put in the hard yards by training his men to meet his expectations and standards. This is his command voice, and the platoon is his tribe. Alone, a command voice can work on a short-term basis or in emergencies. But stretched over a long period of time, relying solely on command voice breeds resentment and dissent. Particularly in the modern world, people have a low tolerance for being treated as a mere tool to achieve someone else's goals, even in the army where there is an expectation of hierarchy and following orders. A switched-on sergeant instinctively knows that it is the *heart* that amplifies his command voice.

You came to the pub to clear your head of all this outer voice and leadership reach ancient history stuff, only to find it alive and well in your local pub. Why hadn't you noticed it before? Perhaps because you weren't looking.

Waiting in line for a drink, you see a familiar face. It's Natasha – from your job with your previous employer. You haven't talked since you changed jobs, and you should have stayed in better contact. You're sure that it was probably your turn to organise a coffee catch up. You really like Natasha. You were so close when you were working on that project together. You both chatter excitedly. She's about to resign for the same reason you did – that overbearing boss. His antics continued after you left, and now he has lost a great team member. She's running late and you have to get the drinks order, so you part with a vague arrangement to catch up next week. It was great to run into her and have a chat. Can't say that about many other people from that joint.

Of all the people in the world that you would recognise if you ran into them in a pub, how many would you want to stop and have a chat to like you just did with Natasha? Some you would pretend you didn't see; some you would give a little waive or a dismissive hello. How many would you *really* want to talk to?

Turns out the answer for the average person is 150; our magic number for a commune. This is not just confirmation bias at work. Academic studies confirm that the intra-cog commune is a natural group size for humans. One study looked at Christmas card lists. You remember that quaint practice of sending Christmas cards, don't you? The study found that, on average, people had 150 relationships that warranted taking the time to send a Christmas card.[1]

Time to say your goodbyes and head home for a well-earned sleep. You are exhausted. In the space of a single day you have undertaken evolutionary travel with sapiens, Neanderthals, and chimpanzees. You have watched our modern brain being built piece by tiny piece on top of our ancient brain. You have studied the societies of the post-cogs, intra-cogs, and pre-cogs to observe the nature of leadership. You have led teams of pre-cogs using heartfelt voice and command voice, led teams of intra-cogs by adding your prosocial voice, and teams of post-cogs with your futurizing voice. You didn't even get to work before realising that the same differential leadership skills that you successfully applied in the ancient world are worth deep scrutiny when contemplating how to approach your current leadership challenges. As you pull out your phone and flick across to the Uber app, you are vaguely aware that thousands and thousands of people have cooperated to make that simple task possible. A whole community motivated by leaders and their futurizing voices.

What we have witnessed in the pub is quite remarkable. We inferred by logical extension that there was a possibility of detecting the shadow of our evolution-based group size. But given the tens of thousands of years since the cognitive revolution, thousands of years of "civilisation", hundreds of years of industrialisation, modern communications, and modern lifestyles, we might expect the remnants to be fleetingly hard to detect. Instead we find the evidence all around us.

Takeaways

The group sizes associated with the societies of pre-cogs and intra-cogs are still discoverable in the modern world. By examining what causes the cohesiveness in these different group sizes, we can witness that it is the same mechanisms that existed for our ancient forbears.

Our heartfelt voice holds together an inner circle of around six people and our command voice works across a group of thirty people, just as they did for a pre-cog leading a tribe.

The indirect communications of our prosocial voice extends to around 150 individuals just as it did for an intra-cog leader of a commune.

Note

1 Hill and Dunbar, "Social Network Size in Humans".

The pre-cog within (and the intra-cog, and the post-cog)

8

Your trip to the pub has left you troubled. While you were on the railway tracks, you were happy to engage in the debate over the behaviour of pre-cogs and the later incarnations of *Homo sapiens*. It was an interesting academic exploration. You were even comfortable starting to contemplate that prehistoric leadership styles might still resonate at some deep level within the brains of modern-day followers. It was interesting to think that *those* people might be unconsciously responding to triggers that were laid down by evolution.

What troubles you is that, all of a sudden, it has become personal. You are one of *those* people responding unconsciously to evolutionary triggers. It is not just *them*, it is *you*!

You felt it acutely in your conversation with your dear friends, Ismir and Jane. You are stuck with a mental image that you can't shake. It is of the three of you sitting around in a tight circle grooming each other like chimpanzees do – running fingers through hair, stroking, patting each other. Then Trevor and Simon turning up and muscling into the circle, breaking the intimacy. Then the others turning up and ruining it completely.

All of a sudden this has gone from academic to personal. Could it possible that far from being a product of your own free will, that your behaviour is significantly influenced by the genetic remnants of your pre-cog ancestors?

Now you're remembering your conversation with Natasha, specifically the former boss that you both despised. With the benefit of your experience on the Eurostar tracks, you start to replay your response to his leadership:

> He had no heartfelt voice. It was like he was a cardboard cutout. There was no one-to-one relationship, and you didn't feel like you could

confide in him. You felt unsupported. You always had to be careful what you said in front of him. There it is – *your inner pre-cog!!!*

He had no command voice either. You were constantly left wondering what he actually wanted you to do. He was always hazy when he wanted something done, and deadlines just seemed to come and go. To be honest, you really slacked off under his leadership, feeling no compunction to work hard for him. There it is again – *your inner pre-cog!!!*

Gossip ran riot in the department. It was weird because the company was in a huge growth industry, but the chatter was always toxic. Lots of bitching about the other departments and spreading of rumours about who was next for the chopping block. There was no social buzz about the place, no get-togethers or cross-departmental contact. The boss had no prosocial voice, and you responded by filling the space with gossip – *your inner intra-cog!!!*

Worst of all was the futurizing. You still cringe even all these years later. The memory of having to stand up in front of the team and recite the vision statement – "I am committed to our vision. We will deliver world-class on-time-in-full performance and a 27 percent return on investment!" Oh my God! Was that the worst day of your professional career or what? What an affront to *your inner post-cog!!!*

It is all so clear to you now you have been down the Eurostar tracks. As a follower, with both feet firmly in the modern world, your response to leadership came straight from the ancient world. And you were completely oblivious to it.

This insight is disquieting enough, but now another one hits you. This one related to you as a leader rather than as a follower. As a result of your trip down the Eurostar tracks, you have had to confront the fact that you were not a good leader when it came to the command voice. As you progressively stripped back your leadership with the decreasing capability of your pre-cog team, it really sharpened your appreciation of what it takes to be good at the command voice. This in turn, shone a light on the fact that back in the modern world, you could do with some work. You have worked on it in the past. Last year, you attended a development course run by the Institute of Management on Delegations Skills. However, you have to be honest with yourself and say that you haven't made much progress.

The skills you learnt from the Institute of Management all made perfect sense. You left the program with a strong resolve to put these new skills into practice. You had lined up your direct reports in a series of one-to-one meetings the next day at work. The task was clear. You had developed a crystal clear set of delegated tasks based on the structure that you learnt via a fancy acronym. Your job in the meetings was straightforward – to get their iron-clad commitment.

But as you fronted up for the first meeting the next day back at work, you could feel the resolve leaking out of you. Then as the moment presents itself, your anxiety started rising. Your blood started pumping faster, and your head was swimming. You felt nauseous and couldn't think straight. You were almost physically ill at the thought of using your command voice. What the hell was going on? It was like something inside you was hijacking your good intentions.

You bumbled your way through the meetings as best you could, and it did have some impact in the short term. But as you reflect now, things have slipped back to where they were. Performance is the same, and your command voice is as weak as it always was. Your course notes are on the shelf covered in dust.

The thing that bothers you now is that feeling you identified – "It was like something inside you was hijacking your good intentions". You now know what that something is. As a leader your command voice was being sabotaged by your inner pre-cog.

Inner voice

To enhance your leadership, we have to get inside your head. It is time to explore a major tenet of the differential voice that we have been alluding to all along – inner voice.

Inner voice? What does he mean by inner voice? What's an inner voice? Hang on. I get it. That's what he has been getting at with all these italicised paragraphs that he has been inserting everywhere. This my inner voice. Talking to me. I'm talking to myself.

Talking to myself about inner voice.

That's my inner voice talking about my inner voice.

Now it's my inner voice talking about my inner voice talking about my inner voice!

To identify your inner voice, just undertake the following exercise. At the end of this paragraph, I want you think about nothing for ten seconds before reading the next paragraph. Not just a pause for ten seconds, I want you to stop thinking altogether. Ready. Go.

How did you go? Were you able to suspend your thinking for ten seconds? Very few people can, and then only after a lot of training and practice. What was going on in your head as you were trying to? Was there an internal conversation going on – a conversation with yourself. That's your inner voice.

Silently speaking to oneself is an almost a universal human experience. For many years, it escaped serious psychological study perhaps because of its oddity, but more likely because it is so embedded in the way we are that it goes unnoticed. The fact that it is ever-present means we never question it. By its very nature, inner voice is also very difficult to objectively study. How do you study something objectively when the only person who can observe it is completely biased? It is referred to in literature by a variety of names: inner speech, private speech, self-talk, covert speech, silent speech, background conversation, auditory verbal imagery, as well as many others. You can tell already, that as a field of academic study, there is constant disagreement about the correct term, as well as the correct definition for inner voice. Frankly, it still lies on the fringe of serious academic study.

This has started to change with the availability of brain-imaging techniques that bring more objectivity to the field. Utilising these techniques, it has been identified that inner voice and verbal speech are sourced from the same zone of the brain called Broca's area. This is interesting. If we are using the same area of the brain for inner voice as for things we say out loud, what's the story? Why is inner voice silent? And why is it that we don't always obey our inner voice?

"Punch him!" it screams as your boss puts on his best condescending tone and dismisses the direction that you have taken with your project – hours and hours of work including voluntary over time. But you don't. You don't punch anyone. Ever. You don't obey your inner voice, or at least not always. People who always obey their inner voice end up in jail. You have another area of the brain associated with volition. Volition is the application of choice to your actions, hence statements like "he acted of his own volition". It lies in the neocortex, the most recently evolved part of the brain. Your pre-cogs with their relatively low neocortex ratio were low on volition. They did a lot of punching. But you can override your urges. Without even thinking, you can evaluate the long-term implications of your actions and choose not to punch your boss right in the middle of that round, pink, smarmy face.

We will examine inner voice in great detail going forward in this book. This is not for the purpose of establishing that inner voice has a special relevance in the makeup of human psychology. You can buy thousands of books on developing leadership through self-awareness that don't mention inner voice. Rather, we are using inner voice as an access point to self-awareness and our leadership development journey. It is not a definitive self-awareness tool, but it is an excellent window on our unconscious. By paying attention to it, we can see things in ourselves that we never saw before. In the same way that we used outer voice metaphorically as well as literally, we shall do the same with inner voice. Inner voice will be a metaphor for our stage of self-awareness development. As we'll see, examining inner voice can generate transformational insights when it comes to our leadership.

For a start, inner voice is a great example of the unconscious. For some of you, this will be the first time that you have noticed your inner voice. How is it that something that has been present in our lives for years and years can go unnoticed? That is remarkable! If inner voice has been unconscious, what else has? The truth is that we shouldn't be surprised. Most of what our brain does is unconscious.

Take a moment to stand up, walk across the room, pick up that hot cup of coffee, and take a sip. Done? The only conscious activities were to decide to act. But think about all the unconscious activity that took place in your brain. For a start, it kept you breathing and your heart pumping, both very complex tasks. It calculated just the right amount of force required across dozens of muscles to take your body from a sitting position to a standing position. Too little force and you would fail to get upright. Too much force and you would topple forward. It calculated just the right amount of force to get our body into the right amount of motion. But the motion must then be counteracted. Taking input from your vision, your motor sensors, and the feel from the force of the floor on your feet, it determined which muscles to activate and did so at precisely the right time to arrest your forward motion. Without pause, it then launched you into your walking regime. When it came to picking up the cup, some truly remarkable things came into play. You had to calculate how to get your hand to the handle, you rotated the cup so the handle was in the right place, and you applied just enough force to prevent the cup form tipping as you lifted it. As you lifted it you made hundreds of tiny corrections to keep it level. As it reached your lips, you were evaluating the temperature and deciding on how far to tip the cup so you took the tiniest of sips to avoid scalding yourself. All of it unconscious.

Eagleman[1] relates the story of Ian Waterman who through a rare disease lost the ability to receive sensory input from his body. He was told he would never walk again, but through amazing determination has taught himself to do so. But he can only do so by visual monitoring of his limbs. Every movement takes conscious thought and planning. Walking is so complex that it completely consumes his concentration. He is fully aware of how much brain activity is required for walking. We just take it for granted. Even though it feels like an incredible effort to Ian, it is not that his brain is doing more coordination. Our brains are doing as much "work", it is just that we have committed walking to the unconscious. We are unconsciously competent at walking and can therefore devote our conscious thoughts to other things while we walk. We have hardwired our ability to walk, so that it frees up our thought for more novel activities.

It is not just the basic tasks that we commit to the unconscious through hardwiring. Most of us learn to drive. As a learner, we used all our concentration on this incredibly difficult activity. Barely a year later we were undertaking complex manoeuvres while our conscious thought was completely focussed on the hot date that we were going on that night.

Einstein donated his brain to science. Examination of the brain found a very distinctive piece of hardwiring, forming a giant fold in his cortex. It wasn't the $E = mc^2$ part of the brain; it was the area associated with the fingers of the left hand. The examiners had seen this before and understood immediately. They were looking at physical evidence of Einstein's passion for playing the violin.[2] Like every other violin leaner, Einstein would have needed to apply a great deal of conscious thought into what his fingers were doing and how it related to the sound that was produced. But as he practiced, his brain picked up the complex repetitive actions and started to convert them to hardwiring. The collection of this hardwiring was so great that the brain had to grow a new section to accommodate it. And as it grew, Einstein's playing improved and improved. The actions became more and more automatic to the point where he hardly had to think about playing at all. The music just flowed.

Elite sportspeople talk of being in the flow when performing at their peak. Brain imaging has confirmed that the high-functioning thinking shuts down. It is their unconscious competence that delivers their peak performance. This should not surprise us that much. A batsman in cricket facing a pace bowler, or a batter in baseball facing a fastball simply does not have time to use conscious thought and translate it into action before the ball reaches them. They rely on the hardwired functions of their brain, forged by hour and hours of practice. They learn that operating consciously is actually counterproductive – start thinking too much and they will "choke".

We are world champions at operating from the unconscious, so we shouldn't be surprised when we discover something like inner voice. Like thousands of other functions, it has always been there, so why would we bother to bring it to consciousness? We have plenty of other work for our conscious thinking.

This begs the question, "if unconscious competence is so amazing, why do we need to meddle with it when it comes to leadership?" Reflecting on Chapter 2, it is time for us to remember that our brain evolved to maximise reproductive fitness in a world that we no longer inhabit. It was not designed for the modern world; it was not designed at all. Some of the functions of our brain are remnants of an ancient world. Evolution trims functions that decrease reproductive fitness but keeps those that are neutral. But what was a positive or neutral trait to your hunter-gathering pre-cogs can be a downright hindrance in our modern world.

Our society has developed and continues to develop at a pace that outruns our evolution. We are not genetically optimised to operate in today's world. This results in many problems, most of them with implications on how we lead. Our inner voice is integrally connected to the unconscious counterproductive behaviours we retain as a result of our evolution. Investigating inner voice gives us access to modify our behaviours and insight into the behaviour of our followers.

"Punch him!" your inner voice screams at you. This instinct has no place in our modern world. And yet there it is. It would be okay if it were merely a distraction that you ignored. But it is so much more. The "Punch him!" part of your brain has sent an urgent signal to your adrenal glands. You are wired for action. Your brain starts shutting down the outer layers; it doesn't need advanced thinking skills in a fistfight! Where does this leave you in your meeting with your boss who you only get to see once a month? The boss who holds the key to achieving the outcome on that project that you are so passionate about. At the very moment that you need to be at your most intelligent and articulate, you've turned into a pre-cog!

But wait a minute. Didn't we say before that you have the power of volition over your inner voice? The power to switch it off. You exercised that choice by not punching your boss. But that didn't switch off the inner voice. Rather than a switch, it is better to think of your volition as a gate. You shut the gate and prevent inner voice moving to action. But your inner voice is still raging behind the gate! And worse, it affects what you are doing.

As the adrenalin kicks in, raising your heartbeat, prepping your muscles, and shutting down the outer layers of your brain, it changed the way that you present yourself to your boss. Your inner voice affected your outer voice. You had planned the meeting carefully. You were clear on your objectives and argument. You knew exactly what you wanted and how to get it. And you knew the professional image that you wanted to project. All coming undone in a spectacular train crash. A train crash that for the next week you replay over and over in slow motion.

But as you replay it, you don't remember the unconscious bits. Of course you don't – that's why they are called unconscious. You don't remember "Punch him!" You just remember that he was a condescending imbecile who doesn't even understand how his own business works. You remember how *he* derailed you. It was *him* that stuffed up your project. Maybe you don't get any further than this – your noble cause thwarted by the imbecile. You don't recall your contribution to the train wreck or your lack of intervention. Or if you do it is in the realm of speculation or conjecture. "When he said X, that's when I should have said Y. That would have brought him down a peg or two". "If only I had brought up Z at that point of the conversation". All you do is obsessively replay the slow-mo. It drives you nuts, but you can't stop it. But the replays and speculation do nothing except consume your energy. Nothing changes, and you are no more effective next time. Your outer voice is unchanged.

The outer voice you wanted was your heartfelt voice. Whether or not you like it, you have identified your boss as critical to your project. You need him in your inner circle. Yes, that's right, an imbecile in your inner circle. It is your objectives that define the group of people that you need to build a heartfelt connection to; you don't get to choose!

The "Punch him!" inner voice obliterated your heartfelt voice. This happens consistently across all layers of leadership. Every outer voice has a corresponding inner voice that either derails or reinforces. This might seem a bit too convenient, but we should not be surprised. We found on our journey along the Eurostar tracks that there were long periods of stability followed by relatively rapid transition to new levels of cooperation, facilitated by a new "layer" of brain functionality. Although the change from generation to generation can't be picked, the cognitive ability reaches a threshold level that is a tipping point. Suddenly, new thinking flourishes and becomes self-reinforcing. The brain has learnt to learn in a completely new way. And as it does it generates a distinctly different inner voice. Each new layer generates an inner voice that is distinct from the previous. Your inner voice is extraordinarily well connected to all parts of your brain, including the parts that you deny. And it acts without filters. That is why it is such a powerful tool for developing self-awareness.

Takeaways

Despite our self-image of our actions being the result of our conscious choices, it is clear that most of what we do is unconscious. This includes what we do as leaders.

If we are to improve our leadership, it is essential that we gain access to our unconscious triggers and automatic responses.

Distinguishing and examining our inner voice can give us access to our unconsciousness. Bringing these to consciousness allows us to exercise choice where none existed before. This practice can be developed into a powerful tool for the development of the self-awareness required to improve our leadership.

Notes

1 Eagleman, *The Brain*.
2 Eagleman.

PART 2

From theory to action

We have reached an important transition point in our journey. To this point, I have positioned you as the researcher, inquiring deeply into the layers of differential leadership. This has deepened your appreciation of the origins of leadership and how our ancient selves still coexist with our modern selves. I have constructed a framework that will serve us well. Now it is time to move from theory-building into action. I want to use this newfound knowledge to help you develop yourself. To do so, I will progressively work through the matched pairs of inner and outer voices starting with the innermost. And as I do so, we can investigate the implications for our modern leadership challenges.

As befits this transition, from this point forward I will end each chapter with "Leadership Development Actions" in addition to "Takeaways". The acquisition of theoretical knowledge is essential for leadership development but is never enough on its own. To develop your leadership, you must *do* something. And the thing that you do must be different to what you would have done otherwise. The purpose of the "Leadership Development Actions" is to give you suggestions of how to put the theory into action.

Primeval shadow hijacks heartfelt voice

Primeval shadow

"Punch him!" is one of the manifestations of an inner voice called the *primeval shadow*, one which is toxic to your heartfelt voice. As the name *primeval* implies, this is the innermost and most ancient inner voice. This the inner voice connected to your base instincts. The primeval shadow is driven by urges identified with the innermost layer of brain functioning as identified in Chapter 2. In this case it is the fear, anxiety, and anger system[1] that has been triggered. Self-preservation dominates this voice rather than conscious thought. "But wait", you say. "I live in a modern, civilised society. I don't see any of that behaviour. We left them behind us. We are civilised. We don't employ savages. And besides, if any behaviours like that turned up at work, we have lots of HR rules to care of it".

This is where we confront the difference between inner voice and outer voice. In the previous chapter, we talked about volition, the "gate" that we have that opens to allow some inner voices to translate into action but also closes to prevent others. The volition gate is more than just a convenient metaphor. In a cleverly designed experiment that measured activity in different parts of the brain during conscious action, Libet showed that our *subconscious instinct* to act occurs *before* our *decision* to act.[2] Because of the controversial nature of this finding, the experiment has been repeated many times in original and modified form. The experimental results are unequivocal: actions taken in the experiment, which were considered by participants to be of their "free will", actually originated from their subconscious (and, therefore, were "not of their free will"). This seems in clear contravention of something that is evident to all of us: that our conscious thoughts do affect what we do and that we are in control of what we do. A psychology researcher, Wegner, was perhaps the most vocal in extrapolating the findings concluding that our actions are not caused by our intentions, that free will is an illusion, a trick we play on ourselves.[3] Not surprisingly, this conclusion is hotly contested (for comprehensive rebuttal, see Mele).[4]

Libet himself, suggested a resolution between his experimental results and the preservation of the concept of free will. He extended his original work to test the proposition that the mechanism of control that we exert over our actions is not an act of "free will" but rather an act of "free won't".[5]

We can think of "free won't" as two separate circuits that converge in one area of the brain, which instructs our motor actions (called the pre-SMA). The first circuit is in our subconscious limbic system, and it is here that action is initiated. After the signal has started racing towards the pre-SMA, our conscious cortical processes start. Crucially, there is enough of a delay in message being sent from the subconscious circuit (about one-tenth of a second) for our conscious circuit to veto the action. It is the veto imposed by our conscious thoughts that is the mechanism of applying conscious thought to action. Hence, it is an act of "free won't" rather than "free will". This all happens so rapidly and automatically that we generally don't perceive the steps involved. We just think that we made a decision to act.

The current research evidence for the "free won't" model of brain operation is far from conclusive. I introduce it here because it accords with specific instances of the human experience. In my experience, most people with a high level of self-awareness can relate to circumstances where they consciously interject to override an urge that seem to come from nowhere. It is not necessary for us to evidence that it acts as a universal mechanism of the application of free will. I believe that investigating the way in which it seems to occur for us on occasions can lead to us understanding our thought processes better. In particular, it seems that "free won't" is our method of operation when it comes to the most basic of our motivational urges.

We are using primeval shadow as the metaphor for the subconscious circuits of our brain associated with these basic urges. Sometimes, it is more than a metaphor and will literally occur as an inner voice ("Punch him!" for example). In other cases, it helps us to just think about the subconscious circuits as inner voices because the metaphor can help us understand ourselves better. We have an instinctual and unconscious inner voice centred in the limbic system, home to our emotions, our memories, and our threat-monitoring functions. We can relate to the fact that our instinctual responses are emotionally charged. This inner voice races towards the "free won't" gate. If unchecked at the gate, it will flow directly into our physical and verbal actions. These physical and verbal actions are our outer voice – all the things that others witness about us. Crucially, though, we get enough time to intervene. That is why your inner voice of "Punch him!" never made it through into action. But although you have trained yourself to apply "free won't" to the action, you cannot train away the inner voice itself; it is just too ingrained. It can be raging away in the background while you model perfect civility.

Maybe "Punch him!" doesn't ever happen to you. Before you dismiss the concept of primeval shadow, consider what *does* happen to you. What happens under stressful situations? What raises your blood pressure, has the hairs on the back of your neck stand up, makes you stumble on your words, makes you shut up when you should be saying something? What's going on when you are avoiding that tough conversation? Or when you felt belittled by a colleague? What are your primitive urges that never make it through to the outside world? Only you can answer the question. Every inner voice is as unique as your brain is.

Asking yourself to identify your primeval shadow is tough, tougher than it first appears. The reason it is so tough comes back to the dominance of the unconscious. We have consigned our inner voice to the unconscious. It rattles away in the background, and we pay it no heed. We spent a large portion of our childhood and adolescence subverting it.

"No hitting" our mother said when we were throwing a tantrum at three.

"Play nicely" said our kindergarten teacher at four.

"Share" said our father at five.

"Don't be mean" said our friends at ten.

"Conform to the group", we told ourselves at fifteen.

A lifetime of subverting our primeval shadow builds the hardwiring in our brain to do so efficiently. We have better things to do with our thinking than be constantly using it on such a repetitive task. Better to consign it to being automatic.

But this efficiency comes at a cost. For a start, it actually doesn't do a very good job. Yes, it triggers your "free won't" to prevent you turning into a savage. But volition is a higher-level brain function. You shut the gate on the urge, but you have not stopped the urge itself flourishing at the lower level. Most of the time this is not a problem. You block the action, and the urge just peters away. But sooner or later a situation arises that supercharges the primeval shadow. You go into a state of extreme internal conflict between urge and volition. This effort shuts down your higher-level brain functioning. You literally can't think. This is why we can always think *afterwards* of what we *should* have said instead of what we did or did not say at the time.

The impacts of the internal conflict are not just cognitive. The neurochemicals released run riot with your physical reactions. Your nervous system triggers the release of adrenalin from certain neurons and also from tiny glands sitting on top of your kidneys. When we talk about a "rush of blood", it is not just a metaphor: your heart rate and blood pressure go up. Muscles tense, hairs stand on end, and we start to shake. This all happens while we (usually) maintain our professional demeanour and socially acceptable behaviours.

The weird thing is that such primitive urges get triggered despite most of us living without the threat of violence, with plenty of food, and a good house to go home to. What is going on? How can all of this be going on unconsciously?

The other problem with consigning the blocking of inner voice to automatic is that it leaves us with no choice. This is hugely significant to leadership development. The very definition of automatic and unconscious is that we are not choosing anything. Our brain is doing stuff beneath our level of consciousness, and choice clearly requires conscious thought. Don't mistake automatic volition for choice. Not hitting someone when your inner voice screams "Punch him!" is a not choice. It is automatic. And where there is no choice, there is no path to development.

Because of the "Punch him!" way that we have introduced ourselves to primeval shadow, you may at this stage be thinking that the concept would be useful only if you are a "hot head". This is not the case. Your primeval shadow is significant no matter what form it takes as we will go on to discover. But we also need to consider that most of us work with at least one hot head. All of us at one stage or another have triggered an outburst that has left us wondering, "What the hell just happened there?" The study of leadership is inherently a study of followership (no, that's not a typo). If we are to become exceptional leaders, we need to become students of our followers. Understanding what is going on with our hot heads is critical to leadership. It turns out that the hot heads in our teams are extremely useful. When a hot head explodes at you in a meeting, for example, you can be pretty sure that you have triggered a primeval shadow in others at the table as well. They might be sitting there in dignified silence or tut-tutting the hot head, but inside they could be seething. Understanding what you trigger in followers is critical to leadership. Be thankful for hot heads. But be even more thankful for starting to understand the inner voices that you trigger in others.

So, if "hot head" is one version of primeval shadow, what are others? The opposite end of the spectrum from fight is flight. For some, this is harder to admit to. The urge to project a tough persona can be very strong. "I never run away from a fight", we say. "I stand up for myself". But do we really?

For some the answer is yes. They consistently respond in fight mode like our hot head earlier. They can then use "I never run away from a fight" as justification for what can be appalling behaviour. It is as if "I never run away from a fight" is something so noble that it trumps everything else. It is used as a rationalisation, a mechanism to combat behaviour in themselves that they would find deplorable in others. We are driven to rationalise the conflicting information, grasping at the improbable if necessary. For an extreme hot head this might be the conflict between their view of themselves as a "good" person and the impact of the actions when acting as a hot head. Their brains are confronted with a massive conflict. A good person does not shout at people, permanently damage relationships, and derail worthy projects. "I never run away from a fight" becomes the resolution – the rationalisation to resolve the internal conflict. "I never run away from a fight" is the rallying cry that sustains a consistent view of the world. Family relationships perish, marriages fail, kids never call, friends move on, and careers stagnate, but "I never run away from a fight".

But what if we do run away from a fight? How can I be a good person but run away from fights? To rationalise this, some people unconsciously ignore the implications of running from a fight. This becomes a strong driver to keep inner voice in the unconscious. Why would we want to make our primeval shadow conscious if it means confronting our cowardice?

If we think about the problem from an evolutionary perspective, though, a "flight" reaction makes sense. Reproductive fitness is far better served by flight than fight. Recall that our pre-cog ancestors resided in the middle of the food chain. An unarmed human is a reasonably easy kill for a pack of jackals. If you have the option, it is far better to run and climb a tree than to try and fight. Flight reactions are common in other mid-tier animals. Attack a wild boar, and it will run; corner it, and it will tear you apart.

We are conditioned to respond to physical threats by running, and we experience a similar response to psychological threats. In the presence of a threat – whether physical or nonphysical – our bodies are flooded with adrenalin, which triggers a fight-or-flight response. It might seem strange that a nonphysical threat would trigger a physical response, but for evidence, we need go no further than the lie detector. The accuracy of the method for detecting lies is dubious, but there is no doubt that it detects a physical response purely to the posing of a question. The lie detector serves as proof that we respond physically to the nonphysical.

We have gotten so used to these physical responses that we don't even think about why they happen in response to nonphysical threats. Of course you sweat profusely before that interview, or clench your fists when someone makes a jibe at you. But a robot with advanced artificial intelligence observing us would find it very curious – our bodies get ready for physical action when no action is called for. Worse than being useless, this is actually counterproductive. Situations that require us to be at our best mentally are hijacked by a physical response.

Our magnificent brains are a marvellous collection of random mutations that enhanced our ability to survive in the world we lived in fifty thousand years ago. Most of these mutations occurred extremely slowly, over many thousands of years. But when nonphysical interactions started to enhance our reproductive fitness, we hijacked the parts of the brain that were used for physical functioning and dual-purposed them.[6] This was a much faster process than building new parts of the brain from scratch and had the advantage of letting humans quickly adapt their skillset to suit nonphysical interactions. Our original responses to physical stimuli weren't completely demolished and rebuilt into something new; they were plastered over the top of. Sometimes, when things get really stressful, we can see the old responses peeking through the cracks in the plaster.

The theory of a dual-purposed brain is supported by our relatively new ability to conduct sophisticated brain scans. In a simple but brilliant experiment by Eisenberger and Lieberman, participants played a game of "catch" on a computer. They controlled an avatar on the computer screen and directed it to throw a ball to one of two other avatars. The participant believed these avatars were controlled by participants sitting in other rooms. In fact, these avatars were controlled by the computer. Initially the computer "played fair", throwing the ball equally to each of the three avatars. But gradually the computer began to exclude the participant from the game and threw the ball only between the two computerised avatars. By programming the computer to exclude the participants, the researchers triggered social pain in the participants. The participants played the game while lying down in a brain scanner (a functional magnetic resonance imaging, or fMRI machine). The resultant images showed that the area of the anterior cingulate cortex (ACC) that was activated by social pain overlapped with the same area activated by physical pain.[7] Social pain and physical pain share the same system of operation.

Our primeval shadow is a result of this oddity of our evolution. Our instincts were honed through evolution to protect us from physical pain. Over time, social functioning became increasingly important in the reproductive fitness of our species. This accelerated markedly during the cognitive revolution. At some point, random mutations in the brains of our ancestors occurred that enabled them to use the physical pain system for social pain. The benefits of this to the species were such that this was rapidly reinforced in subsequent generations. This is the source of our primeval shadow – the connection to our instincts honed in the ancient world. It comes with a baggage as we have discussed earlier, but we need to remember that it has enabled our species to thrive and still continues to serve us well today.

There is more to the primeval shadow than fight or flight. In chapter two, we identified four other systems at play. They were

the sexual desire system,
the grief and distress system,
the seeking pleasure and play system, and
the care and nurturing system.[8]

We do not need to dwell on the obvious. At work, the sexual desire primeval shadow should never make it through the volition gate and manifest itself in our outer voice!

The grief and distress primeval shadow has implications beyond the obvious. We can grieve over more things than just the loss of a loved one. Grief is often triggered by loss of status, either real or perceived. We can become distressed when we lose certainty over our future. This primeval shadow is often triggered in us by change. If we allow it to affect our outer voice, it will disempower our leadership.

Our seeking pleasure and play primeval shadow can be either a positive or negative. If it helps us to imbue our work with a sense of fun, then that is positive. If the fun crosses the line and starts to affect our discipline, or work becomes about monetary rewards to fund our hedonism, then our leadership suffers.

Surprisingly, the care and nurturing primeval shadow can also negatively affect our outer voice. Most of us can recall a time in our career when our care for an individual stopped us doing the "right" thing. Performance conversations are difficult enough, but when they involve a friend, this primeval shadow is not helpful. A care-based primeval shadow might also have us try to protect the structure of our team when the business is best served by a restructure.

In most cases, however, the care and nurturing system serves us well. We want to take this instinct and combine it with our conscious system to create the outer voice, which is the foundation of all the outer voices – the heartfelt voice.

Your heartfelt voice operating across an inner circle of five or six people was the foundation of your leadership style with the pre-cogs. Your pre-cogs were not mindless savages. Yes, they were less intelligent and displayed a higher propensity for violence, but they also displayed empathy and love. They connected deeply with their inner circle and constantly sought the affection of the other members. Later we observed the inner circle dynamics with our friends at the pub and concluded that this pre-cog behaviour was still alive and well in the modern world.

This evidence that pre-cogs were wired for relationships rounds out our understanding of the primeval shadow. As well as being the inner voice of self-preservation and aggression against (mainly nonphysical) threats, it is the voice of belonging, of connection, of acceptance, and of feeling safe. It is the voice that is constantly scanning our environment, evaluating whether it is safe. It is the voice that is testing interactions with others, constantly evaluating and reevaluating relationships: "What does he think of me?" "I don't think she likes me", "She's jealous of me", and "I'm not a part of this group".

The primeval shadow has an impact on our behaviour. We want to be accepted and respected. We want to be able to say things that we are thinking without having to be on our guard. This aspect of human behaviour is incredibly important to leadership. When our primeval shadow is focussed on the warmth of relationships with the rest of our team, high effectiveness follows. We "lower our guard" and interact authentically. We can raise the thorny issues that otherwise would be subverted. We feel supported and important. Our opinions are valued. We can express our fears and seek support. Above all we feel part of something, something worthwhile and important. This is called psychological safety.

The role of psychological safety in high-performing teams has been well established.[9] When people feel safe they will speak up and add their contribution to the task. Knowledge sharing is dramatically increased, and stronger mutual support is created. People are more likely to take personal risks and put themselves "out there". It is an absolute requirement for high performance from a team. Therefore, the ability to intentionally create a psychologically safe work environment is central to leadership.

Hijacking the heartfelt voice

The heartfelt outer voice is the most fundamental of all leadership capabilities in our differential voice framework. This is because our heartfelt voice creates an environment of psychological safety. Furthermore, we have directly related a person's psychological safety to the corresponding inner voice, their primeval shadow. It is time to update our diagram to reflect our newfound insights.

Recall that the diagram represents leadership as a structure. Without a heartfelt voice, there can be no command voice. Take away the heartfelt voice, and command voice topples; take away the prosocial voice, and futurizing voice crashes down with it. This is the fate that befell Australian

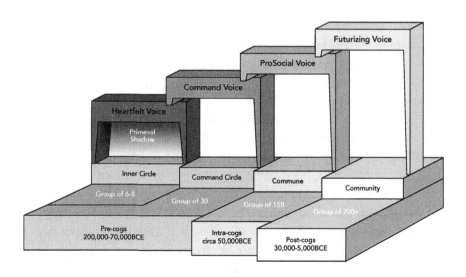

Figure 9.1 Primeval shadow inner voice

Prime Minister Bob Hawke in his attempts to eliminate child poverty. Take away your peoples' psychological safety, and you have no foundation for high performance. They are, quite literally, frightened. They often won't express it, or even know it (remember that most of this is unconscious), but they will be operating on a basis of fear. High performance is simply not possible when operating from fear. As a leader, if your followers' primeval shadow voices are in defensive mode, they will not work effectively. The default position of your primeval shadow is defensive, and it takes active work to shift your position to one of safety.

In our framework, self-awareness is the full understanding of our inner voices. It is your own primeval shadow that is toxic to your heartfelt voice. It is not enough to intellectually understand the concept of primeval shadow and its relationship to psychological safety, because your heartfelt voice comes from your heart, not from logic.

"Punch him!" shouted your inner voice at your imbecile of a boss. It doesn't matter how deeply you understand heartfelt voice, your primeval shadow is overpowering everything with this reaction. Or perhaps your reaction was "Shut down. Don't say anything". There is no room for heartfelt voice here, either. "I don't trust him", "He's out to get me", "Don't mention that thorny issue", and "He thinks I'm an idiot" are all primeval shadows perfectly designed to torpedo your heartfelt voice or, worse, to facilitate an escalation in your "fight" response/reaction.

The primary mode of our primitive brain is defence. Our pre-cogs were an animal of no particular significance, protecting themselves in a hostile world. Being armed for fight or flight was an evolutionary advantage; the ones that weren't so well armed met a sticky end. So, given we use the same hardware of our innermost brain for nonphysical threats as for real threats, it follows that our primeval shadow is defensive.

How does your primeval shadow respond when a stranger approaches you and starts a conversation, even in a perfectly safe environment? Our primeval shadow is wary. It expects the worst until it gets better evidence. Over the years, we have developed strategies to manage these defensive impulses. If we want to approach a stranger, we employ nonthreatening body language before we even get within earshot to signal good intentions. For instance, we often try to telegraph our purpose. When you want a stranger to take a photo of you for your holiday scrapbook, you walk forward with your camera outstretched. You want to let the person know that you are not a threat.

And so it is with your imbecile boss. As you prepare for the crucial meeting, the anticipation of a threat starts to build. Even though you know the threat will not be physical, it is very real to your primeval shadow. After all, your boss has real power over you. Your future prospects are affected by his opinion of you. When you start to allow yourself to imagine all the possible negative outcomes to the meeting, you signal to your primeval shadow that it needs to be on high alert.

Check out the way he glanced at the clock. He's already planning how to get me out of here early.
He's not making eye contact.
Now he's smirking!
There it is. He disagreed with that point. I knew he had an agenda, and now I have proof.
Punch him!

Your primeval shadow is on such high alert that it is picking up false signals, and it picks up pace and intensity. This can all happen in the short span of time it takes for you to walk into the room and greet your boss. You might think you are smiling, nodding, and covering it up well, but are you?

Consciously or unconsciously, your boss has probably picked up your negative attitude. His primeval shadow has been triggered.

She's looking anxious. Something is up.
I know what's coming here! Yet another attempt to send us off on a tangent.
Why can't she stick to the program? If she keeps wandering off like this, we're going to miss every milestone. Man, I'm in deep trouble with my boss when she screws up again.
Let's nip this in the bud, and try to get her back on track . . . again!

The meeting really is over before it starts. The script has been written, and now the actors take their roles. His condescending dismissal of your plan twenty minutes later, followed by your primeval scream of "Punch him!" might appear to come from nowhere, but it's just a line in the final act of the script.

When you leave the room, your primeval shadow is in full song. It is still in fight mode hours and days later, reliving the battle.

When he said X, I should have said Y. That would have wiped the smarmy look off his face. That would have knocked him onto the ropes.

You know it is futile, but you can't stop. Once triggered, a primeval shadow is hard to shut down. Telling yourself to move on doesn't help. Your primeval shadow is still going strong two weeks later as you sit down to apply for that job you found at a rival firm.

Because the default mode for primeval shadow is defensive, we are highly attuned to the signals coming from others. We "pick up the vibes" from others via thousands of minute signals. We forget that in the process of picking up the vibes, we are unconsciously sending our own. These silent, unconscious "conversations" are problematic. Firstly, we can overestimate our abilities in picking up vibes. We are on high alert in defensive mode; we are expecting the situation to be bad. We jump at shadows. Unwitting or unrelated signals are picked up and interpreted incorrectly. The primeval shadow carries no burden of proof. It just gets to run rampant.

Secondly, the defensive mode becomes self-fulfilling. As we start to become defensive, we signal it to others. We think that we have our demeanour under control. We have a lifetime of practice at projecting a mask to the world that presents an untrue version of our self. And we falsely believe that we are good at creating these masks. But we also know that other people create masks of their own, and we think that we become experts at identifying the hidden signals. As we pick something negative in another person's demeanour and react to it, the other party senses our reaction. Their response is to become defensive, of course, and in doing so they send more signals back to us. And so it goes, back and forth in a downward spiral of negative interpretation.

Changing the dynamics of primeval shadow interplay is key to providing the psychological safety that enables high performance. This is the first component of the heartfelt voice. Our heartfelt voice needs to be able to turn down the volume of our primeval shadow. This changes the tone of our interactions with our team from defensive, to neutral, and finally to empathetic, accepting, warm, and open.

Turning down the volume on the primeval shadow

Let's continue this hypothetical encounter with your boss to see how dealing with the primeval shadow would lead to a very different outcome. We will first summarise each of the major components of the heartfelt voice (see *Evolved Organizations* for a fuller explanation) and then see how this would play out.

The first capability of the heartfelt voice is ***unconditional positive regard***. As we have seen, the primeval shadow is defensive by nature due to our evolutionary wiring. Unconditional positive regard is the antidote to this unbalanced view that breaks the spiral of negative interpretations. It is the application of positive energy to generate a positive predisposition towards others" to believe that they have the best of intentions, to see the good in what they do and to believe in their potential.

With respect to your boss, you can start to see that calling him an "imbecile" is part of the problem. When you hold on to those kinds of names, you are doomed to repeat the cycle. At this stage, your primeval shadow has gone so far into defensiveness that it is in fight mode. Your inner voice is ready to attack as you prepare for the meeting, as you walk through the door, and as you exchange pleasantries. And, far from keeping it hidden, you are firing out all sorts of signals for your boss's unconscious to pick up on.

Generating unconditional positive regard for your boss is the first step in remedying the situation. Note that the change starts with changing yourself. There is a logic here that people on a leadership development journey eventually (sometimes begrudgingly) accept. The only psyche that you have direct access to is your own. You can influence others to change, but in the end the choice is theirs and theirs alone. Conversely, you have the power to exercise choice over changing yourself. Get used to this pattern. Exceptional leadership starts with the self. Generating unconditional positive regard towards your boss has the potential to transform your meeting.

Check out the way he glanced at the clock, he is already planning how to get me out of here early.

He glanced at the clock. I notice he does that a lot. Must be a habit.

He's not making eye contact. He's off with the fairies.	*He' not making eye contact. Could mean he's still thinking about his last meeting. I'll pause and check in that he's with me. . . . He is with me. Oh good.*
Now he's smirking!	*Little smile there. That's positive.*
There it is. He disagreed with that point. I knew he was out to get me, and now I have proof.	*He disagreed with me. That's interesting. I've got him really engaged in this but need to understand his position better. Get him talking about his concerns, so I understand them better. That will allow me to circle back later from a different angle.*

You are choosing to have unconditional positive regard toward your boss, and it has moved your primeval shadow to a neutral or positive position. You are now seeing the meeting from a completely different place, one that is much more likely to yield results. The entire nature of the meeting has changed. Having identified your primeval shadow and its negative default mode has given you choice at critical junctures in the meeting. You can choose the positive interpretation of what you see and hear, rather than letting your primeval shadow lead you back to the negative script. This opens the door to your heartfelt voice just a crack. There is still a way to go before it is flourishing, but without primeval shadow undermining your heartfelt voice at every turn, we have made a start.

> *But if I go into the meeting with a positive regard and my boss turns up in attack mode, I'm done for. He'll win.*

Listen to yourself. Who exactly wins a battle of negative primeval shadows? No one wins, but there is certainly a loser. It's a blip on your boss's radar, but a catastrophic plane crash for your project (and probably your career). Ask yourself "What does winning the big game actually look like?"

> *That's alright in theory. If I went in like that to my boss, it would be like turning up to a knife fight with a bunch of flowers.*

One of the things that people worry about when it comes to unconditional positive regards is how vulnerable they feel. We are not used to lowering our guard. It feels profoundly uncomfortable. This goes back to the shared mechanism in the brain with the physical threat system. Feeling uncomfortable when your guard is down is a pretty good survival trait in the ancient world. In our modern world, it makes no sense. Practicing positive regard is an effort at first. You have taken something from the unconscious and started to change it. Your unconscious drivers keep trying to kick in. Your inner voice keeps wanting to butt in with "threat – armour up".

After a time it becomes easier because you are rewriting the rules. Your unconscious is saying that you need to armour up, but you hold this impulse at bay and nothing bad happens. You don't get eaten. After a while you "prove" to yourself that nothing bad happens and the impulse lessens. Your brain has learned a new pattern. You then start to commit it to your unconscious. You find yourself walking out of a meeting saying, "I just held unconditional positive regard for that meeting without even thinking about it. It used to be so hard!" Your heartfelt voice has been released, and your leadership just took a huge step forward.

In moving to unconditional positive regard for your boss, you exercised *choice*, the second major capability of the heartfelt voice. You identified your primeval shadow reactions but chose to take a different interpretation. It was the act of exercising choice that gave you power in the situation. We could say that by exercising choice, you moved from being a victim of the circumstances to being empowered.

As a victim, you had no power to change the situation. The circumstances drove the outcomes. The script was written by the circumstances, and you were swept along. You exercised your choice in a number of subtle ways. The catalysing choice was to be conscious of your primeval shadow. Having your primeval shadow run the show is a natural human condition. When we say it runs the show, we are not blindly following it. We have to constantly exercise our volition to override the impulses of our primeval shadow. If we didn't we would end up in jail. But we allow it to shape the way that we interpret the world. In doing so, we give over an element of control to our unconscious.

Identifying your primeval shadow is pivotal, because it gives you choice over your interpretations. Unconditional positive regard is a choice. You are choosing a new set of interpretations over the ones shaped by your primeval shadow. In the improved exchange with your boss, you chose to interpret signals as positive or at least as neutral, which gave you power in the situation. When you were operating from the interpretation of "he's out to get me", you were helpless – a flailing victim being inescapably sucked into the vortex of circumstances over which you had no control. When you turned that into "he disagreed with me, therefore, he is really engaged", you shrugged off the disabling interpretation driven by your primeval shadow and took on a set of interpretations that transcended the circumstances. You had power in the ensuing conversation to attack the issue from a different angle and deliver the result that you were so passionate about.

When we position ourselves as responsible, it opens the door for us to consider changing something very difficult: ourselves. Consider your two exchanges with your boss.

There it is. He disagreed with that point. I knew he was out to get me, and now I have proof.	*He disagreed with me. That's interesting. I've got him really engaged in this but need to understand his position better. Get him talking about his concerns, so I understand them better. That will allow me to circle back later from a different angle.*

The helpless victim inhabits the left side. You believe that your boss is out to get you, and there is nothing you can do about it. Because of this, you make only a couple of feeble attempts at changing his mind. But because you are coming from an "he's out to get me" perspective, your attempts are one-dimensional and weak.

In the right-hand conversation you take responsibility for the good stuff – "He's really engaged in this"; and also for the fact that you failed to enrol him. Because you are coming from the perspective of "I caused this" rather than from the perspective of "he's out to get me", you have access to action. You resist the primeval urge to put the blame on your boss. It is this choice that keeps you responsible, refusing to be the victim of the circumstances. You are now left with the ability to start inquiring; seeking to understand the key beliefs that underpin your boss's disagreement.

In the larger context, leadership is all about choice. In the absence of leadership, the circumstances are driving the show. Leadership is making the choice to intervene in the system and make something else happen.

What we have distinguished in the preceding section is that this choice is based on another choice: how you choose to relate to the circumstances. If you relate to forces in your organisation as irresistible or obstacles as unmovable, you have chosen to be the victim. You can choose to relate to them differently. And in this choice, your leadership emerges.

Unconditional positive regard and the ability to choose your relationship to the circumstances underpin the third major capability of the heartfelt voice: ***integral listening***.

When you were leading your team of pre-cogs back on the Eurostar tracks, it was a very odd experience. They looked normal, and when you were distracted, you would often fall into the trap of trying to interact with them normally. But they were not "normal". They just did not have the intelligence of a modern human. It made you reflect on how seamless and automatic it was for you to range between the multiple cognitive levels of your brain. As their leader, it was easy to start talking to them in heartfelt voice, but without even noticing you would throw in a bit of futurizing or prosocial voice. You would occasionally find yourself trying to strike up a conversation with them about someone else in tribe or speculating about what the weather would be like next week only to be confronted again by blank faces. They were just too dumb.

But there was one thing that they did that far outstripped the abilities of any modern human. When you had their attention, you really had their attention. They listened to you like there was nothing else in the world going on. They hung on your every word and revelled in your every touch. They never got bored with you or tired of interacting with you. You could say the same thing over and over and over again, and they listened as intently the twentieth time as they did the first. When you had their attention, you were the most important thing in the world to them.

You could see in your pre-cogs how one-to-one relationships were everything. It required their full attention. It defined their place in the world. You could connect this behaviour to the behaviour that we can still see today in chimpanzees where they spend hours grooming each other. Your pre-cogs were practicing a sophisticated version of grooming based on language.

As their leader, it took enormous concentration to maintain this focus. Your leadership was based on maintaining the one-to-one relationships, and you had no choice but knuckle down to some serious one-to-one conversations. If you lost this focus, the relationships started to weaken. You would start to see breakdowns in your inner circle, tribe cohesion started to weaken, and new leadership aspirants started to emerge. You learned to catch this early and refocus yourself on reestablishing the relationships that you had lost.

Even with this insight, you still found yourself wandering off in conversations. There was so much more to think about than the minutiae of the relationship with a single individual. But not for your pre-cogs. Their world was very small. For a start, they spent their entire lives interacting only with their tribe of thirty-odd individuals. There was virtually no interaction with individuals in other tribes. They had no language or inclination to gossip about others, and they didn't think about the future. It was not so surprising, then, that they could focus so intently on the here-and-now conversations with another individual.

Let us think about how this changed during through the cognitive revolution. Each increment in brain capability brought so much more to think about. Intra-cogs lived in communes five times larger than pre-cog tribes. They also traded, socialised, and fought with other communes, giving them much more to think about. The transition to post-cogs brought not only larger communities but also stories, myths, legends, and gods to think about.

We can postulate that the inner voice of a pre-cog would have been pretty simple – the primeval shadow revelling in physical needs, love, and affection while being on the lookout for physical and social danger. Each higher layer of brain functionality during the cognitive revolution introduced new and more complex inner voices. These didn't replace the primeval shadow; they were layered on top. By the time we get to post-cogs, their inner voice is stampeding in all different directions. It is no wonder that pre-cogs were such good listeners, and why we, the information age post-cogs, are so terrible at it.

The pre-cog need to be intensely listened to remains with us today. For pre-cogs, it was life or death. It remains with us today as a strong psychological need. It is at the heart of psychological safety. For leaders, therefore, it is a central tenet of the heartfelt voice.

It was Rogers[10] who coined the term "active listening", the act of focussing our entire attention on the conversation that we are having. The role of primeval shadow and the other inner voices in sabotaging this capability is obvious. Our lack of attention is manifest in our inner voice. We skilfully carry on a conversation with the other person, but our attention is on the conversation we having with ourselves.

As an active listener, you focus your inner voice on the conversation you are having with the other person. You have your total focus in the conversation; paying attention, monitoring and continuously refocussing, providing feedback, paraphrasing and replaying to the speaker what they said, listening without judgement, using open questions, and listening for possibilities. In short, you are focussing all of your attention, including your inner voice, on the conversation. You are listening for *everything* that is said.

Fulfilling this long list of requirements might seem like an ultimate state of listening. It would certainly make you exceptional as a leader. Integral listening goes even further. When you master integral listening, you not only hear *everything that is said*, you also hear *everything that is unsaid*.

More often than not, there is more to be learned from the things that normally go unsaid than from what is said. There can be layer upon layer of shrouding that obscures the issue or the opportunity. Only through integral listening can you get to them. Integral listening is the purest form of inquiry, totally devoid of bias, judgement, and personal position. Operating from this place inevitably reveals the speakers values, beliefs, and worldview. The speaker finds themselves digging far deeper into the topic than they even planned for, often revealing a hidden truth for them. This is a powerful tool for change.

The obvious question, then, is how do you crank up from active listening to integral listening to tackle the unsaid. Again, we examine inner voice for understanding. We translated active listening into our differential voice language by observing that active listening results in total focus of inner voice on the task of listening. By "total" we mean total – there is not an extra level of focus above this. Integral listening is not more focus of the inner voice; it is the *total absence of inner voice*.

Inner voice is an almost ubiquitous human experience. In most functional people, it is ever-present. That does not mean that it can't be stopped temporarily. The practice of applying mindfulness in a business setting has expanded rapidly in recent years. Mindfulness borrows techniques from meditation and applies it in a nonspiritual way. Through consistent practice, the aim is to calm the frenzied activity of the brain and to bring one's focus entirely into the present. When in a mindful state, the inner voice is silent or at least heavily subdued. In a similar way, through practice, it is possible to be so "in the moment" of listening that inner voice disappears temporarily.

Having worked hard on active listening we have reigned in our rampant inner voice, which had dozens of ways of impeding our listening. Having done that, our newly focussed inner voice has become our ally. So, why now would we want to now eliminate it?

Rather the answer that question, let us reframe it. The aim of the exercise is not to eliminate your inner voice. The aim of the exercise is to become an integral listener – a world champion at listening. When you achieve that, one of things that you will notice is that your inner voice was not present for the conversation. The mention of "world champion" is appropriate here. We noted in the previous chapter that elite sportspeople go into a state of "flow", where nothing else in the world exists for them except the moment. We seek the equivalent state with our listening. We want to make the transition from

"I am practicing integral listening. I am concentrating hard on listening",

to

"I *am* integral listening. Nothing else exists for me right now except listening".

You will almost certainly have to confront a couple of fears as you as you move towards this goal. The first is a really practical one. One of the things that we generally use our inner voice for is to prepare ourselves for when it is our turn to talk. A conversation between two people has certain social protocols, honed from our very first exchanges with our parents as a baby. One of these is that we are required to take turns. It is like a game of tennis. Someone serves, and from then we take turns on the returns. As we speak we send out a combination of tiny signals as to how long we are going to speak for, giving the other person the cue that it is coming up to their turn. We do this unconsciously. As you become a student of your inner voice during conversations you will become acutely aware of these signals that you previously gave no conscious heed to. You will be doing a great job focussing your inner voice (or even be in flow) when you'll get the signal that your turn is coming. You will promptly lose control over your inner voice because it will jump to preparing for what you are going to say. You will immediately notice how you have lost your listening power. Worse still, your inner voice arrives with all of its biases and pollutes what you had already heard. Your objective is to hear everything that is said; you cannot accept losing that last thirty seconds of every exchange and downgrading the rest.

The impulse to prepare your return is very strong and counteracting it is quite scary. You feel like you are rushing toward the edge of cliff with no brakes – "What if it gets to my turn to talk, and I've got nothing to say? How unprofessional and embarrassing!" Over time, you can train yourself out of this instinct. With every practice just hold your focus for longer and longer. When you finally go "right to the cliff edge" and don't do any inner voice preparation, you will find out something quite bizarre and hugely enlightening. You won't find yourself stranded. You will know what to say. Furthermore, you will find that the quality of what you say will be much better. It must be so, because you listened fully; you listened to everything that was said and didn't pollute it with your inner voice biases. It might be instinctual that we use our inner voice to prepare our returns, but it turns out that it does a pretty poor job.

The other fear is more bizarre. You may experience a fear that by being an integral listener, you are dropping your guard and leaving yourself vulnerable. It is almost as if you are exposed for the other person to take control of your mind. This sounds a bit sci-fi, but it is a consistent experience.

Achieving mastery at integral listening will teach you a lot about yourself. One thing it will teach you is just how many layers of protection you put up around yourself. Every layer of protection is a shield to protect the innermost you. The shield is formed by our experiences of the world – your worldview, your points of view. When it comes to listening, each of the layers acts as a filter. You can imagine each layer as being solid like a shield but with holes of in it of specific shapes, say, hexagons, triangles, and crosses. When we are listening selfishly, we hold up the shield to the incoming flow of information. We accept the information that fits our worldview – the hexagons, triangles, and crosses. We reject anything that doesn't fit our worldview – circles, squares, octagons, and so on.

One way that we experience these shields is through our inner voice. In fact, the two are inseparable. So, when I ask you to reign in your inner voice, I am asking you to drop your shield. I want you to take in *everything*. I want you to take in the circles, the squares, the octagons. I want you to accept, in the moment, information that your inner voice shield would have rejected in a nanosecond. This is the part that can trigger anxiety. After all, who are you without your shields? Dropping your shields can feel like you are giving up yourself – your principles, your values, and your beliefs.

This might sound nonsensical. It should sound nonsensical, because it is. Your self is much stronger than that. You don't need to protect it with shields of inner voices. If you let something in that violates your personal values, it won't stick. If anything, the deep inquiry will centre and strengthen your self. The trouble is that we muddle and confuse our values with our points of view. Integral listen requires that you drop your point of view and are temporarily open to having it changed. If you haven't prop-erly distinguished between your values and your point of view, you feel extremely vulnerable.

The trick here is not to be scared off at the first sign of anxiety. Paradox-ically, the more you push through the anxiety and open yourself up, the stronger your sense of self becomes. You learn to distinguish between your shields (inner voice/worldview/points of view) and your self (values/princi-ples/beliefs). Deep inquiry allows you to examine the finer nuances of your values, deepening your understanding and fully centring your self.

Operating from this stronger sense of Self is very powerful. It creates a reinforcing cycle. Opening yourself up to inquiry strengthens your sense of self. The stronger your sense of self, the more confident you are to open yourself up in inquiry. This acts, in turn, to further strengthen self.

Dropping your inner voice shield to fully engage in inquiry requires that you suspend your point of view. You must be 100 percent open to changing your point of view. This again can cause anxiety. We can be very committed to being right about things. The thing to remember is that being 100 percent open to having your point of view changed is very different from actually changing it. This is because at the same time that you are 100 percent open to changing your mind, you are also 100 percent open to picking your point of view back up again. Integral listening requires that you understand every-thing that is said and everything that is unsaid. It doesn't require you to agree with everything that you hear. If you did that, you would not be much of a leader.

By distinguishing and applying **choice** to your primeval shadow, you are now exceptionally well armed. Applying **unconditional positive regard** and **integral listening** skills will build the relationships that underpin a powerful heartfelt voice. But let's face it – who has the time to invest that level of investment into everyone they deal with at work. This brings us to the final capability of the heartfelt voice – **being ruthless in selecting an inner circle**.

The word *ruthless* would not seem to fit well with the heartfelt voice. Let us be clear that I am not talking about treating people ruthlessly. If you apply the skills we have discussed so far, quite the opposite is true. People will never feel so valued as when you are being an integral listener.

Instead, we are talking about you valuing your limited time as a leader and being very deliberate about where you put effort into building the deep relationships of an inner circle. A thought experiment often helps here. Think about one of your biggest objectives. Define it clearly and succinctly. Now list all the people who have influence over the outcome – all your "stakeholders". For even modest endeavours, this is usually a long list, far too long to endeavour to build inner circle relationships with all of them. You need to focus your relationship building time on just the first few in the line; the ones with the most influence over the results.

Yet again, the primeval shadow can run subterfuge on this. The primeval shadow, being deeply connected to our pre-cog brain, will draw you to "quick win" relationships to quickly establish a coalition. It will lead you to invest in the relationships with those that you are naturally drawn to. These people are friends or potential friends, and you are inclined to allocate more of your relationship-building time to these people.

Allowing your primeval shadow to decide which relationships to invest in as a leader is a poor strategy. Your primeval shadow is loaded with bias and conflicting motives. It is driven by a skewed retrospective of emotional scars of past relationships that has nothing to do with the people you currently work with or to your current challenges.

Exceptional leaders have a knack for apportioning their relationship effort according to their objectives. Along the way, a funny thing happens. Firm friendships often develop with people they were not initially drawn to! Frequently, these relationships are deeper and longer lasting than the apparently "natural" ones. The development and working towards a mutual purpose can build a depth to a relationship beyond what is possible from initial attraction. As a leader, these types of deep relationships are pivotal to exceptional performance.

Takeaways

An inner voice can act to invalidate our outer voice.

In the case of the heartfelt voice, the invalidating inner voice is called the primeval shadow, a remnant of our pre-cog ancestry.

The primeval shadow is associated with the primitive motivations and functions of our brain: the care and nurturing system, the grief and distress system, the fear, anxiety and anger system, the sexual desire system, and the seeking pleasure and play system.

The original purpose of these systems was predominantly physical, but through evolution, they are also triggered in us by social triggers. The primeval shadow can cause us to be on guard and fearful. This psychological stress impedes performance both in leaders and in followers.

The heartfelt voice is the leadership capability of creating a psychologically safe workplace, one where people feel valued and safe.

The heartfelt voice encompasses the capabilities of unconditional positive regard, choice, integral listening, and being ruthless in selecting an inner circle.

Leadership development actions

- Observe the nature of your inner voice in stressful situations. Come to understand the nature of your primeval shadow and how, for you personally, it invalidates your heartfelt voice.
- When you observe your primeval shadow, make a conscious choice not to act on it.
- Act from the perspective of unconditional positive regard for the person that you are dealing with. Deliberately take the most generous perspective that you can.
- Practice integral listing – listening with total focus for everything that is said and everything that is unsaid.
- Be deliberate with the focus of your heartfelt voice. As leader, there is a limited size of inner circle that you can maintain, and deep relationships take time.
- Choose your inner circle based on their contribution to your purpose as a leader, not on who you get on with best.

Notes

1 Azmatullah, *The Coach's Mind Manual*.

2 Libet, "Unconscious Cerebral Initiative and the Role of Conscious Will in Voluntary Action".

3 Wegner, "Précis of the Illusion of Conscious Will".

4 Mele, *Effective Intentions*.

5 Libet, "Do We Have Free Will?"; Obhi and Haggard, "Free Will and Free Won't Motor Activity in the Brain Precedes Our Awareness of the Intention to Move, so How Is It That We Perceive Control?"

6 Williams, Forgas, and Hippel, *The Social Outcast*.

7 Eisenberger and Lieberman, "Why Rejection Hurts".

8 Azmatullah.

9 Edmondson and Lei, "Psychological Safety"; Collins and Smith, "Knowledge Exchange and Combination".

10 Rogers and Farson, "Active Listening".

10 Tribal shadow undermines command voice

Tribal shadow

Remember back on the Eurostar tracks as you "stripped back" your layers of leadership until you hit on a success formula for pre-cogs? You relied heavily on your inner circle; your trusted coalition. But you quickly discovered that to manage a group of thirty pre-cogs required some discipline. Without discipline, your pre-cogs lacked order and direction and were quickly attracted to the latest upstart trying to take your place as leader. You needed to maintain order by exercising your power.

We all still have a pre-cog resident deep within our brains. It didn't go away just because we went through the cognitive revolution. Our brains are much higher functioning than our pre-cog ancestors, but this new functionality is built on top of the same basic building blocks. Evolution can only ever move forward from a current state. It doesn't get to design the ultimate organism for the new environment. Evolution is a process of reinforcing infinitesimally small random changes to an existing organism. It helps us to think about the pre-cog as a starting point (although, the pre-cog itself was the result of evolution from more primitive creatures) with new capability being layered on top. As we witnessed on the Eurostar tracks, however, infinitesimal changes led to large step changes in capability. The likely explanation is that some of these small pieces of new capability were tipping points, which allowed for existing capabilities to be repurposed. This would explain the common system for physical and social pain as discussed last chapter. This has ramifications beyond a simple brain-layering model. We don't have a discrete pre-cog brain beneath a discrete post-cog brain. Our post-cog capabilities are a result of how we use our whole brain, including the repurposed pre-cog capabilities. We don't get to leave our pre-cog brain behind – it is an integral part of us.

The idea that we are always operating, in part, from our pre-cog brain is helpful in explaining behaviour in the modern world. A platoon works in the modern world even though it is illogical that it should be better or worse than a larger or smaller unit. Part of our brain is the bit that kept us alive as a species on the savannah, and in this case, it continues to enhance our performance on the battlefield. We shouldn't therefore think of it as "primitive" or in any other negative way. It is just part of who we are, bringing both positives and negatives, depending on the context that we are placed in. That is why it is so important in leadership. We will seek to understand it through the mechanism of inner voice. This is our ***tribal shadow*** – the other inner voice of our pre-cog brain.

Let us imagine a scenario in the modern world where your tribal shadow might emerge. Say a board member is in town and is having one of those "fireside chats". You've been invited, even though you are three levels down the organisation from the CEO. You are determined to make a good impression. Right on cue, you get the opportunity to turn the conversation to your chosen topic and launch into . . . ***BAM*** . . . Susan from marketing cuts right in on you, and before you know it, you are completely side-lined. You are furious. Furious!!!

We are so used to this type of interplay that we don't see just how bizarre it is. If you applied logic, it would be clear to you that the potential impact of making a good impression with a board member is zero. He's a waffling twat who gets tolerated on the board because he doesn't make waves. Everyone ignores him, especially the CEO. The only way that your interaction with the board member would make even the slightest impact on your career is if you defecated in his sherry glass.

And yet you are furious. Susan is not even a "direct competitor", and yet you are furious. Power plays are important to us, even when they are not particularly significant to our well-being. People can carry a grudge for years over an incident that disempowered them. Establishing our place in the "tribe" is core to our being, even though the tribe doesn't exist in our modern world.

The command voice is the responsible use of leadership power to achieve reliable results and deliver disciplined performance. All the differential voices are a demonstrations of leadership power, but with command voice it is more explicit. It follows that the tribal shadow, the inner voice that is

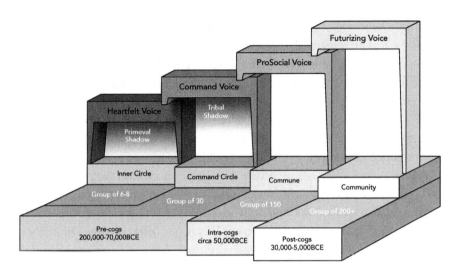

Figure 10.1 Tribal shadow inner voice

triggered by power dynamics, will be significant. Like the primeval shadow, the tribal shadow is usually unconscious or at least triggered by the unconscious. In updating the meta-model diagram, therefore, I have placed it in the shadow beneath the command voice.

We carry our tribal shadow as a consequence of our genetic makeup, as do our bosses, our peers, and our subordinates. It is important to understand this inner voice and the catastrophic impact it can have on your command voice. It occurs differently for different people. Yours is unique to you, but there are some general categories. None of these categories are better or worse than any others. They all have the ability to disempower your command voice or to reinforce it. It is also important to understand the modes that you don't identify with personally. The ability to deduce what is going on in someone else's subconscious is a powerful leadership tool.

As we have already identified, the origins of the tribal shadow lie in our pre-cog tribal past. Tribes work when everyone knows their place in the power structure. A pre-cog tribe on the savannah with a very defined power structure would have been better organised and thus more successful than one where the power structure was unclear. It is easy to see how this tool contributed to enhancing the reproductive fitness of *Homo sapiens* and thus why we still carry the trait today. Let us identify the different roles in a tribe and translate them into the nature of the tribal shadow for different individuals.

Instead of starting with the leader, let's start at the bottom. After all, in the prototypical pre-cog tribe, there are twenty-nine followers for every tribal leader. It is also useful when reflecting on your leadership to also reflect on your followship. Your characteristics as a follower usually play out in some way in your characteristics as a leader.

At the bottom of the power structure is the disengaged follower. For this individual, the tribal shadow speaks of the unfairness of the status quo. It is triggered every time a situation reminds the individual of their lowly station in the tribe. The unfairness could be a result of their own previous attempts at taking power or a general lack of drive. For a disengaged follower, work is often a delicate balancing act between doing as little as possible (because, of course, it is unfair that they have to do all the work when the boss is just swanning around wasting time), and doing just enough to avoid consequences. For the thwarted leadership aspirant, their tribal shadow might have them continually trying to seek power by sneaky means. For example, they will seek to get control of a scarce resource and dole it out in a way that enhances their standing. They will also act to undermine the power of those above them.

It is easy to downplay the role of the disengaged follower. But in a tribe where the power structure is working well, they contribute to the well-being of the tribe. There is work to be done, and given sufficient command, they perform this work. It is not necessary for them to be happy about it. We can see this aspect of the tribal shadow in play in our organisations in the behaviours of the people. The consistent laggard will be watching the clock while arranging her excuses for not achieving the work quota. The sneaky power thief will be putting himself at the centre of a work process such that he has veto power over progress. The underminer will be scheming ways to make their boss look ineffective.

You may have already recognised the characteristics in someone you work with, but what about you? Recognise yourself at all? It's not a pretty thing to confront, but your honesty with yourself will be rewarded. An "it's not fair" mind-set triggered by power dynamics is the tribal shadow sabotaging a command voice. Coming as it does from the disengaged follower in us, it is a disempowering or oppositional voice. Neither is helpful. The ability to identify it and choose to act from a different place can transform our command voice.

It almost goes without saying that in every disengaged follower is the potential for a turnaround. Being disengaged is not a natural state. It is often the case that while disengaged at work, they will be highly engaged in another sphere of their life. As leaders we should consider the disengaged follower as untapped potential.

Next, we move on to an empowered follower. Here the tribal shadow is positive. These are the people who deeply connect their identity with the tribe and respond accordingly. They are not burdened by their own expectations of being a leader. In fact, they are empowered by knowing their place, understanding the expectations, and delivering their part of the purpose of the tribe. In the modern world, these people are gold. You could do with a whole team of these people. However, there is a downside to this tribal shadow. When it comes time for change, the gold turns to mud. With so much of an empowered follower's identity wrapped up in their place in the tribe, any suggestion of change to the tribe is very confronting. The tribal shadow triggers fear, and the engaged follower falters and falls. This is when we get reactions that are "out of character". We should be saying that they are entirely within character. Understanding this dynamic will make you a better leader of change.

The last follower we will examine is the leadership aspirant. For our pre-cogs, tribes were in constant flux. Lifespans were short, and leaders grew old quickly, predators took their toll, and accidents that we would shrug off today were fatal. A leadership vacuum could form at any time, leading to adverse results through disorganisation. Reproductive fitness was enhanced by always having a line-up of aspirants for leadership positions. Furthermore, because of unpredictability in attrition rates, it was better to have more aspirants than positions! A leadership aspirant in a pre-cog tribe was always looking to get ahead in the social pecking order. Ultimately, this would culminate in a challenge, but this was only a small part of the picture. Remember that leadership did not go to the most physically powerful pre-cog but to the one with a strong command voice and the strongest inner circle. Strength of coalitions was the winning formula. So, the behaviour that we are interested in was not associated with the challenge – it was about the tactics to gain favour. A leadership aspirant would either work from outside the leader's inner circle or from within. Working from outside meant building an alternate coalition to rival the leader's inner circle. This meant building relationships with other powerful members of the tribe and trying to win over individuals from the leader's inner circle one by one. When the power shift was sufficient, the challenge would come. Alternatively, an aspirant could work their way into the inner circle by ingratiation or fulfilling a vital role for the leader. They would then start to undermine the leader and win over the inner circle. Along the way, the aspirant will be constantly looking to subvert and disempower the other leadership aspirants.

Today, we see this tribal shadow at work in similar ways. If your tribal shadow takes on the form of a leadership aspirant, then it will be constantly scheming to build power. It will seek to win favour with others who are higher in the power structure, and it will seek to invalidate rivals. In doing so, it will sometimes do things that defy logic. It is this very illogicality that is the reason why a tribal shadow impacts negatively on your command voice. This tribal shadow hijacks your purpose as a leader. For example, you find yourself doing things to invalidate rivals when they could be allies. You display a lack of generosity when others succeed. In fact, you are just downright jealous and start scheming their downfall, all while their achievements are helping you achieve your goals! You should be pumping them up, not bringing them down. No modern organisation thrives from these types of tribal behaviours, and you fail to thrive accordingly. The trouble is that sometimes it can feel like success. We tend to assess our success by comparing ourselves to our peers, rather than in absolute terms. Rapidly climbing a power structure can feel good, even when the ship is sinking.

One particularly nasty manifestation of this inner voice is the tribal shadow manipulator. This is a person who instinctively understands and encourages tribal behaviours in their team. They effectively bring the tribal behaviour out of the shadows and encourage it. This leader will continually exonerate and build up their own team at the expense of other teams that they are supposed to be working with. "We're a great team. We could be even better and deliver even more if it wasn't for those incompetent people in engineering". The more that other teams are invalidated, the better. These leaders build a very strong social connection within the team. This spreads the poison as members of the team follow suit and start to bag the other teams. If you wonder why this behaviour is tolerated by senior management, you don't have to look very far. These leaders often deliver good results within their area. Our tribal tendencies are still very strong, and a leader playing on them can build localised high performance. Where they don't deliver, they are very clever at pointing out how it's another team's fault. Thus, the leader can end up being admired as a high performer who "runs a tight ship" while "saying it as it is". But the impact of the transmitted negativity on the overall organisation can be catastrophic. This behaviour needs to be weeded out of organisations, not encouraged. An exceptional leader takes a collection of tribes and turns them into a commune. This is one of the functions of the prosocial voice, which we will cover in the next chapter.

Having switched from the tribal shadow in followers to one aspect of leadership, let us categorise the tribal shadow more broadly. We will think about this as a continuum and approach it from opposite extremes. At one extreme is the bully. This is a leftover pre-cog behaviour that, personally, I would rather that we had left behind. Humanity's progress and violence are intimately linked, whether or not we like it. All other things being equal, the tribe that wins out in violent conflict will succeed. Also, given that pre-cog leadership included physical interactions, a certain level of bullying to keep everyone in their place actually enhanced tribe functionality. The propensity for violence prevails today in a proportion of the population. The connection between our physical and emotional brain processes means that it plays out in nonphysical ways as well. Although we rightfully focus on eliminating bullying from our workplaces, bullies are getting smarter in the way they go about it. The tribal shadow for a bully says, "I have power over you – attack". There is pleasure in inflicting pain on others. It is massively disabling to their command voice, a huge burden on organisations, and leaves a trail of broken lives behind. Like all manifestations of the tribal shadow, the bullying voice can be controlled (which we will discuss shortly). But it can only be addressed if identified. The shame associated with exposing our bullying (if it exists) means that it is often heavily obscured within the unconscious. However, breaking out of the shadows and bringing it into the light can be enormously empowering and life changing. After all, there should be no shame in having the impulse to bully – we don't get a choice in that. The true shame is in continuing to fool yourself or consciously choosing to act on the bullying impulse.

At the other extreme of the tribal shadow lies the reluctant leader. Where the bully is hungry for power to use as a weapon, the reluctant leader sits uncomfortably with power. You might think that this book is for people that are into leadership, not those who are reluctant – they wouldn't be reading it. Let's remind ourselves, however, that it is our inner voice that we are talking about. It is perfectly normal for an outwardly confident and ambitious leader to have a reluctant leader tribal shadow. For that person, naming the tribal shadow and dealing with it can be transformational to their command voice. And for the rest of us, it can explain otherwise puzzling behaviours in others and give us access to coaching approaches.

The tribes of our pre-cog forebears functioned better when the members knew their place and got along with the other members. This led to greater cooperation, which enhanced reproductive fitness. It is not surprising then that the "fitting in" trait has endured. As a specific example, most of us are susceptible to the so called "bystander effect". The study of this phenomenon was precipitated by the horrifying murder of Kitty Genovese who was stabbed to death outside her apartment in Queens, New York, in 1964. Newspapers at the time reported that thirty-eight separate individuals witnessed the prolonged attack, none of whom intervened or called the police. Subsequent investigations have questioned the accuracy of this report, but there is no doubt that at least some of these people could have taken action but chose not to.

Regardless of whether the reports at the time were exaggerated, they were certainly successful in launching a new line of psychology experiments. Many such experiments were undertaken to investigate this tendency to be a bystander. What was discovered was that it is heavily influenced by social pressure. The larger the group of people involved, the less likely it is that any single one of them will intervene in a situation. The experiments typically simulate a situation that demands intervention, such as someone having an accident or smoke starting to fill a room, and measure whether or not a subject responds. The experiment is repeated a number of times to compare people's response when alone to the responses of other subjects who are in groups with other people. The other people are actors whose instructions are to ignore the situation. The results are highly consistent, highly repeatable, and quite depressing. People's tendency to be a bystander and not respond to a situation that clearly requires it is highly correlated to increasing group size.[1] In a situation that clearly calls to a person to break ranks with the group and be a leader, most people turn their back

We would like to think that we are better than the subjects in these experiments, but statistically we are wrong. When put to the test we fail to live up to our own expectations when part of a group. Our tribal shadow is completely attuned to the behaviour of the others in the group. It is saying, "Someone should do something. How is everyone else reacting? They aren't doing anything! If I do something I will be out of line. I will look weird in front of them".

Given how pervasive this tribal shadow is, we should not be surprised about the reluctant leader. By definition, the leader is the one being weird. She is the one breaking the group norm. It is natural that this will be uncomfortable for a lot of people. The tribal shadow will tell them "don't stick your head up", "don't cause friction", "just go with the flow".

Command voice – lead your tribe

For the large proportion of us with a "don't be weird" tribal shadow, the first step in developing our command voice is to step fully into the "weird" – to confront our tribal shadow and choose to act from a different place. This takes courage and perseverance. Going against a strong tribal shadow will cause anxiety. You will notice a physical response: a churning stomach, sweating, and increased heart rate, which is where the courage comes in. It takes courage to inflict "pain" upon ourselves. And it takes even more courage to try it again if the first attempt goes pear-shaped. For those who persevere, however, the impact on their command voice is extraordinary. With perseverance, the action becomes less confronting. We are rewiring our brains to understand that being a bit weird doesn't actually cause us harm. In fact, it has a positive payback. The tribal shadow may never go away (the wiring for that is very deep), but the anxiety that goes with choosing to ignore it does.

Let's consider a real example from a client of mine we will call Peta, a departmental general manager in a large utilities company. Peta had been finding some aspects of the command voice very confronting. Giving an order, making a direct request, or holding someone to account for failing to deliver on a promise – all induced high anxiety levels for Peta. This exchange took place after I had been a silent observer while Peta conducted a team meeting.

Me: Peta, can I give you some feedback on what I observed in the meeting?

Peta: I know what's coming.

Me: What?

Peta: My command voice was crap.

Me: What do you think was missing?

Peta: Everything that you taught me! I started OK when I singled out Mary rather than just vaguely asking the whole team. But then it went pear-shaped. I wasn't clear on the deliverable, I said, "management need this" rather than being clear that I was making the request, and I was vague about the time frame rather than being specific.

Me: What was going on? What was your tribal shadow saying?

Peta: As soon as I tried to be direct, it wasn't just a voice – it was screaming at me!

Me: Screaming what?

Peta: That I was disrespecting her by being direct, that she didn't like it, that she hated me for treating her like a child. We have such a great relationship – we get on so well. My tribal shadow was screaming that I was jeopardising it all.

By analysing this exchange, we can distinguish how the tribal shadow is invalidating the command voice. Part of Peta just wanted to be loved, to fit in with the crowd, to not be seen as different, and not to rise above her station. By naming this a tribal shadow, we can create a language set that brings insight into the catastrophic impact that this was having on Peta as a leader. Until Peta addressed her tribal shadow, teaching her better delegation skills would always be ineffective.

It is important to realise that none of this was apparent to Peta prior to her identifying her tribal shadow. She was experiencing the frustration of poor delivery from her team but was puzzled as to why. She had concluded that she was part of the problem (hence the request for coaching) but could not pinpoint anything. In identifying her tribal shadow, Peta took a huge step in self-awareness. She now not only understood that she needed to be more direct in her requests but she also understood the cause. By identifying her tribal shadow, she could address the self-sabotaging behaviour that was completely unconscious to her previously.

The other thing to note in this example is Peta's seniority. She was not a recently promoted team leader; she was a general manager with nearly two decades of experience in a large listed company. She enjoyed an excellent reputation and steadily risen through the organisation. Identifying your tribal shadow might not be as transformational as it ultimately was for Peta, but in my experience, almost everyone benefits from engaging in the inquiry for themselves.

As you practice stepping into the lead and exercising your command voice, you will notice something else happening that happened to Peta. Power will start to migrate to you. It is a self-sustaining cycle. As you increase your leadership power through exercising your command voice, people increasingly give you more power. They will start to preferentially defer to you. Power attracts power. What you may realise as a result is that there was a lot of power out there that you had not taken up. Power that is not exercised does not disappear – it's given over to others. If a thorny issue arises connected to your area of responsibility and you take no action, you will soon find one of your peers taking it over. What you realise as your command voice grows is that you have not been fulfilling your obligations as a leader. As a leader, it is always your obligation to fully take up the power associated with your position.

We might ask whether the converse is true if you have the tribal shadow of a bully. If you are a bully, you will have taken up all the power you can. Once you have identified the catastrophic impact that the tribal shadow is having on your command voice, should you give up some of your power? The answer is no. To repeat what we said above, as a leader, it is always your obligation to fully take up your power. The path for you if you have a bullying tribal shadow is to consider how you apply your power. For a bully, the motivation for exercising power is not about achieving common goals but about inflicting hurt. Identifying the motivation behind wielding your power is the key. Whenever the behaviour is masked by the unconscious, you won't see any change in behaviour. After your behaviour is identified as being driven by your tribal shadow, change can begin. The choice is between a destructive form of leadership that is inherently limiting and the opportunity to overcome the impulse and act from a higher level of consciousness. Only then can your command voice maximise its potential.

The command voice consists of a number of complimentary capabilities summarised below (see *Evolved Organizations* for a more detailed description). In each case, let's explore how the tribal shadow can invalidate the command voice.

A leader with a strong command voice uses their command voice to get the people with the right capability matched to the roles required by the challenges. They "***get the right people on the bus***".[2] Leaders who struggle to do this are often weighed down by a tribal shadow that wants to avoid the conflict and difficult conversations that this necessarily involves.

The command voice thrives on explicit mutual understanding of what needs to be done. Leaders learn to use their ***speech as action***; they make things happen with their words. They are deliberate about what they say and how they say it. They make strong, unambiguous requests and demand absolute clarity in the responses to their requests. They make their expectations clear. This level of forthrightness is not the language of everyday speech. In everyday speech, a lot of meaning is inferred. It has complex nuances and shortcuts. Rarely do we say exactly what we mean; to do so in everyday speech is seen as abrupt and rude. When leaders are called to state exactly what they want and when they want it by, then the tribal shadow is often triggered. If this inner voice is allowed to run the show, then the leader will "water down" the request. The resultant weak request becomes the playground for misinterpretation, both deliberate and inadvertent, and ultimately fails to deliver completed tasks on time.

Having established clear mutual understanding of requirements, a leader with a strong command voice always **honours their commitment** by following up and by supporting the outcome where required. Using direct language to make strong requests creates a one-to-one contract for delivery of a specified task by a specified time. Contracts are not one-way; they always bind two parties. Both parties have obligations. The leader has delegated the task but remains equally accountable for delivery. Their part of the contract is to follow up and also to be there when things change or go wrong. Only through robust follow-up does the direct language of the original strong request make any sense. The command voice is always on the lookout for how they can support the request and never lets a deadline slip by unacknowledged. The tribal shadow can intervene here. For many people the act of checking up on the promises of their people feels disrespectful. The tribal shadow can encourage leaders to let things slip by.

Having a nonnegotiable stance on following up inevitably leads to the need for **discipline and consequence**. The command voice is explicitly connected to leadership power. Failure to follow through with consequence is a failure to take up this power. Repeated failures to follow through will permanently erode the leader's capability to deliver the required outcomes. The tribal shadow can play havoc with this dynamic, leading people to avoid difficult conversations or to water down the follow-through to the point of ineffectiveness.

Applying these concepts more broadly, we can observe that **disciplined operations** are a hallmark of a strong command voice. Structure is important; legislative compliance, company rules, budgets, reports, plans, targets, and schedules are respected and acted upon. If you look at some of the key metrics and cycles in your organisation, you will be able to quickly spot the disparity between leaders when it comes to the command voice. If you zero in on a team that has no overdue action items, you will find a strong command voice. You will then also observe that their reports are on time and that their budget preparation starts well ahead of the deadline. As you look deeper again, you find a respect for plans and the planning processes, that they investigate thoroughly when things go wrong and that they are champions at lean operations and continuous improvement. As you look to the leader of this area, you will find someone who does not answer to their tribal shadow complaining about all the "boring stuff".

We can start to see how distinguishing our tribal shadow is important. When we distinguish it, it gives us the opportunity to make a choice rather than to be unconsciously enslaved by it. In practice, this takes more doing than might be imagined. We quickly notice that its hold over us seems to amplify when the situations become most critical. Let's explore why this might be.

The pre-cog choice

Patterson and his colleagues[3] start to open the door on this more complex question of why we are at our worst when we need to be at our best. They call it the "fool's choice" for leaders when they confront crucial conversations. A fool's choice is a leader asking themselves, *"Will I address this negative behaviour now and ruin our relationship, or will I let it pass and suffer the long-term effects?"* It is a fool's choice, because the question itself reflects a series of false beliefs.

We will take this one step further because we now understand that the command voice is heavily anchored in connection to pre-cog brain. So, I will rename the choice the "pre-cog choice" and in doing so rewrite the choice as it really occurs – *"Will I address this negative behaviour now and ruin our relationship, or will I let it pass and ~~suffer the long-term consequences~~ just hope that things will improve?"* We know that this is the question that is truly being asked because we understand that the pre-cog brain doesn't engage with *"long-term consequences"*. It deals purely in the choice to be made *now*. If we are to master the command voice, we must understand how our own tribal shadow influences our decision processes.

Pre-cogs did not have the ability to envisage the future. This ability developed during the cognitive revolution. Remember that as you were walking along the Eurostar tracks, working out how to manage your teams with steadily degrading capabilities, that your futurizing voice was the first to go. Later, you dropped your prosocial voice as you left your gossipy intra-cogs behind you. Your pre-cogs could not engage in abstract future concepts like the post-cogs, nor could they even gossip about who might do what to whom at the festival tomorrow. They purely responded to your command

and heartfelt voice. This pre-cog brain never got left behind as we evolved. And today when you use your command voice, it is highly triggered, both in you and in your followers.

It is logical, therefore, that the pre-cog influence will be to dismiss potential long-term consequences. In fact, we can go one step further. *"Will I address this negative behaviour now and ruin our relationship, or will I let it pass?"* ~~and just hope that things will improve~~*"*. Even hoping about the future is beyond pre-cogs.

Pre-cog society and leadership was dominated by direct relationships. The leader was not the best warrior; he was the best relationship builder. When you are in command voice mode, your tribal shadow will anchor immediately on relationships. This inner voice is not concerned with long-term consequences or even hoping that things will improve; the tribal shadow will fixate on relationship. And it will invariably lead you down the wrong path if you choose to follow it. For a reluctant leader or one with a "don't be weird" tribal shadow, the answer to the pre-cog choice is simple – let it pass. You are not happy with the behaviour or lack of delivery on a strong request, but the immediate impact on you as you stand in the moment is small. As you let it go, you give tacit support to undesired behaviour. But the pre-cog tribal shadow has no look-forward capability; it deals in relationship preservation in the here and now.

The command voice is not a slave to the tribal shadow – quite the opposite. It is the voice that takes up its power and exercises it judiciously in the service of long-term goals. It works in concert with our heartfelt voice, working from a place of safety and care. It recognises that there is no pre-cog choice. Letting poor behaviour pass is damaging to long-term relationships, not protective. The real choice to be made is *"Will I let my tribal shadow drive the show, or will my heartfelt and command voice be in control?"* The command voice never lets bad behaviour pass. It understands that whatever it walks past, it condones. And the heartfelt voice understands that the little piece of resentment that you carry towards the person displaying the bad behaviour will grow like a cancer. Deep relationships are built on total openness and honesty. Deep relationships are often built in the repair. Addressing the issue in the moment from a place of true care and a commitment to the person's success builds relationship.

The power of the command voice is rooted deeply in our pre-cog brain that didn't get left behind. Pre-cog leadership was built on one-to-one relationships. The leader may have led a tribe of thirty, but it wasn't through a connection to group goals – it was thirty one-to-one relationships. This ultimately led to the limitation of the size of a single tribe because the leader simply ran out of time to foster one more relationship. Similarly, your command voice is limited to your command circle. This can vary in size significantly in the modern world. But it can't be effective at scale. Remember your experience at the pub talking to your friend Trevor who explained how it was a platoon of thirty-odd soldiers that underpinned the modern military. Grow this number too far, and the command voice starts to break down as the number of direct relationships grows. Similarly, your command voice will top out, and you will have to do something different. After all, you are not leading a group of pre-cogs. But don't be tempted to flick forward in the book to find out. Remember that a strong command voice is a prerequisite for the higher differential voices.

Command voice and gender

We need to explicitly address a nagging thought that you may have had. If the command voice connects to the pre-cog brain that still resides within us, and pre-cog leadership was based around an alpha male, are men genetically predisposed to be better command voice leaders than women?

The answer is, unequivocally, **no**.

Pre-cog behaviours have no place in our world. The command voice finds effective ways to connect with an inner layer of our brain that is a remnant of *Homo sapiens* evolution, but it is only a remnant. You lead people, not pre-cogs. If you lead like the pre-cog alpha male, you invalidate all the development that has happened to our species since the pre-cogs. In other words, you invalidate everything that we regard as human.

The remnant that the command voice connects to is the part of us that takes security from knowing our place in the tribe, understanding our role in the tribe, and seeing how our contribution leads to the tribe being strong and resilient – all tribal shadow responses. The command voice is the use of leadership power to organise the work to provide this security. It does so in a thoroughly modern context, where people have sophisticated intelligence and free will. This is why the focus throughout this chapter has been on the exchange of commitments between a leader and a team member, not on how leaders should issue orders. Issuing orders has low leverage in today's workplace. Holding people to what they genuinely said they would do has very high leverage.

Of all the outer voices, the command voice is the most explicit use of leadership power. It is, however, a quiet use of power. When coaching people in the command voice, I insist on people keeping the speech volume at normal levels. The nature of their speech changes (from indirect speech to direct speech), but the volume remains the same. One leader that I worked for had the knack of lowering her volume when she shifted to command voice, almost to a whisper. Somewhat counterintuitively, the room would become hyperfocussed in response.

There is no correlation between strength of a command voice and gender. There is no correlation between the strength of any of the differential voice layers and gender. Based on the evidence that you see every day at work, you will conclude that men and women can be equally accomplished or equally inept!

Takeaways

The tribal shadow acts to invalidate our command voice. It is the inner voice associated with evolutionary remnants of pre-cog brain functioning.

Our tribal shadow is triggered by situations that get interpreted by our pre-cog brain as impacting our social standing within a tribe.

The tribal shadow has many manifestations, the most common one being that we feel that our social standing is under threat. Other manifestations range from the bully trying to dominate others through to a reluctant leader who feels unworthy of leadership and is reluctant to take up their power for fear of losing their relationships.

The command voice requires that leaders always take up their leadership power and use it responsibly.

The command voice is based on one-to-one agreements: a "contract" for delivery of tightly specified outcomes by specific times and agreement to follow explicit expectations. These agreements bind both parties to the outcome. The tribal shadow can act to water down the language and thus the power of the "contract".

The command voice requires that the leader consistently follows up on commitments and verifies that key processes are being followed. It establishes disciplined operations delivering reliable outputs.

Leadership development actions

- Observe your tribal shadow, and come to understand how it invalidates your command voice. What is your inner voice saying at the times when you are (or should be) exercising your leadership power? What is it saying when it feels like your status in the organisation is under attack?
- Make the choice to not to act on your tribal shadow. Act consistently with your purpose as a leader.
- Observe the operating discipline within your area of influence, and take responsibility for it. Make your expectations clear, both to yourself and to others. Verify personally what is really going on with mandatory process and rules.
- Analyse your effectiveness in making requests, and make the changes so that all requests you make are a clear contract between you and a single individual, that the specification is crystal clear and the time frame explicit. Do not accept vague responses – only accept a "yes", a "no", or follow-through a counteroffer.
- Follow through. Always. No matter what your tribal shadow is saying.
- Always act respectfully to those that you have power over. No matter what your tribal voice is saying.
- Apply appropriate consequences promptly. Never get sidelined by your tribal shadow into the false "pre-cog choice" – thinking that you have to choose between applying consequences and preserving a relationship.

Notes

1 Fischer et al., "The Bystander-Effect".
2 Collins and Collins, *Good to Great*.
3 Patterson, *Crucial Conversations*.

Shadow gossip incapacitates prosocial voice

Most definitions of leadership can be disputed, but one thing we can all agree on is that leaders have followers. Many contemporary researchers such as Haslam and Reicher[1] argue persuasively that for too long, approaches to leadership have focussed far too much on the characteristics and psychology of the leader and far too little on the psychology of the follower. We won't fall into that trap. In moving to the prosocial voice, we mark the transition from direct relationships to indirect relationships. The ratio of followers to leaders triples and quadruples. As a leader, we need to be spending a lot more time thinking about how we are impacting the psychology/psyche of our followers.

Another important transition takes place with the move to the prosocial voice. We cease to treat people as people. Or at least we cease to treat people as individuals and instead treat them as context. With the heartfelt and command voices, we relate to people as unique individuals. We seek to understand their personalities. We work out their distinctive attributes, their strengths, and their weaknesses. We value their unique contribution and work on our direct relationship with them. When we set out to achieve our goals, we prioritise winning their hearts and minds. With our heartfelt voice, we will work hard to get them individually enrolled and then with our command voice we will create a one-to-one contract to deliver the results we need.

Now let's contrast that with the prosocial voice. This was the leadership capability that emerged to take us from pre-cogs to intra-cogs – the ability to exert power through *indirect* relationships. Put yourself back on the Eurostar tracks with your gossipy intra-cogs. As you moved outside of your inner circle, you related to your intra-cogs in an increasingly impersonal way. By the time you got to the outer limits of your 150-strong commune, you were lucky to remember their name. And yet they were doing what you wanted them to do.

The same applies to us in the modern world with our prosocial and futurizing voices. We treat the people outside of our immediate circles impersonally, as part of the system. They need to be motivated and directed en masse. They are critical components in the giant machine that we oversee, and they need to be managed as a collective. We have been somewhat conditioned to enthusiastically exclaim that as a leader we are a "people person" and therefore identify ourselves with direct relationships of the heartfelt voice. Treating people as context sounds brutal – something from a management textbook from the Industrial Revolution!

The truth of the matter is that treating people as part of the system is an essential part of being a leader, just as treating people as individuals is important. Don't believe me? Just click on your document management system icon and go to procedures. Procedures exist to standardise human input – there is no room for the individual. What about the safety rules that you impose? They are expectations set for the masses. Maybe you want to revisit the last restructure where you sat with the rest of leadership team for days, drawing and redrawing organisation charts from a "clean sheet".

At least we have HR. They'll be all about relationships, won't they? Or will they? We find standardised pay grades, position descriptions, competency frameworks, communication plans, and engagement strategies – completely devoid of individual relationship. "Because of my son's medical treatments, it suits me better to be paid on the second Tuesday of the month rather than the last Friday". "Sorry, here's the policy".

In 1958, Martin Buber[2] summed it up beautifully when he defined the different worldview that we have when we engage from the perspective of I-YOU (relationship) and from the perspective of I-IT (context). We make our choice in the first words we say, and it sets the path of the subsequent discussion. As Buber said, "when a primary word is spoken the speaker enters the word and takes his stand in it".

Nearly sixty years later, Buber's statement still rings true for us. Contrast the "primary word spoken" at the most recent meetings you ran. If you started the meeting with a statement like "Let's go over the agenda", then you have started down the path of context. If you started with "Has everyone heard the news? Tennille had her baby – a gorgeous little girl!" then you are on a direct relationships path. Of course you can change the tone of the conversation, but it takes conscious redirection. The conversation has a natural flow that you need to interrupt. Tennille's baby will lead to other direct relationship conversations until you stop everyone by changing tone and saying. "OK. I guess we had better get on with the agenda".

One thing to notice is how much easier it is to go one way rather than the other. Transitioning from the I-YOU conversation about Tennille and her baby to the I-IT conversation of the agenda item requires conscious redirection but can be done naturally. But transitioning the other way is awkward. "Right, that completes agenda item 4 on the sales forecast. Now let's move to agenda item 5 – Tennille's baby". This is more evidence of the layered nature of the differential voices. Layering a prosocial and command voice on top of a heartfelt voice works. But switching the other way is weird.

Buber's "primary word" also applies to leadership development. Go to your favourite ebook site and search "leadership". Select any book and read page 10. By the end of the page you will be able to categorise the entire book to either direct relationships or context. Very, very few books will cover both; the path is set when "the primary word is spoken".

Exceptional leadership ranges through all the differential voices and therefore ranges between I-YOU relationships and I-IT context. It ranges up and down the differential voices. To maximise their leadership reach, exceptional leaders are powerful shapers of context who use their prosocial and futurizing voices. But they never forget that these voices are built on the foundation of I-YOU relationships. To paraphrase Buber, "Without IT, a human cannot live. But an individual who lives with IT alone is not a human".

Shadow gossip

You might have wondered about why I have used the word "shadow" to name the inner voices so far – primeval shadow, tribal shadow, and now shadow gossip. Here's why. We are often aware of something that is present in our thoughts, but we can't quite make out what it is. It lives in the shadow. This is our inner voice. Naming the inner voice helps to bring it out of the shadows. Maybe this is what Carl Jung was imagining when he coined the term "shadow" in his seminal works of psychology.[3] Jung was a student of Sigmund Freud but struck out in his own direction, one that is infinitely more useful to us. He identified that there exists in everyone a "dark side" to their personality that the conscious ego will either not acknowledge or remain ignorant of. He believed that there are positive as well as negative aspects to this "dark side". He even postulated that, in spite of its function as a reservoir for human darkness – or perhaps because of it – the shadow is the seat of creativity.

When Jung came up with his theory of the shadow, he did not have the extensive psychology research base or the knowledge of brain morphology that we have today. His theories were driven by his relentless observation of human behaviour. It is testament to his genius that he would come to categorise this element of the psyche and link it to the remnants of our ancient animal instincts. The primeval shadow and tribal shadow are associated with our remnant pre-cog brain.

Our remnant intra-cog brain is more sophisticated and takes the inner voice that accompanies it to another plane. Remember back on the Eurostar tracks as we observed the change from pre-cog societies of thirty-strong tribes to 150-strong communes. We related this to the more sophisticated use of language. Your intra-cogs had mastered the art of indirect communication, including the propensity for gossip. To understand the inner voice associated with this piece of brain development, we need to examine how our intra-cogs thrived as a society. But more importantly, we need to think about how individuals thrived in that society and what traits we still carry as a result. Given the pervasiveness of gossip and its power in shaping the social structure of an intra-cog commune, I have named this inner voice the *shadow gossip*.

Referring to our meta-model, I have added in the shadow gossip as the inner voice associated with intra-cogs and update the model accordingly. The shadow gossip is the inner voice that either reinforces or invalidates our prosocial voice and so is placed in the shadow under the prosocial voice.

Thriving in an intra-cog society was a far more complex than in a pre-cog society. There were a lot more people to interact with. The key was to be good at managing your own reputation and evaluating the reputation of others. The intra-cog was constantly checking in on what other intra-cogs thought of her. And she was constantly evaluating the worth of others and sharing it with her friends. It is important to give this the seriousness that it deserves. This was not some idle pursuit. Intra-cogs literally lived and died by their reputation. If the gossip about an individual got bad enough, they would be expelled from the commune. And it is not as if they could just move down the road to the next commune. Without the mutual support

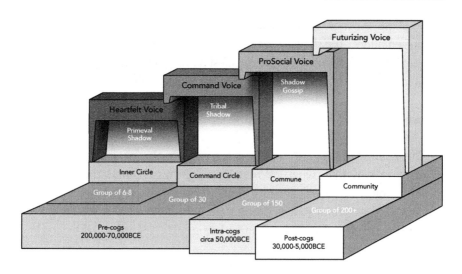

Figure 11.1 Shadow gossip inner voice

of the commune, an outcast would die from starvation or animal attack. If they did wander into the territory of another commune, they would almost certainly be killed.

Intra-cog society became all about perception: how an intra-cog was perceived by others and how they perceived others. We all know that with gossip, facts are few and far between. As an intra-cog, it didn't matter how good you actually were; it mattered how good you were perceived to be. Over the long term, the art of managing perceptions became a key component of reproductive fitness for the species. Gossip had changed human evolution!

This is the engine room of the shadow gossip: image, reputation, perceptions. These are not just some remnant of a long-forgotten time; these things are critical to our success today. The shadow gossip comes from a place that is much closer (in evolutionary terms) to who we are today than the primeval or tribal shadow. Our shadow gossip is constantly checking our standing in other people's eyes.

For intra-cogs, their very survival depended on their reputation – on the way they were perceived by others. Is that so different for us? We value our reputation extremely highly, perhaps even illogically so. We can be our own harshest critic, and it is the shadow gossip that is doing the talking. Our shadow gossip thinks it is a world champion mind reader. "I know what my boss thinks of me", "I know what my colleague thinks of me", "I know what the finance director thinks of me", "I know what they are saying about me after that incident during my presentation". The shadow gossip seems to know quite a lot based on very little information. There are many manifestations of the shadow gossip. Here are some of the major ones and how they show up in both modes.

Shadow judge:

> The shadow judge analyses our character. It is also much more interested in why than what. "Why do you always do that? You are an idiot. You'll never get ahead in life". it says to us when witnessing a repeat mistake. It judges our performance and is quick to reach a verdict on our qualities as a human being.

Shadow critic:

> Closely related to the shadow judge is the shadow critic. Where the judge is quick to analyse our character flaws, the shadow critic in turns the microscope onto our work. It is the voice that says that what we produce is never good enough. It is the voice undermining us as we present a proposal, telling us that we didn't put enough work in.

Shadow cynic:

> "Am I really doing this charity work for the benefit of the sick kids, or am I just narcissistically addicted to the accolades?" The shadow cynic is brutal on our underlying intentions.

Shadow sceptic:

> "It'll never work", says Glum in *Gulliver's Travels*. "It'll never work", says Eeyore the donkey in Winnie the Pooh. "It'll never work", says shadow sceptic quite a lot. It is particularly brutal on our new ideas or on telling us that we are not creative.

Shadow racketeer:

> A racketeer is a person who engages in dishonest business dealings. They operate behind a "front": a seemingly honest and ethical

business. Behind the front, there is fraudulent and corrupt activity. It is a strong suggestion, therefore, that you might be engaged in dishonest, fraudulent, and corrupt business dealings with yourself. We will leave the exploration of this touchy subject to the end of the chapter.

To be fair to our shadow gossip, we should acknowledge that it can have a positive side. We can judge ourselves fairly or give ourselves the benefit of the doubt. Our shadow critic can emphasise some positives. But overwhelmingly, the shadow gossip is the worst kind of gossip. And because it happens in the unconscious, we don't correct it. It presumes the worst in all its juicy glory. Why would this be so? After all, it appears to have some serious downsides.

One way to think about this is to remember the way that brain functioning is virtually identical for physical and emotional stimuli. As social interactions became increasingly important for our reproductive fitness, evolution took a shortcut. Instead of developing a whole new set of brain functions for social functions, it just dual-purposed the system it already had. And this system was already wired for negativity, which leads to caution. For physical survival, it was always better to jump at a shadow than to wander into the shadow and find a tiger. Jumping at shadows a hundred times had no long-term consequences. Finding a tiger just once had consequences. It may be that this predisposition for caution was carried over when the social functions muscled in to the same brain region.

Bringing the gossip out of the shadows

Whenever your shadow gossip is having a disempowering conversation about you, your prosocial voice will never reach its full potential. You will back off when you should be fronting up. You will recede to the shadows when the stage is rightfully yours, and you will be very, very careful when the situation calls for you to be bold. The first step is to shine a light into the shadow.

Amy Cuddy gave a TED Talk on body language that has been viewed over 40 million times, making it one of the most popular TED Talks ever. Her insights on body language are worth reflecting on (remember that the outer voices are more than just what we say; they are metaphors for all observable leadership characteristics, including body language). But what makes the talk so powerful is her personal reflections on the feeling that she always had of "I'm not supposed to be here" as she progressed through her career. She advocates for people faced with this situation to do as she did and "fake it 'til you make it", or more specifically, "fake it 'til you become it".

The popularity of the talk is testimony to the extent to which the fundamental feeling of inadequacy resonates with human kind. Clearly "fake it 'til you become it" has helped many people – continually confronting your fears and having things turn out well will eventually re-wire your brain. The disadvantage is that it takes time to do this. Distinguishing the feelings of inadequacy brought on by your shadow gossip gives you an alternative path to access this change.

The shadow gossip is profoundly connected with our deepest secrets. When psychology researchers started exploring people's deepest secrets, they were in for a surprise. This is amazingly difficult research to conduct, because people will go to extraordinary lengths to hide their deepest secrets – not just from others but also from themselves. Only in the presence of complete psychological safety, built over a long period of time and with ironclad confidentiality, will people start to open up. What is the heavily guarded thing most often held as a deepest secret? It is a deep conviction of basic inadequacy. That despite appearances and external evidence, one is basically incompetent, a fake, a phoney. That one is just holding together a thin veneer of competence that might crumble at any minute to reveal the "truth".[4]

This is the playground of our shadow gossip. It is self-judging-self, self-criticising-self, and self being cynical and sceptical about self. Until this is acknowledged, the prosocial voice is shackled and constrained. As Jung said, "the less it (the shadow) is embodied in the individual's conscious life, the blacker and denser it is".[5] The more we try to ignore the shadow gossip or push it further into the dark, the more it weighs us down. So, we start by simply naming it. There is power in language. Naming it forces the shadow gossip into the light where we can look at it in all its ridiculousness. We can deal with it explicitly, rather than experiencing it as a constant gnawing that saps our energy and never goes away. But most of all, naming the shadow gossip gives us access to choice. Once we name it, we get to choose whether or not we act on it.

You are not bad for having a shadow gossip; you are a well-adjusted human having a very human experience. Now that you have identified the shadow gossip, telling yourself to "stop it" is not helpful. It just adds fuel to the fire. You can't stop it. Your shadow will just start to gossip about how useless you are for not being able to stop your shadow gossip!

A shadow gossip is part of our lived experience. Accept it for what it is and what it isn't. It is an inner voice that loves to gossip. You don't have to listen to gossip. Observe it, name it, don't make it wrong, but don't be beholden to it. Make a choice. It is part of you, but it is not "who you are". "Who you are" lives in your conscious brain, not in an unconscious gossiper. You have put yourself in the position to make the choice – the choice to act from your highest possible brain function, from your commitments, from your values, from your heart.

The prosocial voice and social identity

A distinctive characteristic of a strong prosocial voice is the way that it builds large cohesive groups. Back on the Eurostar tracks, your pre-cogs responded to your heartfelt and command voices. But this mode of leadership, based on direct communication, was limited in terms of the size of the tribe that you could lead. Pre-cog tribes operated independently at best and often with open hostility. The breakthrough came when intra-cogs developed the ability to use indirect language. This allowed for communication at a distance, the ability to share information widely, to send messages, and to keep abreast of any emerging disruptive forces. Society transitioned rapidly from tribes to communes. The leader's approach changed from "power *over* individuals" in the tribe using direct relationships to an approach of "power *through* individuals" in the commune using indirect relationships. The prosocial voice causes us to reconsider leadership power. The prosocial voice is "power through" rather than "power over".[6]

From your session in the local pub, we remember all the evidence that groups of around 150 are still natural group sizes in today's society. We now understand that indirect communication is the mechanism of holding such a group together, but that is not sufficient to fully explain the cohesiveness of the commune. Merely having access to information through indirect communication will not in itself cause someone to become a follower. The information must cause something to happen for that person. We need to understand this process because it is the essence of leading with the prosocial voice.

A commune is created when the individuals in the group develop a shared *social identity*.[7] A shared social identity is created when we identify ourselves with a group. We start to refer to ourselves as "we" rather than "I". In social identity theory, the "we" becomes the ingroup, and the creation of an ingroup consigns everyone else in the world to the outgroup. Importantly, we not only identify with the ingroup but our actions change to support the group goals rather than our personal goals.

The power of the prosocial voice can therefore be measured by the degree to which it creates a "we-ness" amongst the team. It sets up the dynamic where the team say "we are different from (and therefore better than) them".[8] This is a very different form of leadership from the command voice, which is based on a leader using their leadership power in one-to-one direct relationships. The prosocial voice, by contrast, is based on one-to-many indirect relationships. Even this statement is understating the transition. Social identity is created between followers as much as it is created between leader and follower. The prosocial voice is a one-to-many relationship, but the final shaping of the social identity of the group is a many-to-many relationship.

It is for this reason that the prosocial voice is a very distributed form of leadership. Its mechanism is one of shaping context to influence followers rather than the explicit use of leadership power. It is an egalitarian form of leadership, where followers are looking as much to their peers as to their leader. It invites the group to share in the leadership.

This should make perfect sense when we reflect on the social-identity-driven transition from pre-cogs to intra-cog leadership. Society transitioned rapidly from tribes to communes. The leader's approach changed from power *over* individuals in the tribe using direct relationships to power *through* individuals in the commune using indirect relationships. Lots of people got a say at the communal campfire. Overt displays of power or wealth by the leader were frowned upon. A successful prosocial leader of an intra-cog commune went out of their way to display their humility and generosity. These practices have been observed by anthropologists studying ancient cultures that survived to modern times. In Chinook Indian communes, for example, a practice called potlatch involved a formal distribution of wealth from the leader across the commune.

Today's potential followers are still connected to their inner intra-cog. They will also frown on showy displays of power or authority when it comes to joining a social identity. Any power that you exert through the prosocial voice exists only because followers have given you that power of their own free will. It is a very democratic sort of power and very egalitarian. Anyone at any level in the organisation can influence social identity.

It is for this reason that, as a leader, your shadow gossip is so important. As a prosocial leader you are shaping the social identity of the group. To do so, you must put your social reputation on the line, knowing it will become the source of gossip. It makes sense, then, that any insecurities that live in your shadow gossip will weaken or even incapacitate your prosocial voice. Let us think about how this might occur when as a leader you set out to implement some of the practices associated with prosocial leadership (see *Evolved Organizations* for a detailed exploration of these practices).

The prosocial voice recognises the sophisticated mechanisms of language and personal interactions that enable strong social identities to form. The mechanism might be sophisticated, but it is generally put to an unsophisticated use – idle gossip. The prosocial voice is deliberate in wrestling back control of these communications. It **usurps the gossip**.

The origin of "usurp" is from the Latin *usurpare*, meaning "seize, for use". This is a perfect description. As a leader with a powerful prosocial voice, we are seizing control of the social communications and putting them to our use. We know that we can't stop the gossip – it is too powerful a force. Instead we appropriate it for our use.

Many leaders are reluctant to step into this space and hold themselves aloof from the gossip. This is easy to rationalise because gossip can be dismissed as a time-wasting triviality. But even when leaders accept the power of the prosocial voice and the need to usurp the gossip, their inner gossip runs interference. Why? The reason is not hard to find. A lot of the gossip centres on the leader themselves, and it is not all positive. You may have an inner gossip that seeks to protect against this uncomfortable scrutiny and steer you to be ignorant of what people are saying about you behind your back.

Far from being aloof to the gossip, some leaders are fully immersed in counterproductive gossiping. They are active participants. The gossiping trait is very strong, and it doesn't magically disappear when people get promoted. For these people, their inner gossip wants them to continue to join in or even use the privileged knowledge that they have as a result of their position to be at the centre of new waves of gossip. It goes without saying that these people must usurp their own inner gossip first and foremost. The prosocial voice is the responsible use of the social communication channels – a leader engaged in harmful gossip has no place.

Once a leader has usurped the gossip and taken up their responsibility for the social channels of communication, they can start to work on building a social identity. One way to do this is through **rituals that lead to common beliefs**. Well-designed rituals can be a powerful driver of common belief systems, which become part of the fabric of the social identity. An example is the way that many companies engaged in the construction industry adopted the practice of running a "safety moment" at the start of every team meeting in the company. There was obvious benefit in sharing knowledge about safety, but this effect was secondary. The more important outcome was that the ritual helped drive a change in belief system from "Accidents just happen, and I have no influence over whether or not they happen" to "All accidents are preventable, and my personal actions determine whether or not they happen". This became core to the social identity of the company, and dramatic improvements in safety outcomes followed.

This makes it all sound easy; it is not. By necessity, the initial introduction of a new ritual needs to go *against* the existing social identity. This is guaranteed to supercharge the leader's inner gossip. The inner gossip is highly attuned to fitting in with the existing social identity and will undermine the leader's resolve. Any shadow critic insecurities will be amplified in these situations and the leader will shrink from the task at the very time that the prosocial voice should be at its strongest.

When it comes to a social identity, people look to the prototypical in their group to model their behaviours on. The prototypical is a person who represents the group and whose behaviours perfectly reflect the ideal behaviours for the group. They are exemplary. They are the archetypal model. It follows, therefore, that if as a leader you want to change people's behaviour, you need to *promote the prototypical*.

It is fairly obvious that if you are setting out to create a new social identity, you must personally be prototypical of the new behaviours that you want. What is less obvious but critical to changing the social identity is that you need prototypical behaviour to emerge in others within the group. The prosocial voice is egalitarian in nature; leadership is shared amongst many. You must foster this attention on others within the group.

The inner gossip, however, is obsessed with protecting your personal reputation, not building the reputation of others. It is hard for people to acknowledge, but the shadow gossip would rather run others down rather than build them up. Our inner shadow is constantly judging our worth, not in absolute terms, but relative to others. By running others down, or at least by not promoting them, our inner shadow can position us as superior. If unacknowledged, it can subtly intervene to turn the spotlight away from others. This is bad for commune-building. Leaders with a powerful prosocial voice are adept at recognising the self-promoting aspect of the inner shadow and choosing their actions instead from the perspective of building the desired social identity.

With this new outlook for our prosocial voice, we need to expand our ambitions in terms of leadership reach. Almost always, this will require that we move our organisation from **tribes to communes**. We did not leave tribes behind with the pre-cogs. As you witnessed in your trip to the pub and as we explored in the previous chapter, the tribal shadow is still significant in driving people's behaviour. In modern organisations, the tribal behaviours can emerge as silos. I have yet to encounter an organisation where leaders don't bemoan the lost opportunities associated with their organisation acting in silos.

Silos are tribes at work but also a manifestation of the ingroup/outgroup dynamics of social identity. Social identity is a "we-ness", which is powerful driver of behaviour. A strong "we-ness" always creates a "them" – "we are different to (and therefore better than) them". Silos are created when the "them" becomes other departments or offices in the same organisation. A powerful prosocial voice creates a social identity that transcends these "tribes" and builds to a bigger purpose, in effect creating a very large commune from disparate tribes.

The logic of this is irrefutable, but the inner gossip doesn't run on logic. Moving from a tribe to a commune requires giving up a piece of tribal identity. This is as hard for you today as it was for the intra-cog leader trying to stitch together pre-cog tribes. If you allow it to, your inner gossip will hijack your confidence, sending you back to the safety of your tribe.

Freed from the shackles of the shadow gossip, our prosocial voice can create communes from tribes. It is empowered to usurp the gossip and to create social identity through ritual and via the prototypical. When operating unconsciously, our inner gossip can drive us towards behaviours that undermine these capabilities. Yet we don't see this. By distinguishing and then observing our shadow gossip, we start to build our self-awareness. This gives us the choice over our actions, which empowers the prosocial voice.

Shadow racketeer

I have singled out the shadow racketeer for special treatment amongst your arsenal of inner gossips. That is because it entails an extra layer of deception.

131

Shadow judge, shadow critic, and shadow sceptic are all inner gossips you are having about yourself. Shadow racketeer is different. It occurs to you as inner gossip about someone else or about the circumstances you find yourself in. However, once you start to dig, you find out otherwise. It is a little piece of subterfuge that you are running on yourself.[9]

Think of the 1920s Prohibition era in the United States. Fronting onto the street was a charming café, but out the back was the speakeasy bar. Legitimate business at the front; payoff out the back.

Our shadow gossip is a racketeer. The front for our shadow racketeer are our complaints about other people or about our situation. Here is an example:

I don't have the right people in my team. I have to rework everything that they do.

Our shadow racketeer is on the lookout for things outside of our control, things we couldn't have anticipated, incompetent people who let us down and bad people who deliberately sabotaged us. Any of these will serve the purpose.

These are seemingly legitimate complaints; however, the dirty business is in the shadow. When we shine a light into the shadow, a different picture emerges. What appears to be legitimate complaint about others and about the circumstances is a front designed to mask the truths that we are hiding from ourselves. We want to have a lookout the back. What is the payoff?

The first step in our investigation is to notice that shadow rackets are generally lifelong in nature. Let's take the case that you have the previous complaint about the quality of the people in your team. You seem to be stuck at the moment with a team that doesn't have the competencies or drive that you need. But when you think about it, you had the same complaint twelve months ago. Back then, Ange was a particular problem. So much so that you went through the pain of performance-managing her out of the business. You recruited Juan, smart and ambitious, to take her place. But on reflection, your level of complaint hasn't dropped. You still complain with the same intensity; it just seems to have morphed across different people. And when you really reflect, you had the same complaint with the last team you had before your promotion. And the team before that. . . .

If this were you, you would almost certainly be running a shadow racket called "my team are never good enough". The complaint is the front. To all appearances it seems legitimate. You have masses of evidence that supports the case. You have a catalogue of deficiency against each and every team member that you can show the police when they turn up at your speakeasy. But there is dishonesty out the back. When you extract yourself from the complaint, you are confronted by the fact that it is statistically improbable that you have had below-average teams for your entire career. On average, you will have had teams of average capability. And yet you rate your current team in the bottom quartile, as you did for the last team, and for the team before that. You are running a shadow racket. You are getting some sort of payoff for this dishonesty, but it is shrouded and obscured by the complaint.

This can all seem quite odd. How could there possibly be a payoff for this behaviour? What possible benefit could there be in holding your team in artificially low regard? It makes no sense.

It makes no sense because the payoff is not visible or even conscious. It is a psychological payoff to a hidden aspect of your identity – a hidden stroke to your own ego. In some way, you are bolstering your own esteem.

Let us consider a few different social identity strokes that could be fuelling your imaginary racket in this case.

Complaint: My team are never good enough.

> **Surface Inner Voice:** Because you are so weak, I have to do the work myself.

>> **Shadow Racketeer:** If I make you weak, I make myself indispensable.

>>> **Identity Stroke:** I am important. I am needed.

Complaint: My team are never good enough.

> **Surface Inner Voice:** Because you are so weak, I can't deliver on the stuff I want to get done.

>> **Shadow Racketeer:** If I make you weak, I make an excuse for not getting things done that I committed to do.

>>> **Identity Stroke:** I am not responsible. I am off the hook.

Complaint: My team are never good enough.

> **Surface Inner Voice:** I have to compensate
> for your weakness.

> > **Shadow Racketeer:** If I make you weak,
> > I make myself look good (in my own
> > eyes).

> > > **Identity Stroke:** I am better
> > > than you.

Complaint: My team are never good enough.

> **Surface Inner Voice:** You have
> brought me garbage again.

> > **Shadow Racketeer:** If I make you
> > wrong, I make myself look good.

> > > **Identity Stroke:** I am right, you are
> > > wrong.

If you think that the identity strokes identified here belong in kindergarten, consider where it was that your brain wiring associated with social settings got started. We still get a kick out of being the best, being right, looking good, and not being responsible when things go wrong. It is a short-term endorphin rush. It is like a drug. And just like a drug, it is addictive. When you live inside a racket, your view of the world will be through that racket. Because you are predisposed to finding it, you will gather more and more evidence that your complaint is valid. And every piece of evidence is another "high". But, just like a drug, there is a long-term impact on your health. The accumulated burden of limited ambition, thwarted goals, and unfulfilled potential takes its toll. As you live out your complaint, wallowing in increasingly shallower "highs", you shrink and die from the inside.

You get the short-term benefit of a stroke to your self-esteem from your shadow gossip. But there is a long-term cost. Perhaps you think that you hold your complaint private. It doesn't work like that. Your shadow racket will manifest itself in multiple ways. But by far the most catastrophic impact will be to your prosocial voice. History is not full of great outcomes achieved by leaders who invalidated their team's abilities. Leaders achieve great things working with the team they have, not the one they wish for. Your prosocial voice withers and shrinks with every syllable of complaint, regardless of whether or not it is spoken.

It can be quite difficult to get to the nub of a shadow racket. If you have a consistent complaint that is having a long-term cost (as most persistent complaints do), then it will be a shadow racket. There will be a short-term payoff related to social identity, but it won't necessarily be clear what it is. Two different people carrying the same complaint can be running two entirely different rackets.

That is all heavy stuff. At this stage, you are glad that this was an imaginary scenario that doesn't apply to you.

Are you sure? Here some common conversations that are certain manifestations of rackets;

"I'm too busy".

"They just don't get it".

"Why does it always come down to me?"

"The IT department is completely incompetent and preventing me from. . .".

"I'm on top of this. If only it wasn't for engineering (or marketing, or Bob, or that government department, or . . .), I'd be able to nail this".

There is no magic required to deal with a shadow racket. Out it, then take an unbiased view on the long-term implications of what you are doing. Then just give up the short-term fix to achieve the long-term benefits. You must give something up, something quite addictive.

You must give up being right.

You must give up rationalising your own behaviour by invalidating others.

You must give up (mentally) putting others down so you look good by comparison.

. . . actually, just give up "looking good" and "not looking bad" altogether.

Give up on squirming out of your responsibility by (mentally) blaming others.

. . . actually, give up blaming others altogether.

Give up the excuse associated with others as to why you can't take action.

Truly understanding your shadow rackets represents a highly advanced level of self-awareness. With your eyes open to previously unconscious motivations, avenues for action open up that never existed for you before. With your prosocial voice released from constraints, your impact on the world is transformed.

Takeaways

The shadow gossip is the enemy of the prosocial voice.

The shadow gossip is the inner voice associated with the evolutionary remnants of intra-cog brain functioning.

Our shadow gossip judges unfairly, is critical, is cynical and is sceptical. In doing so, it weakens our prosocial voice.

The prosocial voice is based on the innate urge for individuals to associate themselves with others to form social identities. A social identity is a strong driver of behaviour and is characterised by its "we-ness", the feeling that "we are different from (and therefore better than) them".

The prosocial voice works to create new social identities or reshape old ones in a way that results in people's behaviour being aligned with the goals; it is the architect of a social identity.

To create new social identities, the prosocial voice usurps the gossip, creates rituals to create shared beliefs, and celebrates and rewards prototypical behaviour in others.

Because a social identity inevitably (and always) creates a "them", it can be used counterproductively to enhance local performance at the expense of the broader organisation. The prosocial voice counteracts this by creating a social identity that is inclusive and consistent with delivering the organisation's goals. The prosocial voice works to take tribes and deliver communes.

Leadership development actions

- Observe your shadow gossip. What is it saying about you?
- Note any self-criticisms that disempower you or have you behaving counterproductively.
- Make the choice not to act from your shadow gossip. Observe the occurrence of your shadow gossip, but then put it aside and act consistently with your purpose as a leader.

- Notice the flow of gossip in your organisation. Start to anticipate when your leadership will trigger this gossip. Usurp the gossip – put it to positive use.
- Working back from the behaviours that you want to change or culture that you want to create, describe for yourself the social identity that you are working to create.
- Be the architect of the new social identity. Enrol others. Create new rituals that underpin the desired social identity.
- In all ways, at all times, be the prototypical of the social identity but refrain from "putting on a show" about it.
- Look for the prototypicals amongst the group, and publicly celebrate their actions.
- Identify where counterproductive local tribes are forming within the organisation. Create a new social identity that moves tribes to communes that support the highest-level objectives for the entire organisation.
- Note the judgements, criticisms, scepticisms, or cynicisms that occur about others in the absence of objective data. Identify any patterns of compliant that might indicate a shadow racket.
- Analyse the shadow racket. Identify the short-term payoff. Identify the long-term cost. With the shadow racketeer exposed, make your choice!

Notes

1 Haslam, Reicher, and Platow, *The New Psychology of Leadership*.

2 Buber, "The I-Thou Theme, Contemporary Psychotherapy, and Psychodrama".

3 Jung, *Psychology and Religion, Volume 11*.

4 Yalom and Leszcz, *Theory and Practice of Group Psychotherapy*, Fifth Edition.

5 Todd, "The Value of Confession and Forgiveness According to Jung".

6 Turner, "Explaining the Nature of Power".

7 Tajfel, "Social Identity and Intergroup Behaviour"; Haslam, Reicher, and Platow; Turner, "Towards a Cognitive Redefinition of the Social Group".

8 Haslam, Reicher, and Platow.

9 Berne, *Games People Play*.

Daemon invalidates futurizing voice

Because you have inherited the post-cog trait of insatiable curiosity, an obsession with cause and effect, and the ability to project forward in time to anticipate outcomes, you have already deduced some important things about the futurizing voice. Take a moment to look at the differential voice diagram and consolidate your predictions about what's next.

Combining the visual references on the diagram with the contents of the previous chapter, you are probably predicting

- that there will be an inner voice to match the futurizing voice,
- that the futurizing voice will be based on the leadership of large groups of people, and
- that the futurizing voice will have something to do with the belief-in-the-supernatural.

You will be pleased when I tell you that you are correct. How on earth did you deduce all that?

Easy. The diagram is a sequence that you have been progressively filling. And each time you've done a chapter on outer voice, you've given me the inner voice. You've matched heartfelt voice to primeval shadow, command voice to tribal shadow, and prosocial voice to shadow gossip. Clearly now you are going to give us the inner voice for futurizing.

Large group size is obvious from the progression of group sizes in the diagram.

Every time you've done a differential voice, you've referred back to pre-cogs and intra-cogs. Futurizing lines up with post-cogs, which was

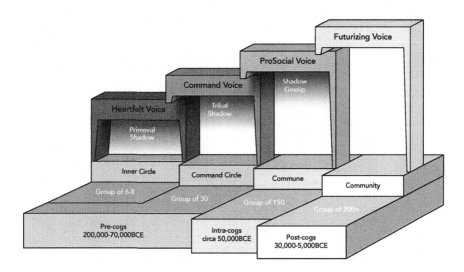

Figure 12.1 What's next?

all about religion and belief-in-the supernatural. Of course, you going to circle back and connect – you wouldn't leave it open.

That is an extraordinary skill that you have. You have taken disparate data from the past and analysed and extrapolated to accurately predict the future. That is superhuman. You are a superhero of prediction. All good superheroes deserve a name – I'm going to call you

The Daemon

In modern storylines, superheroes are not the squeaky-clean characters that they used to be. Some have a dark side that they must overcome to triumph against the villains. And so it is with your superhero, the daemon. The daemon is the inner voice that invalidates your futurizing voice. We can now complete the matched pairs of inner and outer voices on our diagram.

The daemon

Imagine that you were a young man studying at Cambridge University in late 1687. You had just attended a lecture by Isaac Newton. He had just

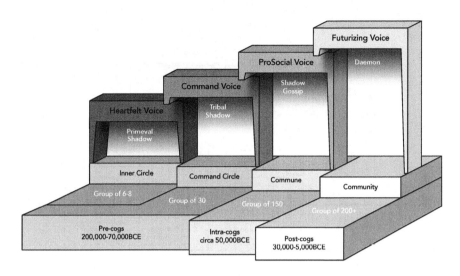

Figure 12.2 Daemon inner voice

had his book *Principia* published and was outlining the principles behind planetary motion.

It is difficult for us to imagine just how mind-blowing this moment would have been. With just a few very simple equations, you can now predict – with amazing accuracy – the motion of the planets, moons, and asteroids. You have been raised as a devout Anglican Christian. For your entire life, you have carried a deep belief that the motion of all the celestial objects is the will of God. But in less than an hour, you have learnt a mathematical technique that allows you to predict the future based on observation and calculation. In an instant, the entire universe has transformed for you. The universe has just lost its mystery. Understanding it is no longer beyond human comprehension. Instead of "moving in mysterious ways", the universe has started to become understandable by mortals. It has become an enormous machine. A machine to be measured, analysed, and understood.

Newton did not just make a scientific breakthrough, he created a discourse for scientific endeavour that prevails to this day. No one would dream of using Newton's work to calculate the parameters of a satellite launch, and yet our dominant way of looking at the world is through "Newtonian" eyes.

Perhaps the ultimate expression of this worldview belongs to Pierre-Simon Laplace, the French mathematician of the late 1700s. Laplace described an imaginary creature that he called a *daemon*. This creature has a vastly superior intellect to humans. Laplace contended that if the daemon could observe every single element of the universe, every miniscule detail of every single entity, and understood their precise location and momentum, then it would be able to calculate the past and future values for any given time. The daemon would be omnipotent, understanding the cause of the current state of the universe and able to accurately predict the future. To the daemon, the future is laid out in minute detail.

I will use Laplace's daemon rather than the more commonly used "Newtonian mind-set" when referring to our insatiable need to explain the world as direct cause and effect. When I refer to your daemon, I am referring to your "direct cause and effect" mind-set. I have chosen Laplace because although the dramatic breakthrough was Newton's, he couldn't quite take his own work to its logical conclusion. Though he was instrumental in submitting the universe to human analysis and understanding, he still clung strongly to the role of God in holding the ultimate secrets. Laplace dispensed with this "irrelevance" and positioned the universe as ultimately understandable. "I have no need of that hypothesis", he is quoted as saying when questioned by Napoleon Bonaparte about the role of the creator in his work.

Generations of scientists have worked tirelessly to disprove the premise of Laplace's daemon. The scientific fields of thermodynamics, evolution, and quantum mechanics have progressively debunked the Laplacian view of the world. But the journey is not easy, even for those with massive intellects. "God does not play dice", said Albert Einstein when confronted with Heisenberg's uncertainty principle, one of the defining moments in daemon slaying. Even the man with the abstract-thinking ability to warp time, gravity, mass, and energy could not bring himself to accept that the world was intrinsically indefinable. And how interesting is it that he immediately reached for the supernatural in his repudiation of the idea.

No matter that the daemon can see for an infinite distance and at the minutest detail, it cannot predict the future based on the current state. The universe was created from a sea of nothingness. It is the fundamental uncertainty that exists at the quantum level that gives rise to our universe. Our world is not just unknown, it is unknowable. The daemon should be dead and buried.

However, the concept of something being unknowable is profoundly uncomfortable for us. Our post-cog ancestors thrived through their ability to understand cause and effect and then apply their own agency. They were unique amongst the animal kingdom in their ability to connect two events and understand that one caused the other. By reversing the flow of time in their minds, they became the first detectives. They could look at a situation and work back in time to deduce what the cause had been. No other animal came close. Have you ever wondered why no other animal has the ability to look at the marks left by on the ground and use it to track their prey when it would be a huge advantage to their survival? It is a feat of an extraordinary brain.

With this skill finely honed, post-cogs went looking for the cause of everything. As discussed in Chapter 6, this was the probable origin of religion. With a driving need to understand the cause of everything as direct cause and effect, post-cogs turned to supernatural causes. It is hugely ironic then that despite his outspoken dismissal of the existence of God, Laplace himself was driven by the same insatiable urge to explain everything as direct cause and effect. It is also telling that he felt the need to invoke the supernatural (the daemon) to explain it. Even though he never asked anyone to believe that the daemon really existed, this ardent atheist needed a supernatural entity to enable his theory to resonate with people.

A post-cog is defined as a post-cog because of her ability to extend cause and effect beyond the physical world and into the imaginary. A post-cog could believe that if they stole desperately needed food from their rich neighbour who had plenty, this would be the cause of eternal damnation in the afterlife. Pre-cogs would not have been so compliant. It is ironic that the very ability that made us masters of the earth also gave us a mind-set so at odds with the very world that we created. The trap was preloaded by our evolutionary history. Isaac Newton just set off the trigger.

And so it is that we enter the world today. Preloaded by our DNA, we set about discovering the cause of everything that impacts upon us.

> We learn about physical cause and effect – running and tripping over on the gravel will result in pain.
> We learn about social cause and effect – being nice to your aunty will result in getting a cuddle; being mean to your friend will result in them playing with someone else.
> And very quickly we learn about imaginary cause and effect – you had better be good if you want Santa to bring you a present on Christmas Day.

We embark on our formal education, still structured according to the classical lines established more than 300 years ago, and learn classical mathematics and sciences. Even the study of physics is done along classical lines first. Introduction to modern physics (which overturns classical physics) is generally left to university study. By this time, we are talking about a minute proportion of the population. The rest of us are turned loose to shape a nonlinear world with linear mind-sets. We bring our daemon to a circus.

If any field should have started from a daemon-free place, the science of human behaviour should have. Taken to its logical conclusion, the daemon does not allow for free will. After all, if it knows the attributes of all the atoms of all the brains in the world, then the future state of these brains could be calculated. And if that were the case, you wouldn't bother with trying to modify people's behaviour – it would all be preprogrammed! This paradox did not occur to early human behaviourists, and they cheerfully followed down the path of replicating the rigorous scientific methods of the "hard" sciences. Confoundingly, they continued to do so even as the so-called hard sciences of physics and chemistry started to recognise that uncertainty is a key parameter.

Ironically, the social and behavioural sciences are undergoing a revolution by adopting complexity science from physics. It seems that, having been sent down the wrong road by classical physics, social and behavioural sciences have had to wait for one hundred years of modern physics to pass before it could be rescued. We should not be that surprised – we all have our daemon.

Complex systems

Our daemon is the enemy of our futurizing voice and must be contained if we are to be successful at catalysing major change. Our daemon thrives on predictability; our futurizing voice thrives on complexity. To start to understand this we must first define what we mean by complexity that is more specific than the general use of the word. We are interested in complexity in the same way that complexity scientists are. For these scientists, complexity is about the study of complex systems. Complex systems are

Nonlinear – in a linear system, cause and effect are in proportion. Big changes require big inputs, and small inputs will result in small changes. Organisations and other social systems are not like this. A massive culture change program with a multimillion-dollar budget and teams of "change leaders" and "communications experts" changes nothing, whereas an offhand comment by middle manager at a team meeting sets off a chain of events that changes the culture of the organisation.

Emergent – things happen in unexpected ways in unexpected places. They take on a life of their own. A small group of nerds, working in secret after hours, produce the product that becomes the mainstay of the company's operation.

Adaptive – shortcuts are established within hours of the introduction of a new rule designed to stamp out a shortcut.

Evolutionary – a set of company rules and practices are applied to a newly acquired business. Even when fully compliant, the new business has a different "flavour" to the rest of the organisation and outperforms it in every measure.

Spontaneously ordering – some sort of order (rarely the one that you would want) will form out of chaos. Deprived of access to their union by court order, a group of blue-collar workers stack the safety committee to disrupt the workplace and promote their agenda.

Open, not closed – influence comes from outside of the arena. Neither the origin nor the impact can be predicted. The risk management system for the project has nine hundred identified risks, all documented with mitigation plans. Unexpectedly, localised rioting associated with upcoming elections in a small country in Asia prevents transport of critical equipment, and the project is delayed by months.

Your daemon wants to approach all of these situations as if the world were a giant machine; pull the right lever, engage the overdrive, and open the throttle valve. Before too long, you figure out that it wasn't that simple. Organisations exist as complex systems operating in a society that is even more complex.

Let's put you in a hypothetical situation (while hypothetical, it is based on a real event). Say you take over the running of a public transport business. You want to increase revenues on the train service that you run. Your daemon gets to work reverse-engineering the cause and effect diagram (Figure 12.3).

You can now attack the root cause with relish. You analyse the potential to apply your agency to influence this system. Soon, you are deeply engaged with negotiations with the train drivers' union. Months later, and you have nailed it. There were plenty of issues on the table to resolve, but you held fast on this one. The new agreement contains a mechanism for determining

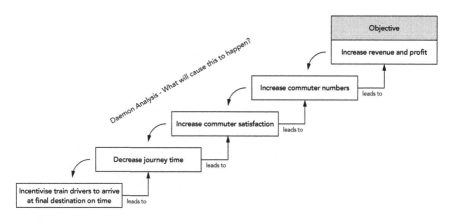

Figure 12.3 Daemon analysis of agency, cause, and effect

the quantum of an incentive payment. If the train arrives at destinations on time, they get the payment; for every minute late, the payment reduces.

On the day that the new agreement goes into effect, you watch the data with anticipation. Nothing extraordinary happens. The next day is the same. And the one after that. At the end of the first pay cycle there is no improvement against the historical levels of timeliness. Your daemon is not concerned. Of course, it will take a bit of time to register. Sure enough, there are murmurings of discontent from the drivers – their pay didn't include the bonus. Your daemon is pleased as you communicate the data backing up the pay determination. Now they will get the message. Over the next few days, you start to see improvement. Until the day that every single train arrives at its final destination on time. The same happens the next day. You and your daemon celebrate wildly.

On the third day, you get some disquieting news. The number and severity of complaints to the customer complaints line has increased markedly. It takes you no time at all to figure out what has happened. The drivers are responding to the incentive. Every time that they start to fall behind the schedule, they skip stations to keep on track for an on-time arrival at the destination. Passengers are left standing on the platform while their train whistles through the station without stopping.

You and your daemon have taken on a complex system.

It is *nonlinear* – a new incentive does not linearly transfer up the tree to increased revenue.

It is *emergent* – an unanticipated behaviour emerged from the chaos.

It is *adaptive* – the organisation did not respond like a machine. It morphed and adapted to the new context that you created.

It is *evolutionary* – your daemon took account only of the here and now. It went over the wages agreement with a fine-toothed comb. You had lawyers and highly qualified consultants advising your daemon, but your daemon was stuck in the context of the present. It ignored history. Your company only took over the train service a couple of years ago. Previously, it had been government-run. There is a long history of political and class-based antagonism with the union. They form the precursors for the way that the drivers will respond to the change.

It spontaneously orders itself – the union hierarchy did not issue an instruction to the rank and file to skip stations. In fact, the union negotiators were taken by surprise as much as you were. It was a movement that spontaneously grew amongst the drivers when prodded with a new stimuli. Before long, it had settled into a very ordered set of behaviours – albeit ones that you don't like!

It is open, not closed – at the same time as the drivers were checking their first payslip, a major story was breaking in the news as the prime minister took aim at excessive executive salaries. It was a calculated response to polling data, which showed that the opposition was gaining ground on an accusation that the government was serving the fat cats of industry rather than serving the hard-working populace. By extraordinary coincidence, your company was holding its annual general meeting that day, and this included a vote on awarding $3 million of preference rights to the CEO. Your CEO's executive remuneration package was splashed across every major news outlet in the country. Your train drivers were reading their payslips that included no bonus at the same time as their CEO was pocketing millions, and their anger grew. They were influenced by something outside the system that you had no control over and could not have been predicted.

Having suffered such an experience, of course, you immediately ditch your daemon, right? Wrong!! Mind-sets don't work like that. They are literally your worldview, the way that you see the world. So, you are only able to analyse your failure from within that mind-set. Your daemon swings into action by analysing the failure. How could you have been so stupid? Of course, this was a predictable outcome to what you did. You forgot to include a quality measure in the bonus mechanism. A simple clause that required drivers to stop at every scheduled station would have prevented this. You won't get caught out next time. And so, you march forward to the inevitable failure that waits for you as long as you continue to treat a complex system like a machine.

This is the power of the daemon. Because cause and effect are always obvious *after* the event, we look back and think that were negligent in not predicting it *before* the event. "If only I had thought about it a bit harder, I would have picked that up", we say to ourselves. Or perhaps we say it to our boss at annual performance review time. But complex systems do not work that way. In a complex system, *hindsight* does not lead to *foresight*.

When you operate from your daemon, you are almost always frustrated by this aspect of complex systems. There is never enough data. People act illogically. The world seems designed to unhinge your well-thought-out plans. But every now and again, some small action that you took results in a large positive outcome. Your daemon is a bit puzzled. Small actions should cause small impacts, not big impacts. This should be a signal that your daemon has a faulty view of the world, but in the same way that disproportionally large negative impacts are rationalised away with the gift of hindsight, so are positive ones. In hindsight, it is pretty obvious why a small action led to big results because you can replay a chain of events that led to the outcome. Again, your daemon mistakes the fact that something is obvious in hindsight, for the idea that it should have been obvious in foresight.

When you view an unpredictably positive event through your daemon, you may latch onto a new cause-and-effect model and look to apply it again. You quickly forget that it was a complete surprise to you and go looking for opportunity to use your newly discovered leadership skill. Alas, you are doomed to failure. The complex system has morphed, and the next time you try the same thing, it fails. The original event is characterised as an anomaly by your daemon, and you continue your frustrating journey look for the big actions to solve your problems.

Your futurizing voice is different. Where your daemon sees frustration, your futurizing voice sees power. Far from being frustrated by the responses of the complex system, the futurizing voice embraces complexity to deliver extraordinary outcomes.

Harnessing the power of complexity

Conditioned as we are by Hollywood and other forms of fiction, it is easy to be drawn to the conclusion that the futurizing voice is like the superhero of differential voices: a voice so powerful that it came overcome the forces of a complex system. This is daemon thinking.

Indeed, the futurizing voice is amazingly powerful in its impact, but it doesn't achieve this through brute strength. The futurizing voice does not overpower a complex system. The futurizing voice gets its power from within a complex system. It works with the forces already at play. It experiments and plays with them until it works out how to subtly change the landscape such that the forces align.

The futurizing voice catalyses change by creating a movement within a complex social system. I will define a movement as follows:

A movement is a large community of people with a shared social identity acting in a coordinated way that causes large-scale disruption or change in a complex social system.

Examining each of the elements of this definition we can observe the following:

Large community: Movements may start small, in fact they always do. But to qualify as a movement for our purposes, they must grow into something big. From the preceding chapters, we already know how to motivate a tribe and a commune to take coordinated action; our focus with the futurizing voice is to motivate a community.

Coordinated action: Movements are more than just a group of people with a common mind-set or belief system. The futurizing voice must ultimately create activists working with other activists in a coordinated way.

Large-scale disruption or change: The futurizing voice is the leadership capability of making big things happen. We engage it when leading through big change. If the organisational objectives do not call for big change, then the heartfelt, command, and prosocial voices are most effective. It is not just that the futurizing voice will be less effective in this circumstance; the futurizing voice is defined by the need for large-scale change. Attempting to engage it in the absence of big challenges will guarantee failure.

Complex social system: As we covered in the preceding section, the futurizing voice taps into the energy of a complex system. Its power is generated from within the complex system, not imposed from outside. If the system is not complex, then the futurizing voice has no energy to tap into. The heartfelt, command, and prosocial voices should prevail.

This leaves us with *shared social identity*. We have already covered the power of social identity in the previous chapter. The prosocial voice is fundamentally founded in social identity. We need to investigate what is different about the shared social identity created by the futurizing voice.

The shared social identity created by the futurizing voice is more than that which is cultivated by the prosocial voice. Recall that a social identity can be characterised by "we-ness" – "we are different from (and therefore better than) them". The prosocial voice cultivates a social identity by establishing rituals and celebrating the prototypical – building a larger social identity that honours the different tribes but binds people together into communes. Where the prosocial voice cultivates, the futurizing voice creates.

The futurizing voice creates the belief in a new ideal. Instead of a "we-ness" of

we are different from (and therefore better than) them,

the futurizing voice creates a belief that

we are different from and better than them, because we hold a higher purpose.

This is the golden elixir of leadership that has written our history as a species. It has created civilisation itself.

Andy Warhol has been quoted as saying

I'm impressed with people who can create new spaces with the right words.

Warhol was not referring to leadership when he said the words, but I think that it is an extraordinary description of the futurizing voice. It is also extraordinarily fitting that it should come from a master of creativity.

The futurizing voice creates something new that wasn't there before, and it creates it in language. It is an act of creating collective imagination through outer voice. It weaves a story that enthrals people and has them collectively believe. It is the act of a master storyteller.

The storyteller

It might seem initially that I am trivialising such a world-defining capability by relating it to storytelling. This might escalate to outrage when I go one step further and say that it is all fiction. However, a "higher purpose" is not real. A "higher purpose" is supernatural; you can't see or touch a "higher purpose". The success of a futurizing voice is directly proportional to the leader's ability to get followers to believe the supernatural, to believe in a story, to believe in a fiction.

The telling and interpretation of fictitious stories is one of the most advanced functions of the human brain. In fact, stories and religion (a particularly powerful form of storytelling) appear to be the *only* activities that require the full capacity of our very advanced brain.[1] We have already discussed just how costly it is for humans to have such large brains. The energy consumption of a large brain is a significant disadvantage to an animal struggling for survival in a world of limited resources and hostile predators. So why would it be advantageous to the reproductive fitness of the species to develop such advanced capabilities? Why is storytelling so important, and how did the benefits to society outweigh the disadvantages of feeding a brain big enough to support it?

Let us rebase ourselves on our Eurotrack journey, travelling west. It is no coincidence that the massive societal transformation taking place as we walk back towards St Pancras leaving the last of our intra-cogs behind corresponds with the emergence of fiction. Your team of 150 intra-cogs responded well to your prosocial voice, but your leadership reach could not extend any further than this. The ability to communicate indirectly through social interactions broke the constraints of direct communication, but this too had its limits. As the population increased beyond 150, social cohesion broke down. The web of relationships became too great to manage.

Looking ahead you can see an amazing transformation as people start to cooperate on a much greater scale. The age of kings, czars, emperors, and presidents is approaching, where leadership reach grows exponentially. You look for the clue in the behaviour of your forebears and quickly identify the changed behaviour. The post-cogs have developed imagination. They have developed their belief-in-the-supernatural. They have invented fiction. They have become storytellers. But more importantly from a leadership perspective, now they can jointly believe in the same fiction. This is an extraordinary capability.

Let us examine the concept of jointly believing in fictions into a modern-day business context. In doing so, let's get more specific about a certain subset of fictions called *institutional facts*.[2] Institutional facts (I will use the term *ifacts*) are things that exist only because we all say that they do. They are distinct from "real" facts because they cannot be physically proven. Ifacts are so ever-present in our lives that we have ceased to discriminate between them and real facts.

As an example, you might think that it is a fact that you have ten dollars in your wallet. You pull it out and show me, and I agree that it is worth ten dollars. Whenever you and I agree that it is a ten-dollar note, then it has a value of ten dollars. Your ten dollars is an institutional fact because you and I agree. I offer to give you an ice cream for the ten dollars, but you decline – you can get a better deal at the ice cream shop down the road. You go down the road to the ice cream shop. The owner of the shop looks at your ten-dollar note and says, "I'm sorry, but this note is counterfeit. It is worthless". In an instant, your ten dollars no longer exists. It doesn't matter whether the note is actually genuine. As soon as the joint agreement was lost, ten dollars was lost. No ice cream for you today. The ifact is gone, and you are left with the real fact – you have only a piece of printed, plasticised paper.

Printed banknotes are an institutional fact created to allow strangers to cooperate. You and the owner of the ice cream shop are perfect strangers, and yet if you had turned up with a banknote that he agreed was genuine, he would happily have swapped real food for an otherwise worthless piece of paper. Because we all agree that the piece of paper is ten dollars, you have purchasing power. It can get you real things. As soon as agreement is lost, the system breaks down. The owner will not give you (a stranger) ice cream unless you give him something real of equivalent value.

Money is an example of the power of ifacts. Its power is recognised almost universally. Ecommerce is based on the strength of joint agreement – we do not even have the token piece of paper to represent the ifact. Governments are giving up maintaining their gold reserves, replacing it with numbers in a database. (The value of gold is itself an ifact. If its value were based on supply and demand for industrial usage, the value would plummet. It is our collective agreement that defines its high value.)

Your fixation on certain ifacts will stand in the way of your futurizing. Ifacts sit beneath all of our most powerful institutions. These institutions are not physical entities, they are *social constructions*. In other words, you cannot physically locate the essence of them, but you agree with most other people in the social system that they are real. The company you work for is a social construction. That's right, the company you work for is not real.

To test this through an example, let's pretend that you work for a bank. You go to work every day in the financial district to a multistory building with the bank's logo emblazoned across the top. The bank operates internationally and has millions of customers. How on earth could we say that it is not real?

You cannot locate the essence of your bank. You can't find it in your head office building – the building is leased anyway. If that building burnt down, the bank would survive. It is not in the chairman or the board of directors or the CEO – they get changed out regularly. It is not in the incorporation or registration documents – banks can be deregistered and survive to be reregistered later. Your bank exists because we collectively say it exists. We socially construct its existence.

I will refer to social constructions as a network of real facts and ifacts tied together by the stories we create and agree upon. Although this does not strictly line up with academic interpretations (of which there are many), it is helpful for us to think about it this way. Your bank is underpinned by real facts (physical assets and people) and ifacts (debt, equity, valuations) tied together by strong stories (accounts must balance at close of business each day).

Every now and then, the social constructions get a shake-up. One of the surefire signs of imminent societal collapse is when people lose faith in the currency. They rush to get their money out of the bank and convert it to something of physical value. Unfortunately, they are then confronted by locked doors at the bank. A "story" has broken down – the one that says that our money is safe in the bank. For many people, this illusion is complete. They actually think that the bank has their money. In a failing economy, people are starkly reminded that a bank is a broker between depositors and lenders – it doesn't have their money. "Safe as a bank" is a powerful story.

During the global financial crisis of 2008, the "story" of banking came under extreme stress. In the midst of the chaos, people's commitment to the joint agreement started to waiver. In response, governments around the world rushed to guarantee bank savings and underwrite failing banks. The irony of course is that "governments" are also a social construction. Fortunately for all of us, our collective story about government held. But everyone was shaken to the core by having witnessed just how fragile the social construction of global banking was.

The point of reinterpreting our organisations as social constructions is not to invalidate them. These things have real power over your life. Reinterpreting your zero bank balance as an ifact will not mean that you won't go hungry or be evicted from your home. The judiciary and police force are both social constructions but they will work very effectively to deprive you of your liberty should you break the law (another social construction).

The point of thinking in terms of social constructions is that it gives us access to leadership power. Leadership is a social construction. You have authority as a leader because people generally agree that you have it. Say that your boss dismisses you by email but accidently sends his email to the wrong email address (you have a sloppy and rather callous boss). He then informs HR and leaves on holidays. (You have a really callous boss!) You turn up for work the next day, blissfully unaware that you have been sacked. Luckily, you know the security guard pretty well, and she lets you in in despite the curious malfunction of your swipe card. You go about your business as usual. Your team still respond to your command voice on a couple of issues that happened overnight, your input at the morning operations meeting is respected, and the performance conversation that you have with one of your direct reports goes to plan. You are sitting with a number of others in the conference room waiting for the next meeting to start. Everyone else is checking their emails. You would, too, except that your email has suddenly stopped working. All of a sudden, everyone around the table simultaneously looks up from their smart phones at you. The email from HR announcing your dismissal has hit their inbox. In that moment, you lose your leadership power. All morning, you were a leader because everyone you dealt with agreed that you were the leader. As soon as the agreement is lost, you lose your leadership. Your leadership lives only inside a story. For us, this is a positive rather than a negative, because it can be a very powerful story.

If your leadership is based in the story, then the ability to shape this story is central to increasing your leadership capabilities. As a futurizer, we embrace the power of the social construction of leadership. The futurizing voice is the capability to shape the future by forging new joint intentions and agreements. You might say that the futurizing voice is the architect of new social constructions, through storytelling.

Martin Luther King had a dream – a supernatural experience. If it had merely remained a private supernatural experience, then the world today would be a different place. Martin Luther King used his futurizing voice to leverage his dream, to skilfully appeal to his follower's belief-in-the-supernatural. He wove a story that harnessed the power of existing social constructions by extolling the values of the United States of America, the constitution, the church. He destroyed previously unquestioned ifacts that positioned African Americans as an inferior race to white Americans. His storytelling created new social constructions based on integration and equal rights that people believed in. His social constructions described in enticing detail the attributes of a new social identity. Millions of people were moved to take up this social identity, and the movement was created. A story had changed the world.

Your futurizing voice creates a movement. It uses stories to enrol a large community of people in a shared social identity, which causes the community to coordinate their actions in a way that results in large-scale, but controlled, disruption to the system.

Your futurizing voice will be driven by a future that you authentically commit yourselves to; that encompasses your values; that integrates rather than alienates; and that defines a social identity that attracts a critical mass of people. It creates a new centre of gravity within the complex system that changes it irrevocably.

The biggest story of all – your defining identity

I would be surprised if you weren't at least a bit bothered by the concept of the futurizing voice being about a story (and not just any story, but a fictitious story!). It is disquieting to recategorise things that are really important as a social construction – a story. It can also seem manipulative, perhaps even immoral, to be speaking so frankly about a leader using her futurizing voice to sell a story. After all, isn't this just conning someone? Isn't it a trick that a fraudster would play?

Your futurizing voice operates from your authentic self, not from duplicity. There is no "selling" to others involved in the futurizing voice. The futurizing voice is not the act of manipulating others to a point of view that benefits your objectives. It is inviting them to be a partner with you in something that you passionately believe in. When you passionately believe in something, it will not occur to you as a story or a social construction or an ifact. It will occur to you as an expression of your true self, as your defining identity.

Your defining identity describes your primary motivation and the centre of your every action. It is the source of your power. It is irresistible to others. It is your highest purpose. It is you at your very best, delivering to your highest potential. It is you as a force for good in the world. It is, however, not yours alone. It exists only in the context of your relationships. It encompasses you, but it is not exclusively you.

It is a *defining* identity because defining is what it does. It defines who you are: your identity. It defines who you are becoming. It defines the social identity that you have created that draws in your followers and creates a movement. It inherently defines the actions of members of the movement: the culture and behaviour of "us" as distinct from "them".

It is a defining *identity* in deference to pivotal role of developing a shared social identity in the futurizing voice. However, the shared social identity is not something separate to us. Your defining identity also describes your personal identity in the context of the movement.

Fundamentally, your defining identity is illogical. It is supernatural in nature and can neither be evidenced today, nor predicted by extrapolating the current trajectory of things in today's world. It is certain, therefore, that your daemon inner voice will be triggered when you try to engage with it. Your daemon is the enemy of your creativity, and the futurizing voice is creativity personified and put into action.

Banishing your daemon is incredibly liberating to your futurizing voice. You effectively remove the "rules". These rules (mostly unwritten) are very effective in saying what is not possible. These appeal to your daemon who believes that rules govern everything. Your defining identity steps beyond your daemon giving you permission to break the rules, to play in areas that shouldn't exist, and the create things that shouldn't have been possible to create.

All great acts of futurizing leadership have created things that shouldn't have been possible. Now it is time for you to live your defining identity and create your own impossible future.

Takeaways

"The daemon" was created by Laplace as a thought experiment to support his argument that the entire universe can in principle be measured and understood and its future state predicted.

Daemon is the inner voice based on this mistaken assertion. It is, therefore, the invalidator of the futurizing voice.

In contrast to daemon thinking, the world we inhabit is a complex system. A complex system is nonlinear, emergent, adaptive, evolutionary, spontaneously ordering, and open (not closed).

The futurizing voice is *not* leadership that overcomes complexity.

The futurizing voice *is* leadership that harnesses the power of complexity.

The futurizing voice uses storytelling to create a shared belief-in-the-supernatural called a common purpose. Shared belief in the common purpose creates a very strong social identity.

The social identity created by the futurizing voice storytelling creates a movement – *a large community of people with a shared social identity acting in a coordinated way that causes large-scale disruption or change in a complex social system.*

The access point for a leader to empower their futurizing voice is to generate their defining identity that embodies their highest purpose as a leader. This necessarily requires the leader to overcome their daemon.

Leadership development actions

- Reflect on your previous attempts at leading change in an organisation. Identify for yourself where the organisation had the characteristics of a complex system.
- Reflect on where your leadership had unintended consequences or disproportional outcomes, either good or bad. Don't allow yourself to be tricked by your daemon; it may seem logical in hindsight, but was it really predictable at the time that you took action?
- If you currently have a big project or major change initiative, identify your daemon. Are you approaching a complex system with a linear mind-set?
- Create your personal defining identity. What are your values, what is your personal vision for your future, and what do you unequivocally stand for?
- Have you been acting consistently with your defining identity *in the moment*?
- Examine the "purpose statement" or "vision" for your organisation. Does it align with your personal identity? If the answer is no, then set about changing it, or resign.

- Is the purpose statement the basis for a great story that will create the right social identity? Rework the story so it does. Think creatively about how you will tell the story to create the shared belief.
- Identify mini-movements within your organisation that support the change. Think creatively about how your storytelling will cause the movement to grow.
- Identify counter-movements or pockets of resistance. What is the local shared belief system that is causing it? Think creatively about how your storytelling can reshape the shared belief system to align with your goals.

Notes

1 Dunbar, Barrett, and Lycett, *Evolutionary Psychology*.
2 Searle, *The Construction of Social Reality*.

13 Bringing it all together

We have now brought together all the elements of our trip down the Euro-star line: the size of the societal groups through different period through the cognitive revolution, the outer voice mechanism of leadership for each of the groups, and the inner voices we experience today as remnants of this evolutionary journey.

Having made a case for our modern brain retaining characteristics of the brains of our ancient ancestors,

and

having made a case for the origins of the differential voice being directly correlated to the size of the populations being led at points through the cognitive revolution,

and

having made a case for these population sizes still being relevant in the modern world,

and

having shown how the differential voice applies in the modern world,

it is tempting to put the pieces together to give an elegant model of lead-ership based on group size. This model would say that a leader simply observes the number of people in the group that she is interacting with and picks the appropriate outer voice. Such a model would look like this.

Such a model would be nicely ordered and be (relatively) easy to under-stand. The only problem is that it would quickly fail in application. As I said at the outset of this book, leadership is not easy. We need to dig into its complexity if we are truly going to make a difference. We have uncovered evidence that the natural group sizes that mark the cognitive revolution still emerge in today's society. That doesn't mean that as soon as your inner

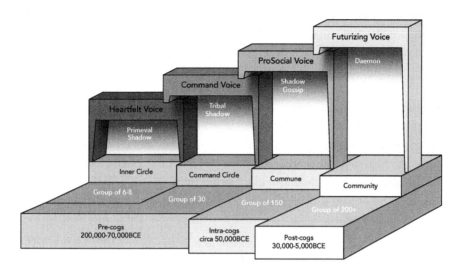

Figure 13.1 Evolutionary basis of the differential voice

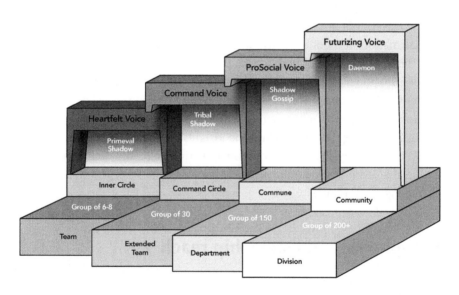

Figure 13.2 Oversimplified application of differential voice

circle are all together at your team meeting that they suddenly turn into pre-cogs!

Reflect on your own experience. The heartfelt voice is the mainstay of your inner circle, but it will never be exclusive. It is obvious that there are situations when you will want to be using your team meeting to explore future possibilities using your futurizing voice or need to use your prosocial voice to communicate the implementation of a new policy.

The differential voices map directly to group size in the ancient world for two reasons that don't apply any more. Firstly, the individuals in the group had limited mental capability. Pre-cogs did not have the mental capability to engage in gossip or futurizing. There was no expectation of being engaged in prosocial or futurizing discussion because there was no mental capacity to do so. Not so today. People do have the mental capacity to be engaged prosocially and through futurizing. Importantly, this means that they also *expect* to be engaged by prosocial and futurizing leadership. The heartfelt and command voices resonate strongly with people today just as they did with pre-cogs. But if you treat them like pre-cogs and exclude the prosocial and futurizing voices, they will be unfulfilled and uninspired by your leadership.

The second reason why direct mapping of leadership style to group size is not the full story is that the context in which we operate is far more complex than it was for our ancestors. Our context is dominated by massive volumes of information, the connectivity of the world, the speed of travel, money, government control, legislation, and dozens of other things that were completely unknown to our forebears. As complexity increases, the need for higher-level differential voices increases. Even a small team needs prosocial and futurizing leadership if operating in a complex system.

We are looking for a way to take the insights gained from our tour of leadership through the cognitive revolution and bring them into modern context. Group size is still important in selecting a differential voice, but we need to also recognise complexity.

Complexity and leadership reach

We carry the evolutionary traits of our prehistoric ancestors, but that does not make us behave prehistorically. We are a blend of pre-cog, intra-cog, and post-cog traits. We still respond to the heartfelt voice and the command voice of our pre-cog ancestry but never to the exclusion of being a modern human. We set out to recognise this in the differential voice framework.

It is the complexity of the modern world that weakens the direct correlation between group size and outer voice. For example, you might be progressing the renegotiation of a labour agreement with a team of only twenty-five workers operating in a remote, standalone environment, but if you happen to hit upon a hot-button issue of the trade union's national executive, then the speed of modern communications will ensure that the complexity of your situation skyrockets. The group size might not grow by more than a few people, but complexity has increased significantly.

The determinate of appropriate outer voice is no longer solely dependent on population size. Rather it is the combination of the group size and the complexity of the operational context that dictates the extent of required leadership reach. Increasing either group size or complexity results in the requirement for the higher differentials. This incorporation of complexity into the differential voice framework is an important step towards a meta-model.

I represent the incorporation of complexity into the differential voice diagram as follows. In doing so, I redefine leadership reach as including both group size and complexity.

In decreasing the granularity, I hope to discourage the use of the diagram to approach leadership like it is a formula. A highly granular diagram is an opportunity for our daemon to run wild. Our daemon would have us

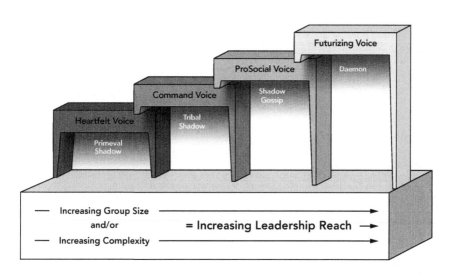

Figure 13.3 Differential voice and leadership reach

measure the group size, measure the complexity, move along the x-axis to the point defined, and move up the y-axis to determine the outer voice required. We need to remember that our daemon is the enemy of exceptional leadership.

Exceptional leadership lives in the inquiry. In completing the differential voice meta-model, we have a new frame for that inquiry. Let's put it to use.

PART 3

Traps and pitfalls

We have reached an important milestone in the book. The differential voice meta-model is now complete and ready to support your leadership development journey. There is no new theoretical content from this point forward. The remainder of the book is devoted to the application of the differential voice rather than introduction of new theory. Because leadership in the real world happens in application rather than theory, there is much to learn!

Part two concluded with a plea from me about not letting your daemon turn the differential voice into a formula for leadership. I have tried to clearly structure the buildup of the meta-model in logical steps supported by evidence (although *Evolved Organizations* is a better source for evidence). In a way, I have structured the book to appeal to your daemon. Now, I appeal to your newfound knowledge of complex systems to put your daemon in the right box.

With this overarching guidance established, I believe there is a lot to be learned about the misapplication of the differential voice. Let us start by talking about differential disfunction.

Traps and pitfalls

14 | **Differential disfunction**

Failure to launch

Bob Hawke set out to end child poverty in Australia. Instead of creating an enduring legacy, he created his biggest mistake.

In attempting to engage his futurizing voice in the absence of the lower differentials, Hawke failed to respect the hierarchy of differential voices.

- By revealing his "bold declaration" on the election dais rather than in collaboration with his inner circle, he invalidated his heartfelt voice.
- By having no immediate plan, no immediate deliverables, no allocation of accountability, and no governance structure, he invalidated his command voice.
- By making no attempt to engage stakeholders in positive informal communications, he invalidated his prosocial voice and inadvertently triggered a tsunami of negative gossip.

Without the lower differentials, the futurizing voice is empty and devoid of substance. It is perceived as "spin" by potential followers – just another leader caught up in hubris of thinking they can manipulate their followers through their flowery language.

In *Evolved Organizations* I look at the issue of hierarchy in more detail. Nokia's vision of the future of mobile devices makes for freaky reading – they had it 100 percent spot on. Their spectacular collapse was a failure of prosocial voice: the lack of ability to collaborate across four incredible powerful "tribal" silos within the organisation. This was not so for Enron. Enron was unmatched in the power of its social identity driven by compelling futurizing and prosocial voices. This was backed by an awesome ability to deliver results through command voice. It was, however, entirely devoid of the heartfelt voice. Without this foundation, Enron was always a house of cards.

To complete the picture of leadership disfunction through disrespecting the lower differentials, let us look at the other manifestations.

Command without heartfelt – the heartless commander

Have you ever had a boss that was a real #$&@%$# (insert your preferred profanity here).

One of the worst kind of bad boss is the heartless commander; a leader that rules by fear and intimidation. This a perverted form of command voice implemented without a heartfelt voice, represented on our meta-model diagram by removing the heartfelt voice block and having the command voice block topple over.

The heartless commander comes in a few different forms. At an extreme there is an outright bully, where the tribal shadow says "attack". This is a psychotic form of the command voice because the objective is to inflict pain rather than get the job done. So much better, then, to deliberately leave requests vague and expectations unclear. The bully is not a committed partner in any request because the lack of clarity serves their purpose. They get their reward by inflicting the unfair consequences against invisible expectations. The bully has a complete absence of heartfelt voice. As a result, they have nothing to offer in terms of long-term value to their organisation. Their short-term results are poor because of their secret (often even unconscious) objectives and their long-term impact is toxic.

A step up from the bully is the barking drill sergeant. As you learnt in the pub from your friend Trevor, platoon sergeants can be excellent examples of a command voice based on heartfelt voice, but we want to pick out a sergeant who runs drills and nothing else. He makes his expectations very clear, in a very loud voice, and rides the troops relentlessly in pursuit of the target. He never gives an inch when it comes to judging performance and delivering consequence. He consciously avoids relationships with the troops because that could compromise his impartiality. This works well for his limited set of objectives. The approach doesn't work anywhere else in the military or anywhere at all in civilian organisations. The barking sergeant is a one-trick pony. As soon as the situation starts to stray beyond the straightforward, he fails. Without a connection to his inner circle and without a psychologically safe environment, knowledge goes unshared and mutual support is absent. And people rapidly tire of being shouted at (either literally or metaphorically). They vote with their feet.

Next, we can consider the aloof leader. This is a leader who avoids building relationships because they are frightened by the situations that could result. They cannot reconcile close relationships with their responsibilities as a leader. They decide that it is better not to form close relationships at all. An aloof leader can have all the attributes of a strong command voice, but her leadership lacks soul. Her followers may perform their tasks reliably, but they will not be connected to a shared purpose. They will lack the feeling of support from their team. An aloof leader can never really develop a feeling within a team that "we are all in this together".

Your command voice is an essential part of your armoury as a leader, regardless of position, rank, organisation, industry, or culture. It is the most explicit of the voices when it comes to exercising your leadership power. The command voice requires that you fully take up your leadership power and use it responsibly.

Using your leadership power irresponsibly inevitably results in potential followers being repulsed by it. The result is long-term harm even if short-term objectives are met. Conversely, the command voice can be the responsible use of power, which attracts and motivates followers. This occurs because the command voice is built on the foundation of the heartfelt voice. When people feel safe, are mutually supported, and connect to a shared purpose, they seek the opportunity to make a difference. They not only accept the application of your leadership power through the command voice, they actively seek it out.

Magnifying your command voice is pivotal in your journey toward being an exceptional leader. Start with the heart.

Prosocial without heartfelt – the shallow popularist

The shallow popularist is often the biggest personality in the room and often the most popular (at a surface level anyway). They revel in the presence of large groups. When social situations start to feel awkward, they are the ones cutting through awkwardness with some banter and a funny joke. Seeing them walk around the workplace is a pleasure to watch. They seem to have the ability to remember the names of everyone, even the ones they met only briefly twelve months ago. A bubble of excited chatter seems to float with them wherever they go. In cultures where alcohol features strongly, they will be encouraging everyone to drop by the pub for a drink on Friday afternoon. There you will find them standing at the bar, two hours before normal close of business, ordering the drinks (from the bar staff who they know by name) and running up the tab on the company credit card. These sessions seem to frequently migrate to boozy dinners and late-night nightclubs. They have no compunction in then presenting this expense claim to their boss with stained receipts duly assigned to "team-building".

When it comes to work, the shallow popularist seems to be in the know on everything and is very open in sharing it. Where other managers are guarded about certain information, say the current direction on the reorganisation, they are happy to share. The breadth of their knowledge is impressive; they are able to connect disparate happenings and weave together a story that explains anything that you throw at them. This ability seems to serve them well when bad stuff happens because they can put a positive spin on almost anything, including bad performance. Using expressions like, "I really respect the way that IT go about their business and they have some incredibly tough challenges but . . ." and "Susan is an incredibly dedicated sales leader, but on this occasion . . ." they seem to be able to shift and spread accountability. Even if they do damage a relationship, they are confident that they will patch it up. They gain a reputation of being "Teflon-coated"; no matter how much mud is being thrown about, nothing sticks to them.

The prosocial voice is mastery of widespread indirect connections. Shallow popularist are masters of these widespread connections, but these connections are all shallow. They have no deep heartfelt connections, either because they are scared of them or get bored with focussing on one person for too long. The heartfelt voice is the ability to directly connect with an inner circle of trusted allies. Shallow popularists either run from these direct connections or wander off looking for more exciting people to talk to.

Prosocial without command – the social director

A leader who has a strong prosocial voice without command voice is the social director. With the social director, there is plenty of back-slapping encouragement but no steel. Underneath the veneer of a happy workplace is poor delivery and a lack of disciplined operation. This is skilfully explained away, of course. Good excuses are easier to manufacture than operating discipline for a social director.

Both versions of the social director, the one lacking heartfelt voice and the one lacking command voice, can be found in most organisations. When both the heartfelt and the command voices are missing, the result is a leader devoid of any substance at all. A social director tries to supercharge their prosocial voice in the absence of the heartfelt voice or the command voice. They are masters of indirect relationships spanning a huge number of people, but the prosocial voice doesn't work that way. The prosocial voice is perilously close to gossip, using the same propensity in potential followers for indirect communications. In the absence of heartfelt and/or command voice, it is little better than leadership by gossip.

15 Differential dark side

There is a dark side to the differential voice. Strong and effective leadership can be used for evil as well as for good. This is evident time and again throughout history and by extension through prehistory. With the communication tools now available to a large proportion of our society, I believe that we have never been better equipped to recognise and stamp out misdirected leadership. Unfortunately, the very same access to communication tools means that we have also never been more vulnerable.

Antisocial manipulation – the dark side

The differential voice approach to large-scale change is through the prosocial and futurizing voice. Both are founded on creating and shaping social identity. An exploration of leadership through social identity is incomplete without exploring the dark side. The very attributes that make the prosocial voice and futurizing voice such powerful forces for good can be exploited for less admirable objectives. Far from being prosocial, it becomes antisocial. It is to the long-term detriment of humanity. This is leadership by antisocial manipulation. I believe that it is our collective responsibility to identify when this is happening and do our best to counteract it.

The antisocial manipulator operates by misusing the power of social identity. Instead of using it in an inclusive way to break down tribal barriers and build communes, the antisocial manipulator builds bigger and bigger tribes. In Chapter 11, we discussed the toxic impact of a tribal shadow manipulator, a leader who instinctively understands and encourages tribal behaviours in their team. They effectively bring the tribal behaviour out of the shadows and encourage it. The tribal shadow manipulator is a counterproductive person in an organisation, but their impact is generally contained to that organisation. The antisocial manipulator, however, uses a tribal form of social identity to expand the toxicity across a vast number of followers.

Recall that a tribal shadow manipulator will continually exonerate and build up their own team at the expense of other teams. "We're a great team. We could be even better and deliver even more if it wasn't for those incompetent people over there". The more that other teams are invalidated, the stronger our team appears. These leaders build a very strong social connection within the team. This spreads the poison as members of the team follow suit and start to "bag" the other teams. These leaders are often strong performers against their specific tasks. Our tribal tendencies are still very strong, and a leader playing on them can build localised high performance. Where they don't deliver, tribal voice manipulators are very clever at pointing out how it's another team's fault. Thus, the leader can end up being perceived as a high performer. But the impact of the transmitted negativity on the overall organisation is counterproductive.

The antisocial manipulator supercharges this toxicity by weaving the tribal behaviours into the fabric of a social identity. In doing so, he can extend his leadership reach to millions of people. While the same psychological processes that underpin the prosocial voice are the basis of the antisocial manipulation, there is an important difference in the way the two are played.

With the prosocial voice, the primary focus is on building the "us" of a new social identity. The predominance of the effort goes into building a cohesive identity based on the possibility for this new "us". This inevitably (and always) creates a "them", and the leader will contrast the attributes of "them" to clearly define the desired attributes in "us". However, the predominance of attention is on the positive attributes of "us".

Conversely, the antisocial manipulator overwhelmingly focuses on "them". This is a leader who understands the power of playing on people's fears. You might say that he supercharges a common tribal shadow. By validating their fear and powerfully focussing it on "them", a power base of "us" is created. Although the prosocial voice is based on the social identity drive that "we are different from (and therefore better than) them", the antisocial manipulator approach can be characterised by "they are the pinnacle of evil, and, therefore, we are united in war against them". The stronger the demonisation of "them", the stronger the power base of "us".

This, then, is the first way to distinguish an antisocial manipulator from a prosocial voice or futurizing voice. By observing that the balance of the focus is on "them", we know that social identity is being manipulated for self-serving purposes, even though it is operating in a similar way. Once you spot it, you will spot something else. Manipulators always unconditionally attribute badness to a specific group. An example of this attribution is "all terrorists are Muslims; therefore, all Muslims are terrorists at heart". Here you can see that by starting with a falsity ("all terrorists are Muslim"), an antisocial manipulator can then falsely assign an unconditionality ("all Muslims are terrorists at heart").

This is a fine line that I am drawing. It could be argued that the prosocial voice and futurizing voice are also fundamentally based on social manipulation. For me to label one example as good and another example as bad could just be my biases being played out in public. It is irrefutable, however, that the manipulation of social identity has been used for evil (Adolf Hitler's demonisation of Jews to validate Aryan supremacy, for example), and there appears to be a strong correlation with whether the balance of the focus is on "us" or "them" and whether badness is attributed to a specific group. I believe it serves the purpose of improving your prosocial voice to contemplate where you will position the balance of your focus between "us" and "them" and whether you unconditionally assign badness to a specific group.

How Donald Trump and Kim Jong-un are the same

At the time of writing, the world stage is dominated by a confrontation between Donald Trump and Kim Jong-un of North Korea. It is ironic that I consider both of these leaders to be powerful antisocial manipulators of social identity, despite their very different ideologies. I need to be clear that I am not saying that they are alike in any other way. I also need to be clear that this categorisation of Trump is not a statement about politics; it is purely about his tactics in gaining and maintaining power. As I said above, this is a fine line. To me, it is an important line.

When Donald Trump swept to power, it was a victory for the social identity that he had created and nurtured. "Make America great again" was a call to the tribal shadow of millions of Americans, appealing to their unreliable nostalgic fantasy that things used to be "better". But how could it be a triumph of social identity? Trump was not the prototypical of his voters. He shared some of the same attributes: he was old, white, and conservative.

However, he was diametrically opposed to other attributes. He was urban whereas his voters were rural. He had a wealthy upbringing, but his voters had low-income upbringings. He went to private boarding school; his voters went to public schools. He attended Wharton, the original Ivy League university, whereas his voters never went to any university.

Trump was extraordinary in the way that he mobilised millions to unite in what they were *against*. Or more specifically, to unite in *who* they were *against*. They were against Mexicans and Chinese who stole their jobs. They were against Muslims, who were all terrorists. They were against the elite with their incredible wealth gained at the expense of the average Americans. They were against the newspapers and TV station, all owned by billionaires, for conspiring to prop up the elite through their fake news. And most of all, they were against politicians – those wealthy leeches on society with their fancy language and broken promises.

The Democrats fell directly into the well-planned trap, fielding a candidate that was the prototypical of everything that this group now despised. Hillary Clinton had moderate views on relations with Mexico and trade with China. She was inclusive towards Muslims. She was the darling of the newspapers and TV stations owned by billionaires. She was not just part of the elite– she was the elite of the elite. And worst of all, she was a politician to the centre of her soul.

Donald Trump swept to power. This was an enormous surprise of the vast majority of observers. The exception was keen observers of social identity who accurately predicted his rise through the primaries, his Republican nomination, and his ultimate victory.[1]

The problem for antisocial manipulators is that they have nowhere to go after they achieve power. This because their overriding objective is the acquisition of power. Once they have the power, there is nowhere to go except to maintain it by any means. This causes them to drive their divisive agenda even harder. For the best current example of this in action, we go to Trump's international rival, Kim Jong-un. As the current situation unfolds on the Korean Peninsula, people are dumbstruck by the actions of Kim Jong-un. Why is he being so provocative towards the United States and its allies? He is hopelessly outgunned. He must be mentally unhinged!

Such observations miss the point. Kim Jong-un's actions are not the actions of a madman. They are the clever actions of an extraordinarily talented and intelligent antisocial manipulator. His objective has little to do with the United States. His objective is to build his power as leader of North

Korea. Kim Jong-un's succession to power following his father's death was far from predictable. Most observers picked that Kim Jong-un's uncle, Kim Jong-thaek, would take the leadership position. Kim Jong-un was considered too inexperienced to take the role. We can presume (we have to work with presumptions as verifiable information is almost completely inaccessible) that there were many other power plays in motion at the time with other family members and within the factions of the military. There was the very real possibility that the unity of the regime would begin to crumble. Kim Jong-un prevailed through this uncertainty, but his initial hold on power was extremely tenuous. This can be presumed from the alacrity of his actions in eliminating potential rivals, including the execution of Kim Jong-thaek for "treachery", and also his suspected involvement in the assassination of his half-brother, Kim Jong-nam.

Elimination of rivals is one way to shore up power, but Kim Jong-un understands that this is short term at best. To rule North Korea for decades, he must have a broad support base from the people even in a totalitarian regime. The model used so effectively by his father was based on a propaganda machine unleashed on a population with ironclad isolation from the outside world. This is breaking down. No matter how much effort his regime puts into maintaining isolation, technology-enabled infiltration is inexorably underway. He simply cannot keep the outside world out. A starving population under totalitarian rule will not remain passive when armed with information.

Starvation is not a problem if you are part of a strong social identity (for example, devout follower of certain Hindu social identities will starve to death rather than eat meat from a cow). Kim Jong-un has been extremely effective at building a social identity where people can connect their hardships to the struggle to protect their social identity. As an antisocial manipulator, he has not had to go very far to identify the "them". Hatred of the Americans was a natural outcome of the Korean War, and it has been fostered by propaganda ever since. His masterstroke has been to amp this up. By developing nuclear weapons and firing missiles over Japan, he has provoked an enormous reaction. Each escalating response from the Americans is played back as a direct threat to the North Korean people. You can see already that in this context, the UN sanctions are not just ineffective, they play directly into Kim Jong-un's hands.

President Trump's threat to rain "fire and fury like the world has never seen" on North Korea was in service of shoring up his own power. In the light of subsequent events it looks like it had a weak impact at best. We can be certain, though, that it was absolute gold for Kim Jong-un. As the "them" of the Americans becomes increasingly demonic, the "us" of the North Korean people becomes stronger. It is an "us" of the righteous North Korea under the inspired leadership of our supreme protector, Kim Jong-un.

The lesson to take from this analysis is that when using your prosocial voice, pay attention to the "them" that you inevitably create. Drawing the line between "us" and "them" is an essential component of your prosocial voice. It can be a powerful motivator to enrol followers into the social identity that you have created. A "them" that comprises "people who don't care about the safety of our people" or "people who don't believe that we can get this project done on time" is an essential part of you positioning your social identity for success. But if the "them" becomes "those people in sales" or "head office" or worse still "the Mumbai office" then you have crossed the line. The prosocial voice takes tribes and delivers communes. A tribe is exclusive, a commune is welcoming to a large audience and inclusive to all. Be a commune builder.

Note

1 Haslam and Reicher, "Trump's Appeal".

PART 4

The ultimate case studies

If the differential voice functions as a meta-model for leadership, then we should be able to map most leadership situations to fall beneath its umbrella. The obvious way to do this is by case study. Throughout the book, I have tried to connect the theoretical concepts with real-world examples. None of the instances really qualifies as a case study, however. They are more like anecdotes. I believe that including them has made the concepts more accessible. In making that choice, I accept the criticism that I am inevitably biased when selecting such anecdotes.

Given my bias towards proving the meta-modelling functionality of the differential voice, I decided to go big. If the differential voice is effective as a meta-model, then you should be able to map the biggest leadership events to it!

In the next chapter, I will focus on religion. Religion and leadership power have been inextricably linked since the cognitive revolution. I aim to identify the functions of religion in supporting societal cooperation and map these to the differential voice to support the case for its meta-modelling capability.

The final chapter of the book is devoted to one of the most celebrated leaders of our time, Martin Luther King Jr. and the American Civil Rights movement.

16 The leadership study of religion

Religion has no place in business leadership today (other than as a contribution to diversity). I contend, however, that it is essential that we undertake a secular study of role of religion in historical leadership if we are to fully understand the differential voice. The differential voice does not have a religious basis, but it fulfils a function that has been almost exclusively the domain of religion for at least the last 10,000 years. By studying how religion underpinned power and functioned as the agent of social cohesion, we can understand how to engage our followers with our nonreligious differential voice.

What is religion?

Religion is based on a belief-in-the-supernatural. Belief-in-the-supernatural does not qualify on its own as religion, but it is a nonnegotiable prerequisite for a religion. A group of ardent Harry Potter fans who believe that magic is real have a belief-in-the-supernatural but do not qualify as a religion. However, *all* religions have a belief-in-the-supernatural. For some the supernatural is manifest as supreme beings such as gods (either one or many). For others, it can be spirits of the dead, of animals, or of other natural entities. In the absence of any of these, there will be supernatural occurrences or supernatural states of mind. Buddha was not a god and his followers do not have gods or spirits, but the path of enlightenment is supernatural by definition – it cannot be observed in the natural world.

Belief-in-the-supernatural is at the origin of religion and is an integral part of religion. However, religion became much more than this alone; there are many other dimensions to most religions. We need to find the other commonalities if we are to discover how it fulfils such a powerful place in the history of social cohesion and leadership. Let's deconstruct religion into its major functions and examine how each of them helped humanity thrive.

There are thousands of definitions of religion, which is not surprising given the hundreds of thousands of religions that have existed in the world. After analysing many of the more respected ones, Jared Diamond came up with his own. I prefer his definition as a starting point because he studied religion from the perspective of its function. He observed that religion can have a high cost on a society (supporting full-time priests, officials, the time devoted to worship, the building of monuments and churches, etc.); therefore, it must have a beneficial function. This is of keen interest to our investigation, because the function will surely be closely related to the benefit of the leadership capabilities that it underpins. Diamond's definition is

> *Religion is a set of traits distinguishing a human social group sharing those traits from other groups not sharing those traits in identical form. Included among those shared traits is always one or more, often all three, out of three traits:*
>
> *supernatural explanation,*
> *defusing anxiety about uncontrollable dangers through ritual, and*
> *offering comfort for life's pains and the prospect of death.*
>
> *Religions, other than early ones, became coopted to promote:*
>
> *standardized organization,*
>
> *political obedience,*
>
> *tolerance of strangers belonging to one's own religion, and*
>
> *justification of wars against groups holding other religions.*[1]

Diamond's definition has the societal-function focus that we seek. This aligns with our interest in religion, which is purely functional. We want to understand the role that religion played in ancient post-cog society and how it became intimately entangled with leadership and power. We will then quite deliberately untangle it and find the nonreligious approaches that fulfil the functions that religion played so powerfully in the past.

When viewed from a leadership perspective, two functions are missing or at least underplayed in Diamond's definition. Religion has a powerful motivational function in society; it causes people to go above and beyond what they would otherwise do. Religion also usually has a lot to say about the structure, role, and values of the family unit within society. We need to add these into the mix.

Putting this all together, I have generated a "leadership function" definition for religion. From this perspective, a religion has eight components. Not all religions have all eight components, but *all* religions have *most* of them. My definition for religion, based on leadership function, is

Religion is a movement based on a shared-belief-in-the-supernatural and fulfils most of the following functions:

> *providing supernatural explanation for things that cannot otherwise be understood,*
>
> *providing a motivational higher purpose, shared with all members of the ingroup, which encourages people to work hard and accept adverse circumstances without dissent,*
>
> *underpinning a strong social identity amongst believers by providing a set of beliefs and rituals,*
>
> *providing a code of behaviour towards the ingroup (including the treatment of strangers) and towards the outgroup (including justifying conflict or war),*
>
> *providing organisation and structure for a community,*
>
> *instilling discipline and obedience,*
>
> *diffusing personal anxiety by providing hope of supernatural intervention and/or an afterlife, and,*
>
> *extolling family values, defining family structure, and encouraging strong personal relationships.*

Separating out the functions this way allows me to propose that religion provides a full suite of leadership voices, not just futurizing. I have aligned the functions with the differential voice meta-model as shown in the next diagram. By analysing religion in this way, we can directly connect the different functions to the differential voices. The components that fulfil the futurizing voice that differentiated post-cog leadership can then be isolated and analysed.

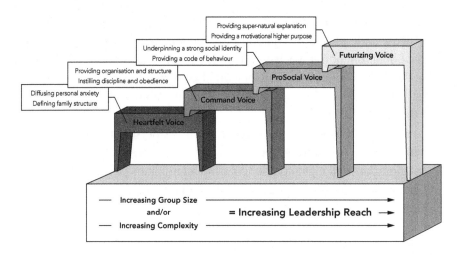

Providing super-natural explanation
Providing a motivational higher purpose

Underpinning a strong social identity
Providing a code of behaviour

Futurizing Voice

Providing organisation and structure
Instilling discipline and obedience

ProSocial Voice

Diffusing personal anxiety
Defining family structure

Command Voice

Heartfelt Voice

— Increasing Group Size
and/or   = Increasing Leadership Reach ➝
— Increasing Complexity

Figure 16.1 Differential voice and the leadership function of religion

Let us consider each of the eight functions in turn to justify the alignment depicted. We will start with how religion fulfilled the heartfelt voice, the lowest differential voice that is a prerequisite for all others. Working up through progressively higher differentials will bring us to the futurizing voice last – the leadership function unique to post-cogs.

(For simplicity of reading, I will use terminology common in some Christian religions: church, priest, congregation, God, and so on. This is to avoid continually having to refer to the multiple terms used by multiple religions. The points I am making however apply generally. Therefore, when I say priest, I also mean imam, cleric, rabbi, shaman, and so forth. When I say church, I also mean synagogue, temple, and so on. When I say Bible, I mean any Koran, Torah, and so on.)

Heartfelt voice

Extolling family values, defining family structure, and encouraging strong personal relationships

Coalitions based on kin relationships have an evolutionary benefit.[2] The special relationship between parents and their offspring would have been clearly observable in pre-cogs. It is reasonable to presume that the advanced language skills of intra-cogs and post-cogs would have reinforced kin-based relationships. At some point in time, we would observe enough cohesiveness in these kin-based groups to loosely classify them as a family. Language would seem to be important in allowing a continuing tightening of family relationships.

We can see, for example, how tightening family relationships has a reproductive fitness benefit to the species through the protection of children and sharing of resources but not if it results in a high level of incest. This would introduce genetic defects, which would decrease reproductive fitness. Sexual competition between siblings would also act to destabilise cohesion. Language is very well suited as a mechanism for creating taboos on incest. This would allow for the benefits of tighter family groups without the detriment of high levels of incest. Some form of taboo on incest is almost universal amongst human societies, and, in most cases, it is inseparably bound in the religious beliefs. It would seem logical that at some point taboos of a practical nature would be bundled in with the supernatural taboos (e.g., thou shalt not enter the sacred cave on the full moon) to form a continuum. This is just one example of religious influence on the family.

Most religions hold the family in a special light. For many communities, the very definition of what constitutes a family has a religious basis (e.g., polygamy is encouraged in some religions and abhorred in others). Religions act as very effective method of extolling family values and strong personal relationships. In a post-cog world where the inner circle was family based, this aspect of religion was performing the function of the heartfelt voice.

Diffusing personal anxiety by providing hope of supernatural intervention and/or an afterlife

> No one laughs at God in a hospital
> No one laughs at God in a war
> No one's laughing at God
> When they're starving or freezing or so very poor
> From the song "Laughing With" by Regina Spektor

The post-cog capability of envisaging the future had a nasty side effect – the anticipation of bad things occurring. Although other animals will get distressed if confronted with a known precursor to danger or pain, it is momentary. Post-cogs, on the other hand, could imagine all sorts of bad things happening, anytime in the future, even in the absence of any stimuli. Almost all religions have rituals designed to diffuse this anxiety. For some this takes the form of an appeal to a supernatural being to intervene – by prayer, for example. Others focus on the acceptance of fate. Many of the rituals are highly repetitive and include practiced body movements. It is clear that repetitive chanting and body movement calm anxiety. In the extreme, this can progress right through to a trance where all anxiety is released.

As far as we know post-cogs were also alone in the animal kingdom in envisaging their own death. We take it for granted, but the cognitive process to extrapolate witnessing death to anticipating one's own death is a large step. Having already established the supernatural realm, we can imagine that it was only a small step for post-cogs to harness it to relieve this anxiety. Most religions feature afterlife or postdeath condition to ease the mental burden of death's inevitability.

Teams function far more effectively when there is a low level of anxiety; we have already explored the power of psychological safety. A key capability within the heartfelt voice is to create a place of physical and psychological safety. It is one of the things that binds an inner circle together. People in a highly anxious state are not in the right mind-set to build the strong relationships needed. Calming the anxiety through ritual and prayer was a way for post-cogs to feel safe and calm enough to engage with each other and the objectives of the leader.

This supports the argument that the religious function of diffusing personal anxiety is well-aligned with the heartfelt voice. Furthermore, the act of jointly participating in rituals itself would have supported relationship building.

Command voice

Providing organisation and structure for a society

There are practicalities associated with running a large religion. Effective worship requires that someone lead it, and there is a physical limit to how many people can be led in worship by one priest. If the congregation of worshippers grows, then it needs to be split between two priests. As it grows further, it will require many priests, which then brings the problem of how to stay coordinated on the practices associated with the religion. An organisation is required to manage this and to implement a host of administrative tasks. Chief amongst these is how to manage the money. Large-scale religions have lots of full-time employees who do not directly produce food. To survive they must, therefore, coopt resources from followers. Religion invented taxes, and with taxes comes rules and administration.

Religion provides the authority to put in place organisational hierarchy. This is necessary to effectively sustain the religion. It is a short step to expanding the hierarchy for the running the whole community. This explanation is slightly misleading in making it sound like a sequential step when in fact their respective growth has always been intermingled. Historically, organisation of the church and organisation of the community were generally indistinguishable from each other.

Instilling discipline and obedience

Establishment of a system of taxation was a big challenge for religions. From the perspective of an intra-cog, taxation is theft (you may personally know some people who are intra-cogs in this respect). It took a post-cog brain to willingly give up hard-earned food to another person who made no contribution to getting it.

Even in post-cogs, it took more than just the threat of retribution from a supernatural being to comply willingly. The system would break down during the first drought if it were all voluntary. Religions drove discipline and obedience into their followers. They set clear expectations and were strict on consequences for nondelivery. This was set within a broader framework of discipline and obedience based around regularity of worship. Again, the practicing of religion and running of the community was integrally connected, and the communities functioning took on a regular cadence.

Prosocial voice

Providing a code of behaviour towards the ingroup (including the treatment of strangers) and towards the outgroup (including justifying conflict or war)

When Diamond visited the remote tribes of Papua New Guinea, he needed to travel across extensive parts of the country to carry out his research. He quickly confronted a problem that we don't give any thought to in our modern world – it was incredibly dangerous. And not just dangerous in the same way that we would need to be careful if we went trekking in another country where we didn't speak the language. To traverse any distance across lands inhabited by different tribes was to write your own death warrant. New Guinea tribesman killed any intruders. This problem could not be solved by hiring some locals. The locals themselves would not dream of traversing other lands. The highlands were a maze of invisible lines that demarcated the tribes. People lived their entire lives within their boundaries. The only time that an indigenous person would cross the line without prior agreement was as part of a war raid.

This natural state of being hostile to strangers was a huge impediment to the growth of religions. Religions required that people cooperate in larger and larger numbers. Very quickly, this meant that people needed to cooperate with strangers. The religions that thrived achieved this by codifying a set a behaviours towards fellow followers of the same religion, a set of moral standards for behaviour that were the same for strangers as they were for kin. This set of rules became part of the identity of the group of followers (ingroup).

At the same time, religions could thrive in the long term only if they outcompeted other religions in wars. They therefore had to manage the paradox that this created. A young man would grow up honouring a code that required him to be kind to strangers, but then as a young adult he was dressed in armour and told to kill as many strangers as possible. Religions very skilfully navigated this territory. The code almost always draws a heavy line between the ingroup of fellow believers who you should be kind to and the outgroup of heretics and disbelievers who you should pity or hate.

Underpinning a strong social identity amongst believers by providing a set of beliefs and rituals

Atheists find the beliefs of the vast majority of religious groups to be bizarre. More interestingly, devoutly religious people find the beliefs of the vast majority of religious groups to be bizarre – that is, every set of religious beliefs other than their own! Even the most populous religion has no chance of winning a worldwide opinion poll on the validity of their beliefs. They are hopelessly outnumbered by nonbelievers. In the face of this overwhelming opposition to their beliefs, you might think that the cohesion of the believers would start to wane. In fact, quite the opposite is true. Opposition actually strengthens the cohesiveness of believers. People's sense of self becomes increasingly associated with the shared beliefs of the group. This is social identity.

The creation of almost any group creates this ingroup/outgroup dynamic: a collective attitude that "we are different from and therefore better than them".[3] The stronger the difference, the stronger the sense of superiority. Hundreds of thousands of people have seen the Broadway musical *Book of Mormon* and laughed themselves to exhaustion at the concept of Joseph Smith being visited by the Angel Moroni who revealed the location of golden plates placed by God in a wooded area near Manchester, New York (golden plates that then mysteriously went missing). Has this mass derisiveness started to undermine the Church of Jesus Christ of Latter-Day Saints? Not according to the U.S. National Council of Churches who rank it on their website as the second-fastest-growing religion in the United States.[4]

Importantly, having a standard set of beliefs and rituals is a way to create cohesion between people who barely know each other. It is a tangible manifestation of something shared, of common ground. Consequently, ingroup members are better disposed towards each other. They are primed to interact with more openness and less defensiveness. This is prosocial behaviour. A leader promoting the shared beliefs and rituals is using their prosocial voice for the building of a commune.

Futurizing voice

Providing supernatural explanation for things that cannot otherwise be understood

As well as being the original source of religion, belief-in-the-supernatural becomes a function of religion. It is not just prehistoric post-cogs that were driven to distraction by their curiosity. Evolution ensured that it stuck through to modern times. Understanding why or who or both is important to us. It is more than just a desire; it occurs as a driving need.

To understand this better we need to put ourselves in the mind-set of an ancient post-cog. Even though ancient post-cogs were close to our intellectual equal, their experience of the world was very different. We are raised with the principles of scientific inquiry, even though we don't generally call it that. From a very young age, we were taught not take things at face value, not to believe everything that we were told, to look for measurable evidence, and to hold open the possibility that our initial theories were incorrect. This is a very modern phenomenon. None of this existed for our forebears. They were also exposed to much less diversity of thought, fewer opinions, and fewer specialists. With no formal schooling, wisdom lay with the elders. The elders had an amazing knowledge of their natural environment, so why would you question their understanding of the supernatural?

Scientific explanations have been supplanting religious explanations for hundreds of years now but still fall short for many people. For example, most people accept that gravitational attraction, not a god, is responsible for the motion of the planets but are still disconnected from the scientific explanation for "Why did the universe come into being at all?" The existence of god/s remains the answer for billions of people.

Providing a motivational higher purpose, shared with other believers, which encourages people to work hard and accept adverse circumstances without dissent

A belief in a higher purpose, often supernatural in nature, is a function of most religions. What makes this so powerful is that this belief is shared with fellow believers. An individual with a belief in a higher purpose might diligently work towards it but, when faced with adversity or personal suffering, is likely to question this belief and stray from the cause. Sharing the beliefs with other believers brings with it an obligation to the others. No one wants to be the one to let the team down. This sets up a self-reinforcing cycle. People work diligently on tasks connected to the cause. They are reluctant to complain; to do so would be to let their fellow believers down. They will accept pain and suffering without straying from the cause. The group dynamic acts to reinforce this behaviour, and very quickly, pain and suffering become intimately connected to devotion. The belief system expands to exemplify "suffering for the cause" as a sign of devotion, often accompanied by the anticipation of reward in the afterlife.

This was an extremely useful dynamic for post-cog societies. As communities became larger, the requirement to coordinate around goals and find new ways to extract hard work out of the population increased markedly. Communities working in concert towards a higher purpose without dissent were simply more productive than those who didn't have this. But perhaps the area where it became most useful was in disputes and wars. By using religion to provide a motivational higher purpose, a new breed of warrior was born: one that would fight with a religious fervour. This was a huge advantage in battle, and the communities that were best at it routed other communities. Religion and war became inextricably linked.

It is obvious that a distinguishing feature of a higher purpose is that it is always in the future – it is the anticipation of getting to a better place. It seems that the best ones are in the distant future, and religions took this to the extreme to offer grand rewards to believers in the afterlife. This approach works only with post-cogs. Looking back down the Eurostar tracks, you can imagine the response of your pre-cog team if you took one-tenth of their food in exchange for infinite food in heaven! And yet this approach was not just tolerated in religious post-cog societies, it was welcomed.

Today we can witness the legacy of this capability. In countless places all over the world, grand mosques, temples, cathedrals, monuments, and pyramids stand testament to the enormous power wielded through religious futurizing voices. All built with the labour of millions of believers engaged with futurizing voices to work towards a higher purpose.

Notes

1 Diamond, *The World Until Yesterday*.
2 Geary and Flinn, "Evolution of Human Parental Behavior and the Human Family".
3 Haslam and Reicher, "Rethinking the Psychology of Leadership".
4 "National Council of Churches USA".

The differential voice of Martin Luther King

In choosing Martin Luther King and the American Civil Rights movement as the case study for the differential voice, I am taking the risk of losing your attention. It is so long ago for one thing; how can it have relevance in today's world? Also, it is so clichéd and worn out; how can I possibly maintain your interest?

It is precisely because it is so clichéd that I want to analyse it. This is because I believe that some of the conclusions drawn in the past about King's leadership are grossly misleading. They have done more to harm the cause of developing exceptional leadership than to help it. By leading you through the way that leadership gets misrepresented, I aim to establish a greater depth of understanding that you really can put to work.

On the issue of relevance to today's world, I concur with the view that the world was a simpler place in the 1950s and 60s than now. However, the scale of what Martin Luther King took on was so great that it nullifies this. The systems that we operate in might be very complex, but it is unlikely that they approach the level of complexity faced by King. Therefore, as a study of the futurizing voice which is always based on leadership in a complex system, it is ideal.

The American Civil Rights Movement is also, arguably, the most successful social movement in contemporary history. This is not because it solved the problem of racial inequality in the United States – according to my American friends, white supremacy is alive and well in the USA (arguably even undergoing resurgence). I regard it as the most successful because it created a dominant discourse which impacted almost every society on earth. As far as I can tell, there is a position on racial equality in almost every corner of the world; a discourse which has been influenced by the events in the United States in the late 1950s and early 1960s.

Because it is so ubiquitous, we take it for granted that we should have a position with regard to racial equality, but in historical terms it is a novelty. For thousands of years up until the mid-1800s, racial inequality was normal. It would have been offensive to most people to suggest that it could be any different. As an example if we read the Code of Hammurabi, the ruling mantra of Mesopotamia in 1770 BC, we find that "if a superior man should blind the eye of another superior man, they shall blind his eye", while "if he should blind the eye of a slave, . . . he shall deliver one-half of the slaves value (to the slave's owner)". This was a code that millions lived by. 'An eye for an eye', except if the eye belonged to a slave. Suggesting to the ruling class that equal rights should exist for slaves would have been laughable.

Overwhelmingly, the public discourse today supports racial equality and tolerance. Even where it doesn't, the influence exerted as a result of the Civil Rights Movement demands that any alternative position be defended. It is impossible in today's world, not to have a position on racial equality and this position is in some way influenced by the Civil Rights Movement. Not surprisingly then, it is the subject of a lot of interest when it comes to leadership.

I believe that many 'lessons' taken from Martin Luther King and the American Civil Rights Movement to be false and misleading. Part of the problem is 'Hollywoodization' – the desire we have for the story to read like a Hollywood script. Putting this aside though and we find that the cause of the misinterpretation is down to our constant companion, the daemon. Examining the misinterpretations therefore has a secondary benefit. We will come to see how easy it is to be seduced by simplistic 'cause-and-effect' analysis in hindsight and thinking that it leads to informed action to take in the future. The purpose is not just to demonstrate how our daemon flounders in a complex system; it will also start to sow the seeds for empowering our futurizing voice through the use of small acts of leadership. To examine this, I have chosen to start with one of the starkest examples of a small act of leadership triggering a large impact: the Montgomery bus boycott.

Civil Rights – Martin Luther King or Rosa Parks

The number of versions of leadership lessons associated with the Civil Rights Movement has already filled a library section with books. In this section, I will focus on two contrasting views, both equally flawed in my opinion.

The first view is that the Civil Rights Movement was an act of great charismatic leadership by Martin Luther King Jr., who mobilised a nation with his great speeches. Here is an example:

> Let us not wallow in the valley of despair, I say to you today, my friends.
>
> And so even though we face the difficulties of today and tomorrow, I still have a dream. It is a dream deeply rooted in the American dream.
>
> I have a dream that one day this nation will rise up and live out the true meaning of its creed: "We hold these truths to be self-evident, that all men are created equal."
>
> I have a dream that one day on the red hills of Georgia, the sons of former slaves and the sons of former slave owners will be able to sit down together at the table of brotherhood.
>
> I have a dream that one day even the state of Mississippi, a state sweltering with the heat of injustice, sweltering with the heat of oppression, will be transformed into an oasis of freedom and justice.
>
> I have a dream that my four little children will one day live in a nation where they will not be judged by the color of their skin but by the content of their character.
>
> I have a dream today!
>
> I have a dream that one day, down in Alabama, with its vicious racists, with its governor having his lips dripping with the words of "interposition" and "nullification" – one day right there in Alabama little black boys and black girls will be able to join hands with little white boys and white girls as sisters and brothers.
>
> Martin Luther King Jr., excerpt of speech delivered 28
August 1963, at the Lincoln Memorial, Washington, D.C.

This is undoubtedly one of the greatest speeches in history and one of the many great speeches made by King. There is power in the vision that King continually creates through his oratory skills. Herein lies the trap that many have fallen into when it comes to trying to develop their own leadership.

The power that is evident in the speech is the power of personal conviction, the power of taking a stand, and the power of committing to a seemingly impossible but enticing future. I was once taught in a high-priced, consultant-led program that exceptional leaders take a stand and then speak the future into existence, that the power of their language will overcome all obstacles. This was 'evidenced' using excerpts of King such as above, along with John F. Kennedy and Nelson Mandela speeches. One had to commit to an enormous stretch target or big audacious goal and talk charismatically about it. I was taught that Martin Luther King started the Civil Rights Movement by mobilising the masses with the power of his conviction and expression.

As usual, it is the half-truth nature of this proposition that makes it so dangerous. Yes, there is enormous power in a leader genuinely committing to a future and speaking about it from the heart. And great speeches have helped change the world. Our daemon loves this version of events as it leads to a cause an effect model – take a stand, commit to a future, and speak powerfully causes people to follow us and deliver the future.

We have explored in detail already how this isolated view of futurizing fails because it is not backed by the lower differentials. Even with these in place, however, it is still flawed. Even the most cursory examination of the facts invalidates this as a complete solution.

Martin Luther King did not start the American Civil Rights Movement. The origins are multi-faceted, but probably the most significant event was the founding of the National Association for the Advancement of Colored People (NAACP) in 1909, 10 years before King's birth. King was a leader in the Montgomery bus boycott which was a significant turning point for the movement, but, contrary to popular belief, did not initiate the boycott. Before we move on to examine how it did start and King's broader leadership role over the following decade, I need to dispel the myths about Rosa Parks.

The Montgomery bus boycott was sparked when on December 1, 1955, Rosa Parks refused to give up her seat on the bus to a white male passenger as she was required to do by law. Most accounts describe Mrs Parks as a quiet dignified elderly lady, with no history of civil disobedience, who was tired after a long day at work and in a singular act of extraordinary leadership decided that she "had had enough" and refused to move. In this account, we now have another super-hero who changed the world in a singular act of defiance. Instead of crediting King, we could alternatively conclude that it was Rosa Parks who sparked the Civil Rights Movement through her small act of leadership; that she created a "tipping point". Other versions are that it was both Parks and King, either independently or together. Or maybe Parks was inspired by King's great speeches to undertake her protest. All these accounts break down under scrutiny.

Rosa Parks was not elderly. She was 42 years old at the time. She was not quiet and compliant; she had a long history of protest against segregation. She began serving as secretary for the local NAACP branch in 1943, twelve years before the day of the bus incident. In the late 1940s, she moved to be secretary for the Alabama State Conference of the NAACP. Four months prior to her arrest she had attended the Highlander Folk School, an institution dedicated to fighting segregation, where she participated in a workshop called 'Race Relations' which encouraged non-violent civil disobedience. The 'fateful day' and 'spontaneous act' are dramatizations; this was not a singular act. In the 1940s she had refused several times to comply with the segregation rules. The very same driver who alerted authorities on the day of Park's arrest had ejected her from a bus in the early 1940s. Mrs Parks is quoted as saying "My resistance to being mistreated on the buses and anywhere else was just a regular thing with me and not just that day".[1] Neither was this non-compliance restricted to Mrs Parks. The Women's Political Council (WPC) who were central to the initiation of the boycott had earlier started to organise a boycott when a fifteen-year-old girl, Claudette Colvin, was arrested for the same crime on March 2, 1955. The plan was dropped on discovery that Miss Colvin was pregnant out of wedlock and would not therefore engender unconditional support in any campaign. Neither was the disobedience by the African American community isolated to buses. For example, members of the NAACP youth council would regularly attempt to borrow books from the whites-only library.

The purpose here is not to downplay the courage displayed by Mrs Parks on that day in December 1955. If you immerse yourself in the context of the time, you cannot fail to be amazed at her bravery. The purpose is to point out that acts of civil disobedience were being carried out all over the South every day by other equally courageous people. The reason that Rosa Parks is famous while the others are largely forgotten is that the Rosa Parks incident was perfectly positioned for Martin Luther King to leverage the non-linearity of the complex system. King's futurizing voice took a small act and magnified it into a massive impact.

Rosa Parks is remembered for the impact that her actions caused. Seeing this large impact our daemon therefore zeroes in to isolate the "causing event" and look to extract the lesson to use for ourselves. In doing so it misses the thousands of other events that caused the system to build to a point where one incident could be used to create a movement. Rosa Parks did not cause the Montgomery bus boycott. Rosa Parks triggered a system that was pre-loaded by thousands of events. Her small act of leadership was at the centre of what was to follow. But as we will see, it was King's futurizing voice that exploited the situation and triggered a change that was completely out of proportion to the Rosa Parks's action.

Do not be misled in to thinking that Martin Luther King was orchestrating from the beginning though. He did not start the Montgomery bus boycott. A Montgomery local by the name of E.D. Nixon, the president of the local chapter of the NAACP, and members of the WPC led by Jo Ann Robinson initiated the boycott. Both had long associations with Rosa Parks as part of the protest movements. The organisational forces of the African American protest movement were already aligned, and they rallied when one of their own was arrested.

The American Civil Rights Movement is undoubtedly a story of successful leadership, but not in a way that our daemon would like. Our daemon demands a starting point (Montgomery 1955), an exceptional leader (either Rosa Parks or Martin Luther King), some agency (organise a bus boycott), and the effect (the Civil Rights Movement). This is a flawed model of leadership. The futurizing voice is powered by non-linear complexity and cannot be a product of daemon thinking. It takes a different view on the events of 1955, the Civil Rights Movement, and more broadly Martin Luther King's role.

The futurizing voice expects that small acts of leadership will result in disproportionally large positive impacts. Its power is based on this massive leveraging effect. Paradoxically though, it does not expect to be able to predict which acts will work and which won't. And critically, it debunks the model of top-down leadership, where the leader calls the shots. To demonstrate this, I will move on to show that Martin Luther King was an exceptional leader, not because of the popular view of him as a 'great man' driven by an inspiring vision, but because he had an incredibly powerful futurizing voice. He used his futurizing voice to harnesses the power of a complex system to cause change by catalysing small acts of leadership.

The Montgomery bus boycott

E.D. Nixon made a crucial decision as the Montgomery bus boycott was mobilising that might seem odd but proved to be incredibly important. He chose not to run the protest through the NAACP, the most prominent organisation of African American protest and the one which he personally held office with. The roots of the NAACP went back 45 years. Over that time, it had grown massively and in the process become highly bureaucratic. Its numerous successful campaigns were largely a result of carefully planned legalistic action. It was largely a 'by-the-book' organisation both internally and externally. Taking action through NAACP would need approval up the line to New York with the risk of over-analysis and debate. Nixon decided that the situation demanded speed, so instead of consulting New York, he picked up the phone and started ringing local Christian ministers. The third phone call he made was to Martin Luther King.

A new organisation was formed called the Montgomery Improvement Association (MIA) and King was elected as its president. Unlike the NAACP, the MIA was agile and proactive. Its power base was fundamentally different. King, a Christian minister, was its charismatic leader, but there was also a large coalition of cross-denominational ministers as an underpinning power base. Together with the large number of informal networks, this allowed for rapid dissemination of information. Coordinated action could be arranged very quickly.

The role of Christian ministers in leadership positions had a number of advantages. Ministers were paid by the church, not by white bosses. They were free of the influence placed on other community leaders who could ultimately be intimidated by threats to their livelihood. Ministers also had the ability to engage the masses in a way that other organisations could not. They had an explicit leadership role across a broad base of the community. An African American with a low level of education would be alienated by NAACP's legal tactics, but highly engaged by the minister who held their attention and their trust.

The boycott faced many challenges, but the greatest one was the most obvious one. People needed the buses to get to work. The Montgomery African Americans were poor. They could not afford to lose their jobs, and they relied on the bus service to get to their place of employment. A lot were in the position to be able to walk to work, but the boycott needed to be universal. Therefore, alternative transport was urgently required. Within a matter of days, the MIA had organised a sophisticated alternative transport operation. African American taxi drivers were co-opted to transport people for discounted fares or for free. The local legislature responded by passing a regulation banning taxis from charging less than 45 cents. This move had been anticipated by King and the MIA, and they had already called on the experience of previous bus boycott attempts in other cities such as Baton

Rouge, Louisiana. This speeded up the implementation of a system based on private vehicles, and within days a sophisticated system of carpooling was in place with forty-eight dispatch and forty-two pick-up locations. The system very effectively transported African Americans all over Montgomery for more than a year.

The boycott was highly successful. Within days the number of African Americans riding the buses reduced to practically zero. Fares from African Americans made up most of the revenue of the bus company. Losing this revenue caused financial distress to the bus company and put pressure back onto the white authorities. The white establishment responded in numerous ways to break the boycott, not least of which was direct bullying and physical attacks on African American boycotters. King's leadership stance of non-violence was critical during this period; retaliation would have escalated quickly and caused harm to the objectives.

On November 13, 1956, a full year after the commencement of the boycott, the U.S. Supreme Court ruled that Alabama's laws on segregation on the buses were unconstitutional. This was a substantial victory for the movement. This was not just a victory for Montgomery African Americans, it was a clear signal across America and indeed across the world that dominated people can cause change by organized collective action.

Foundational differential voices

We are starting to get a sense of how the Montgomery bus boycott and the subsequent direction of the American Civil Rights Movement is a case study into the characteristics of the futurizing voice. A founding principle of the futurizing voice is that it is effective only in the presence of the lower differentials: heartfelt, command, and prosocial. Therefore we need to also be looking for evidence of the foundational differential voices in the Montgomery case study.

Heartfelt Voice – The call to action was initiated by the heartfelt voice across an inner circle that ultimately became known as the MIA. It was not an appointed organisation; it was a very small collective of people who held a shared purpose and had built deep relationships.

Command Voice – The speed and quality of the carpooling operation is testament to the strength of command voice across the movement. This was a disciplined and efficient operation that required coordinated action to be taken, and reliable results to be delivered. "Summing up the effectiveness of the transportation system, King revealed that even the White Citizens Council admitted that the car pool moved with military precision".[2]

Prosocial Voice – Life for the Montgomery African American people revolved around the church. Montgomery, like many southern cities, was subject to extraordinary growth of its African American population as people migrated from rural areas. These newly urbanised African Americans flocked to the churches. It was typical in southern cities for African Americans to own more than half the churches even though they generally comprised less than 30 percent of the population. The church became their social life. Despite his young age, King was intimately acquainted with the social structure of the churches as well as the politics. His father, the Reverend Martin Luther King Sr. was an influential churchman. King grew up emmeshed in church political and social workings and came to understand the church as a whole. The boycott was the opportunity for King to tap into this power that he knew so well using his prosocial voice. By enlisting the support of the church ministers, King tapped into the dominant social identity of African Americans, their Christianity. He set about redefining what it meant to be an African American Christian. For King, if you believed that all people were one within Christ, then it was your obligation to protest the inequality of segregation. He changed the social identity of being an African American Christian from passivity to activism.

Bus boycotts had been attempted in other cities prior to Montgomery. Their 'failure to stick' was not due to a lack of passion or bravery from their leaders, but rather the inability to adequately fill all the differential voices. These 'failures to stick' should not be considered failures, however. It is unlikely that Montgomery would have been successful without the momentum that had been generated by these previous acts of leadership.

The most successful boycott prior to Montgomery was Baton Rouge in June 1953. This boycott led by the Reverend T.J. Jemison successfully galvanised mass action and achieved greater than 90 percent boycott rate for eight days. It was a victory in the sense that it forced the white establishment to change the rules on seat allocation and that this compromise was accepted by Jamison and confirmed by a vote of the masses. The boycott ended because Jamison chose to accept the compromise, not because the white establishment had forced it to end. However, it was a limited victory only, because the compromise still reserved specific seats for whites only – the buses were still segregated.

The success of the Baton Rouge boycott over previous attempts resulted from a strong heartfelt voice (an inner circle called the United Defence League), a strong command voice (effective carpooling and organisation), and a strong prosocial voice (broad, church-based popular support). The futurizing voice of the leadership however was not strong enough to deliver the ultimate victory. This is evident from Jamison's own words – "My vision was not anywhere, at that time, other than to see that Negroes could sit down when they paid the same fare".[3] Without the vision of a Martin Luther King, Jameson limited the scale of his potential success.

It would be erroneous to judge Jameson's leadership poorly as a result of this analysis. He was an incredibly powerful leader who achieved an outcome that a reasonable observer of the time would have considered impossible. And from a capability perspective, simultaneous mastery of heartfelt, command, and prosocial voices is very high capability leadership. We will never know if even more could have been achieved if his futurizing voice was stronger, but we do know for certain that the later success of the Montgomery bus boycott would not have occurred without Baton Rouge. Sometimes great victories need to be won in stages.

We can be certain of the contribution of Baton Rouge to success at Montgomery because of the leadership action taken by King in the first days of the boycott when he picked up the phone and rang Jamison to get a detailed understanding of the practical mechanics of organising a carpool. King may have been working towards an incredibly powerful vision, but he was not lost in hubris. He was not working on his next inspiring speech or lining up television interviews. He was reaching out to a valuable ally using his heartfelt voice, arming his command voice to deliver direct action and contemplating how to engage the masses through prosocial communication.

Martin Luther King was an extraordinary leader for reasons that go unrecognised. He connected deeply with close friends, family, and allies with his heartfelt voice. This inner circle worked tirelessly in the background, corralling his support base and shoring up his leadership. King understood that his charismatic speeches were just words if not backed up with action. He used his command voice to turn passive supporters into workers. He developed organisational structures, and practices focussed on the reliable completion of the thousands of tasks required. He was a leader who understood the power of prosocial communication. By enrolling the networks of church ministers, King could heavily influence the gossip channels in virtually every African American community in the land.

At the same time, Martin Luther King was an extraordinary leader for his futurizing voice. These are the aspects of his leadership which are trumpeted. He held unshakeable convictions. He took a stand on issues of deep significance. He committed himself to a future that others could only dream about. He was unstoppable in finding ways forward when others would have surrendered. He was courageous, literally putting his life on the line for his cause. He was a charismatic personality with powerful oratory skills. He was humble, never seeking personal glory, and yet always willing to push himself into the limelight if it benefited the cause.

The futurizing voice is all these things, but it is more. Again, we need to resist our daemon who would like to take the most obvious observable data and attribute it as the full cause. The futurizing voice harnesses the power of a complex system. To understand the power of King's futurizing voice, we need to not only observe the power of his conviction and skill in communicating it; we need to understand how he interacted with the complex system that he was part of.

Futurizing voice – creating, reinforcing, and accelerating movements through storytelling

The first lesson to take from the Civil Rights Movement about King's futurizing voice lies in its very name. It is instructive that studying the progress of civil rights is the study of a movement. Driving change across an entire community cannot be achieved by a single leader acting alone. We have already witnessed how the direct influence of a single leader 'tops-out' very quickly. Even the pre-cog tribe of thirty individuals cannot be led by one-to-one command; there are just too many relationships to manage. The pre-cog leader needed an inner circle coalition to drive change through even this small group of individuals. The development of the prosocial voice in intra-cogs broke this limitation by utilising indirect communication to build social identities. But this also 'tops-out'. In the modern world with modern communications the size of the commune can be pushed beyond 150 people, but there is still a limit to how many people can be monitored and engaged prosocially from a single leader. How then does change happen across a community of many thousands? The answer is that it happens via a movement.

It was a small act of leadership from Rosa Parks that was a defining moment in the Civil Rights Movement. But particularizing the act itself is misleading. It was a defining moment in the midst of a web of defining moments. Was Rosa Parks's attendance at a workshop at Highfields a few weeks earlier a defining moment? Were actions taken by the Women's Political Council defining moments? Was King's speech a few months earlier at an NAACP meeting a defining moment? Was E.D. Nixon's decision to ring a virtual stranger, King, rather than a trusted ally a defining moment?

All these events and hundreds of others were significant. The lesson is that action was happening across a huge front. Inspired by the movement, thousands of individual small acts of leadership were under way across the South. The role of a futurizing voice is to build movements that catalyse small acts of leadership as broadly as possible.

Recall that I have defined a movement as a large community of people with a shared social identity acting in a coordinated way that causes large-scale disruption or change in a complex social system.

It can be argued that a movement doesn't necessarily need to be a large community, but I have positioned this definition this way to allow us to differentiate between the prosocial voice and the futurizing voice, which operate by very different mechanisms even though the objective of creating a social identity is the same.

It is clear that a shared social identity is still central – a movement is characterised by people giving up their personal identity on a particular issue and taking actions defined by the values shared by other people in the group. We are now looking for the mechanism that King used to create change beyond the leadership reach of the prosocial voice.

The futurizing voice builds a movement by enrolling people in a common ideal through storytelling. The social identity is created by common beliefs based on common values. Importantly, it does so in a way that has people believe that the ideal is achievable if coordinated action is taken. While only successful if built upon a prosocial voice, it functions in a different way. Recall that a prosocial voice creates social identity by creating a 'we-ness'; we are different to (and therefore better than) them. The futurizing voice builds on the 'we-ness'; we are different to (and therefore better than) them because we hold a higher ideal and have a higher purpose.

African Americans of the time already had a very strong set of social identities: their race, their religion, their local church. These social identities did not lead to a movement by our definition because they did not act in a coordinated way to cause change. They existed within the status quo of white domination. The NAACP was causing change by its legal challenges to segregation, but at that stage did not function as a social identity for the masses. The NAACP certainly was a social identity for its members, but with its northern origins, highly educated founders, bureaucratic structure, and legalistic approach, it did not act as a social identity for the majority of African Americans who were poorly educated and working in manual or menial jobs.

Martin Luther King's futurizing voice created a much larger, more inclusive, and more active social identity by connecting the hearts and minds of the masses to a higher ideal. Drawing heavily on Christian values and that of the constitution of the United States, King used his storytelling to create an incredibly compelling social identity. We can get a sense of this from another of his speeches.

> And certainly, certainly, this is the glory of America, with all of its faults. This is the glory of our democracy. If we were incarcerated behind the iron curtains of a Communistic nation we couldn't do this. If we were dropped in the dungeon of a totalitarian regime we couldn't do this. But the great glory of American democracy is the right to protest for right. My friends, don't let anybody make us feel that we are to be compared in our actions with the Ku Klux Klan or with the White Citizens Council. There will be no crosses burned at any bus stops in Montgomery. There will be no white persons pulled out of their homes and taken out on some distant road and lynched for not cooperating. There will be nobody amid, among us who will stand up and defy the Constitution of this nation. We only assemble here because of our desire to see right exist. My friends, I want it to be known that we're going to work with grim and bold determination to gain justice on the buses in this city.
>
> And we are not wrong, we are not wrong in what we are doing. If we are wrong, the Supreme Court of this nation is wrong. If we are wrong, the Constitution of the United States is wrong. If we are wrong, God Almighty is wrong. If we are wrong, Jesus of Nazareth was merely a utopian dreamer that never came down to earth. If we are wrong, justice is a lie. Love has no meaning. And we are determined here in Montgomery to work and fight until justice runs down like water, and righteousness like a mighty stream.
>
> Martin Luther King Jr., excerpt of speech delivered 5
> December 1955, to 5,000 people at the Holt Street
> Baptist Church, Montgomery

King expresses an ideal of justice and righteousness firmly rooted in the constitution and in the Bible. To join with King was to join a social identity that displayed exemplary moral character. It reinforced, rather than invalidated, the other strong social identities already in existence. It appealed to the domestic maid with her social identity founded in her church group as it did to the NAACP constitutional lawyer.

But perhaps the most important aspect of the social identity which King championed was that it appealed to moderate whites. Creating a social identity creates a new 'us', and in doing so always creates a 'them'. King positioned the white supremacists as law-breaking, anti-Christian, anti-constitution criminals. By isolating these groups as 'them', moderate whites were encouraged to join the side of righteousness and justice. King understood that it would be a mistake to promote a social identity that included only African Americans. To do so would create a 'them' that included all whites, even those active in the movement. King understood that race-based divisiveness would hinder the cause. He also understood where power lay in America's democracy. Ultimately, the change in attitude of a vast swathe of white, middle class, Christian America from being ambivalent about the issues to being anti-segregation was required to change the nation.

Against our definition of a movement, we can see how powerfully King created "a large community of people with a shared social identity" using his storytelling skills. To fulfil the definition however also we need to witness that they were "acting in co-ordinated way that causes large scale disruption or change". A movement requires action, and King was a master at catalysing it. He did this through his personal actions of leading protest activity. In doing so he was modelling the prototypical behaviour of a member of the social identity (a prosocial voice capability). King then used his futurizing voice to amplify the impact. Nowhere is this better exemplified than in his writings after being arrested in 1963 for leading a protest rally.

> The Negro has many pent-up resentments and latent frustrations, and he must release them. So let him march; let him make prayer pilgrimages to the city hall; let him go on freedom rides–and try to understand why he must do so. If his repressed emotions are not released in nonviolent ways, they will seek expression through violence; this is not a threat but a fact of history. So I have not said to my people: "Get rid of your discontent." Rather, I have tried to say that this normal and healthy discontent can be channeled into the creative outlet

of nonviolent direct action. And now this approach is being termed extremist.

But though I was initially disappointed at being categorized as an extremist, as I continued to think about the matter I gradually gained a measure of satisfaction from the label. Was not Jesus an extremist for love: "Love your enemies, bless them that curse you, do good to them that hate you, and pray for them which despitefully use you, and persecute you." Was not Amos an extremist for justice: "Let justice roll down like waters and righteousness like an ever-flowing stream." Was not Paul an extremist for the Christian gospel: "I bear in my body the marks of the Lord Jesus." Was not Martin Luther an extremist: "Here I stand; I cannot do otherwise, so help me God." And John Bunyan: "I will stay in jail to the end of my days before I make a butchery of my conscience." And Abraham Lincoln: "This nation cannot survive half slave and half free." And Thomas Jefferson: "We hold these truths to be self-evident, that all men are created equal. . . ." So the question is not whether we will be extremists, but what kind of extremists we will be.

Martin Luther King Jr., Letter from
Birmingham Jail, 16 April 1963

We can imagine the impact of King's futurizing voice that comes through this excerpt on someone who shares the social identity already created. They are drawn to extend their social identity beyond being a passive supporter and become an activist. As you study King's work more broadly, you repeatedly see this pattern. As soon as he puts a 'peg in the sand' of the social identity, he immediately leverages off it to extend it to the next level. We get a sense of this from the excerpt above, but perhaps it his boldness with his moderate white followers that exemplifies this best.

Moderate whites were drawn to the higher purpose of a society united behind non-violence, Christian values, and the American constitution. The majority were supportive. This support on its own was not enough. King understood that to be successful, he needed to turn this passive support into activism. When it came to repealing segregation, the pace of change was inexorably slow. This pace was not about to change just because a large number of people held a philosophical position opposed to segregation.

As the social identity was increasingly adopted by moderate whites, King worked tirelessly to turn this passive support into activism.

> I must confess that over the past few years I have been gravely disappointed with the white moderate. I have almost reached the regrettable conclusion that the Negro's great stumbling block in his stride toward freedom is not the White Citizen's Counciler or the Ku Klux Klanner, but the white moderate, who is more devoted to "order" than to justice; who prefers a negative peace which is the absence of tension to a positive peace which is the presence of justice; who constantly says: "I agree with you in the goal you seek, but I cannot agree with your methods of direct action"; who paternalistically believes he can set the timetable for another man's freedom; who lives by a mythical concept of time and who constantly advises the Negro to wait for a "more convenient season." Shallow understanding from people of good will is more frustrating than absolute misunderstanding from people of ill will. Lukewarm acceptance is much more bewildering than outright rejection.
>
> Martin Luther King Jr. Letter from
> Birmingham Jail, 16 April 1963

In this excerpt, King lambasts his followers for their inaction. This is so severe that you wonder how this didn't cost him support. As you dig deeper you find that his futurizing voice is always backed up by the lower differentials. King could use his storytelling skills to lambast his followers into action because they were more than words. King had control of the gossip channels through his prosocial voice and was the prototypical of the social identity. His command voice continually drove action; the next rally or legal challenge was always being planned as the current one was being executed. And King's heartfelt voice was constantly reinforcing and building his inner circle.

With this insight we see how King's actions created all the ingredients of a movement – a large community of people with a shared social identity acting in a coordinated way that causes large-scale disruption or change. The final element of our definition to examine is the complex social system. We are not looking for evidence that it was a complex social system – that much is self-evident. Instead we are looking for the evidence that King's futurizing voice drew its energy from the complex social system.

Futurizing voice in a complex system

Having previously established the pivotal role that Martin Luther King's futurizing voice played in directing and accelerating the Montgomery bus boycott, let us now examine it from the different perspectives given by the definition of a complex system.

Non-Linear – We have already noted that Martin Luther King did not start the Civil Rights Movement; its origins went back decades prior even to his birth. Neither did he create the modern movement. He did not even create the Montgomery bus boycott. This does not matter in the least. Martin Luther King's futurizing voice was uniquely positioned to take an unremarkable event of an African American being arrested for breaking the bus segregation rules and turn it into a defining moment in the history of a nation.

> Mrs. Rosa Parks is a fine person. And, since it had to happen, I'm happy that it happened to a person like Mrs. Parks, for nobody can doubt the boundless outreach of her integrity. Nobody can doubt the height of her character nobody can doubt the depth of her Christian commitment and devotion to the teachings of Jesus. And I'm happy since it had to happen, it happened to a person that nobody can call a disturbing factor in the community. Mrs. Parks is a fine Christian person, unassuming, and yet there is integrity and character there. And just because she refused to get up, she was arrested.
>
> And you know, my friends, there comes a time when people get tired of being trampled over by the iron feet of oppression. There comes a time, my friends, when people get tired of being plunged across the abyss of humiliation, where they experience the bleakness of nagging despair. There comes a time when people get tired of being pushed out of the glittering sunlight of life's July and left standing amid the piercing chill of an alpine November. There comes a time.
>
> Martin Luther King Jr., excerpt of speech delivered 5 December 1955, to 5,000 people at the Holt Street Baptist Church, Montgomery

In this excerpt, you can see how King is using his futurizing voice to deliberately exploit the non-linearity of the system. The arrest of Rosa Parks was a small event, just one arrest of an African American amongst hundreds for that year. Under other circumstances, it would have gone completely unnoticed. King understands however that all the small acts of leadership by African Americans all across the South have been building pressure within the system. He judges that the system is approaching a critical point, that his futurizing voice can take this small act and use it to deliver a disproportionally large impact. Read the excerpt again to gain an appreciation of the power that his futurizing voice puts behind a simple decision by ordinary person who decides to say 'enough'.

Emergent – The futurizing voice is an opportunist. It has to be. On 1 December, 1955, the day before Rosa Parks's arrest, Martin Luther King was using a powerful futurizing voice. He had been for some years. He was fully committed to an ideal. He had taken his stand and envisioned a future where people would not "be judged by the colour of their skin, but by the content of their character". The vision was clear and the commitment unwavering. He was actively planning his next moves both with his local parishioners and on the bigger stage. He knew that a breakthrough would come; he just had no idea where or when.

One of the ways that King had exercised his futurizing voice was by making a speech as a guest at a meeting of the NAACP a few months before. This was not particularly special occurrence. The speech was enthusiastically received, but if you were to analyse the situation a few days later, you would not say that it had had any significant impact – just one speech among many other 'preaching to the converted' speeches over the years at NAACP events. You would not be able to tell that the speech had made a particular impact on one of the members, E.D. Nixon. The impact was such that it caused Nixon to call King as he was mobilising action after the arrest of Rosa Parks even though they had only met that one time.

In seeding the ground across as many forums as he could, using his futurizing voice, King was using the emergent nature of a complex system to his advantage.

Adaptive – E.D. Nixon made an extraordinary decision when he bypassed the NAACP. The NAACP was at the front line of the anti-segregation fight. It was a very effective and successful organisation. But it was not the right organisation for the challenge. Nixon knew that speed was of the essence and set in train an adaptive approach to organising the boycott.

We can see the skill that King had in shaping adaptive forces in his later work. The Southern Christian Leadership Conference (SCLC) was formed shortly after the Montgomery event and came to lead the Civil Rights

Movement. You can see King's futurizing voice at work in the following quote from a central character in the movement, Stanley Levison:

> It would be very difficult to single out one individual as the originator of the SCLC idea. Many discussions by Dr. King and other leaders such as Fred Shuttlesworth, C. K. Steele, Ralph Abernathy, Mrs. King and with Northern figures who were consultants such as A. Philip Randolph, Bayard Rustin, Ella Baker, and myself were held. In brief, it arose out of a great deal of collective discussion, and if there was one individual who clarified and organized the discussion it was un-questionably Dr. King.

Evolutionary – Martin Luther King didn't create the Civil Rights Movement or even the Montgomery bus boycott, but it was undoubtedly King's futurizing voice that catapulted the movement forward. A complex system is evolutionary; the futurizing voice never starts from a clean slate. In this case King's futurizing voice was building on the work of others. King could see higher and further than most and had the leadership skills to create change, but he did not allow this to result in hubris. He had no need for the Montgomery bus boycott to be his idea. His only interest was to whether he could help shape it in service of his vision.

Spontaneously Ordering – Because of the speed of change associated with a complex system tipping into a new regime, the futurizing voice relies heavily on the spontaneously ordering nature of the complex system it is dealing with. The magnitude of the change in the system at Montgomery over the period of a few days cannot be overstated. Tens of thousands of people used the bus to get to work. A few days later, all but a very few were getting to work by alternative methods. The influence of King's command voice in setting in place the planning was critical to this change, but there was no possible way that this magnitude of change could be planned at any detailed level. Instead, the planning focussed on providing an adequate enough structure that the system could spontaneously organise itself. The structure in this case was the pick-up and drop-off points and the mobilisation of private vehicles. It was King's futurizing voice that then established an entirely new context.

> But just before leaving I want to say this. I want to urge you. You have voted [for this boycott], and you have done it with a great deal of

enthusiasm, and I want to express my appreciation to you, on behalf of everybody here. Now let us go out to stick together and stay with this thing until the end. Now it means sacrificing, yes, it means sacrificing at points. But there are some things that we've got to learn to sacrifice for. And we've got to come to the point that we are determined not to accept a lot of things that we have been accepting in the past. So I'm urging you now. We have the facilities for you to get to your jobs, and we . . . have the cabs there at your service. Automobiles will be at your service, and don't be afraid to use up any of the gas. If you have it, if you are fortunate enough to have a little money, use it for a good cause. Now my automobile is gonna be in it, it has been in it, and I'm not concerned about how much gas I'm gonna use. I want to see this thing work. And we will not be content until oppression is wiped out of Montgomery, and really out of America.

> Martin Luther King Jr., excerpt of speech delivered 5
> December 1955, to 5,000 people at the Holt Street
> Baptist Church, Montgomery

The masses responded to King's futurizing voice. They connected their personal sacrifice of the convenience of transport to the cause of wiping out their oppression.

We can only imagine the chaotic scenes on day one of the boycott; people rising hours before they normally would, the streets full of walkers where normally they would be deserted; people running because they were late, church forecourts a mass of frenzied activity, people shouting directions; people weeping that they would be late to work, car horns blaring.

Within a few short days, the scene was transformed: ordered processions along the various walking routes, demarcated pickup zones, ordered queues of people in logical groups awaiting a car that would arrive at a predictable time. This was not the result of some grand master plan being implemented at minute detail. This was the result of thousands of individual conversations and decisions. The structure had been planned, but it was King's futurizing voice that catalysed tens of thousands to self-organise into a new ordered system.

Open, Not Closed – The mobilisation for the boycott was impressive and the mechanics of its execution remarkable, but it was still an incredibly fragile thing. The initial enthusiasm of the masses was bound to wear off, the overwhelmingly powerful white establishment would respond rapidly, and the money to run the carpool would quickly run out. But by directly linking the bus boycott to the elimination of oppression for all African Americans through his futurizing voice, King had mobilised energy from outside of Montgomery. In a closed system that consisted of Montgomery only, the boycott would quickly fail. In an open system, where Montgomery was seen as the vanguard for the entire Civil Rights Movement, success was inevitable. Money and resources poured into Montgomery from all over the United States. A leader in the Brooklyn NAACP, located over one thousand miles way wrote to King:

> At present our Committee is raising money to buy a station wagon to send to Montgomery. Thousands of people, Negro and White, are working behind the lines to help you who are carrying on the fight on the front lines. All we ask is that you stand your ground, hold fast, and wait. . . . Help is on its way.[4]

The resources were important, but the support was perhaps even more critical. An individual boycotter would likely rapidly tire of walking over an hour to work and then back at the end of a tiring day's work if it was just about standing rather than sitting on a bus. Their resolve was unshakeable however, when asked to 'stand their ground' and 'carry on the fight' for the entire nation. This was the power of King's futurizing voice in action.

Martin Luther King's role in the American Civil Rights Movement was one of exceptional leadership. He created a movement, a large community of people with a shared social identity acting in a coordinated way that caused large-scale disruption and change in a complex system.

Complex systems are non-linear, emergent, adaptive, spontaneously ordering, and open to outside forces. They do not respond with the predictability that our daemon seeks. They also do submit themselves to daemon analysis in hindsight. The mistake that many observers have made in examining Martin Luther King's exceptional leadership is to analyse it through daemon cause-and-effect methodology. In doing so they erroneously point to actions which fail when applied in a different context. The differential voice gives us the ability to examine the whole, rather than analyse by dissection.

Martin Luther King demonstrated mastery of all four outer voices. The extraordinary storytelling talent of his futurizing voice was never used in isolation. He was a leader who created and nurtured deep and lasting connections to his inner circle through his heartfelt voice. His command voice was evident in the way that he elicited action. His actions were prototypical of the social identity he was advocating for, and his prosocial voice also took control of the informal communication channels. Without these foundational voices, his oratory genius would have been perceived as empty words. Instead, with the foundational voices established, his futurizing voice was full of powerful conviction.

King told a compelling story. It was an invitation to share a social identity defined by a higher purpose. To join with King was to affirm your commitment to Christian values, your commitment to justice, your commitment to freedom, and your commitment to the American constitution. The story spoke to white middle America as much as it did to African Americans.

The movement was fully created when a critical mass of followers with this shared social identity moved from being passive supporters to being activists. The shared social identity came to define how people acted, as well as how they thought. King used his futurizing voice to elicit coordinated action on a massive scale, and the world was changed forever.

Notes

1 Morris, *The Origins of the Civil Rights Movement*.

2 Morris.

3 Morris.

4 Morris.

Postscript

The leadership theory of everything

At the start of the book, I promised you a meta-model; in some ways, a "theory of everything" when it comes to leadership. The purpose of this book was to cut through the overwhelming volume that characterises the field of leadership development and offer a framework that brings order. This order is not to enable us to neatly assign every leadership approach to a box and shut the lid. Rather, it is the opposite. By arranging leadership approaches within the differential voice framework, the aim is to give you the ability to look at any approach in the context of many others. This provides powerful insights that can transform your leadership.

Let us look at an example of this in action.

Like me, you may be a fan of the Goleman approach of emotional intelligence.[1] Also like me, you may be a fan of Stacy, Boulton, or Heifetz when it comes to operating in complexity.[2] Both approaches are excellent and give you access to leadership development. But how do you relate the two approaches? You can't . . . or at least you can't by studying the approaches independently. They have completely different languages. You need a bigger frame to position both approaches within.

When viewed from the perspective of the differential voice, a different picture emerges. Emotional intelligence is fundamentally a relationship-based approach. It will certainly, then, be focussed on the lower differentials and centred in the heartfelt voice. But importantly, the emotional intelligence approach is about the understanding and development of self in the context of these relationships. You can now relate to that through the shadow inner

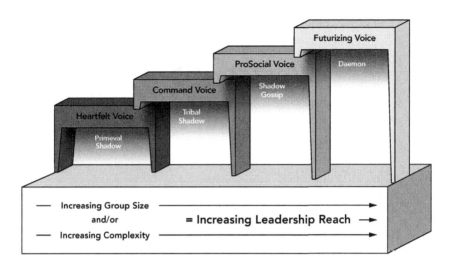

Figure BM1 Differential voice meta-model

voices and how they act to reinforce or degrade the power of our outer voice.

Complexity theory on the other hand cares very little for relationships. It is completely anchored in the context, where people exist only as part of the system. As you brush up on your adaptive leadership skills, you are a million miles from emotional intelligence. You couldn't possibly connect the two. With the differential voice framework, you can. And connecting them enables your development in ways that are not possible from your independent study.

When viewed from the perspective of differential voice, complexity inhabits a very narrow niche within the futurizing voice (despite the massiveness of its reach!). You can learn to be a better futurizer through studying complexity, but you also understand that futurizing fails when used in the absence of the foundational voices. Bingo! You have connected complexity theory to emotional intelligence with a common language. In doing so, you not only have gained a far broader perspective but you are learning things that you otherwise wouldn't. Importantly, you are being more mindful in your application and gathering feedback within the broader frame.

Start trying this for yourself, with your favourite leadership development approaches. You might find that the cognitive-behavioural approaches fit with the shadow inner voices as do the psychoanalytical and Gestalt approaches, that transactional analysis is an interplay of inner and outer voices at the lower differentials, that action frame theory is the command voice, and that social constructionist approaches are futurizing.

If the differential voice framework does tick the boxes for you, please don't stop there. It can truly be successful only if it is a framework for life-long inquiry. Treat it as your own. Rebuild it as a result of your own experiences, and continually test it against the feedback you get.

As I undertake the inquiry for myself, I am confronted by an obvious, critical shortcoming. The differential voice framework is missing something; – something important. Don't get me wrong; I believe that the differential voice functions as an effective meta-model for all aspects of leadership that we have known historically and that confront us today. A leader with mastery of the suite of differential voices would be one of the greatest leaders on earth. The differential voice encompasses the historical and embraces the current. However, it does not yet encompass the future.

Let us take one final look at our long line of ancestors, hand in hand along the Eurostar tracks. This time, instead of walking backwards and forwards along the line, let us get a satellite view. Go to Google maps on your computer. Request the walking directions from Victoria Park to London Zoo. Google maps won't direct you along the Eurostar tracks, but it will give you a reasonable approximation. The route is five miles (9 km). This is the route that we have travelled in this book. Now hit the zoom-out button six times. Paris will appear on the bottom of the screen, and our five-mile journey is no longer a journey; it has become a dot. Remembering that our last common ancestor with chimpanzees is located somewhere north of Paris, we observe the insignificance of the time frame of our journey. When we talk of the cognitive *revolution*, we really mean revolution. In evolutionary terms our journey is the blink of an eye.

Now zoom in, but this time keep London Zoo in the centre of the window and Victoria Park on the far right of screen. We are representing the two major steps in cognitive ability, pre-cog to intra-cog and intra-cog to post-cog, on the right-hand side of the window. These steps set us on the wild ride through to today at London Zoo. However, I have located London Zoo in the centre of your window for a reason – the line goes on into the future.

What might societal cooperation and thus leadership look like on the far left of your screen – say at Wembley Stadium?

Rather than launch into speculation about what leadership will look like in 50,000 years' time, I think that there is a more interesting way to frame the question.

> Will the leadership researcher of the 50,000 ACE look back along their line of ancestors stretching eastwards from Wembley Stadium and conclude that the most relevant step changes in human cognitive ability occurred around 50,000 BCE at Victoria Park? Or will they observe another step change?

The reason that this is such an interesting question is that there is overwhelming evidence that they will observe another step change and locate that step change at London Zoo. We are at the epicentre of another step change in human cognitive ability. This will change the way that humans cooperate and thus how leadership works. This time the step change in cognitive ability is not due to genetic change in our brain; we are causing it ourselves through artificial intelligence.

Many factors have led to our ability to function in larger and larger groups. In this book I have concentrated on cognitive ability as it pertains to leadership. I see this as a fundamental and underpinning ability, but clearly other factors are at play. Our post-cog of 30,000 years ago did not automatically create empires, even though they had the cognitive ability to lead empires. Natural resources were also fundamental to larger societal groups. If the land that post-cogs inhabited could not fundamentally sustain sufficient food density, then group sizes was inherently limited. This is why small group sizes perpetuated into modern times in many arid regions and why the first evidence of large-scale leadership through the futurizing voice are located in areas of high food density. Göbekli Tepe, for example, was in an area with sufficient food density to support cooperation on a larger scale. Sufficient food could be hunted and gathered to support a proportion of the society to be engaged in other activities: leader-priests and builders.

The agricultural revolution was enabled by post-cog futurizing voice but occurred only after a number of other factors converged. Sufficiently fertile land was still a prerequisite as were other natural resources such as having the native animals suitable for domestication. But food density was also increased through harnessing energy and innovation. Energy was in the form of harnessing the motive power of the domesticated animals. It is no accident that the largest societal groups occurred in the regions that had native animals that could be domesticated for meat consumption and/or pull a plow (remarkably, of the millions of animal species, very few are suitable for this task).[3] Ancient post-cogs in America would never be farmers, not because they didn't have the cognitive ability to function in an agricultural society but because they didn't have access to sheep, goats, cows, pigs, and horses (don't be fooled by old Westerns into thinking that American Indians had horses – they were introduced by the Spanish in the 1500s).

Harnessing domestic animals was a required innovation for an effective agricultural society, but only one of many. The agricultural revolution became a revolution only when thousands of little innovations came together. The rate of generation and diffusion of innovation was therefore important. Diffusion can be limited by geographical isolation; ideas are difficult to transport across oceans or over high mountains. But even in favourable geographies there are limitations. It largely becomes a numbers game. On average, the rate of innovation generation would have been proportional to population. In a world before writing, the diffusion of these ideas was a function of population density; the more people who directly saw an innovation or heard about it by word of mouth, the faster the innovation travelled. This creates a reinforcing cycle. An innovation in food production enables a higher population density. This higher density improves the rate at which subsequent innovations can be spread. This again increases density, and so on. At some point, a tipping point occurs, and you have an agricultural revolution. Even in advantageous locations, it took thousands of years to reach that tipping point despite post-cogs having the cognitive ability to lead an agricultural society.

Applying a natural resource, energy, and innovation-diffusion lens to Göbekli Tepe is insightful. At the time, it was an extremely rich natural environment that could support a large society led by the futurizing voice, even with hunting and gathering as its food base. It was located on the edge of the Fertile Crescent, an ideal natural environment for agriculture. It had access to the right native fauna for domestication, both for food production and to harness energy. The rich environment supported a high density of hunter-gatherers for the rapid diffusion of innovation around food production and the geography of the Fertile Crescent offered little physical impediment for those ideas to travel long distances. No wonder the Fertile Crescent became the "cradle of civilisation". At the same time, the American Indians who had the same cognitive abilities lacked important prerequisites and, therefore, never developed the same large societies.

For our line of ancestors on the Eurostar tracks, the pattern is set for the rest of our journey to London Zoo. Our post-cog at Victoria Park had the cognitive ability to lead with the futurizing voice and create societal groups on a large scale, but even with perfect natural resources it would take until St Pancras station for the diffusion of innovation to gather enough momentum to create a tipping point called the agricultural revolution. The same factors continue to define societal progress as you take the walk from the station to the zoo. Diffusion of innovation becomes particularly important in the military context, and you see wars being won and lost as a result.

As you walk inside the zoo perimeter and come within sight of the chimpanzee enclosure, you witness the Industrial Revolution. Accumulation of innovation results in a tipping point, and a step change occurs in the ability to utilise energy. This is the first Industrial Revolution, powered by the invention of the steam engine. Long-distance communication is subsequently transformed with the electric telegraph, also enabling a step change in the diffusion of innovation.

As you pass your great-grandmother and grandmother, you observe the second Industrial Revolution with the widespread adoption of mass production, electric power, and the telephone.

Your dear mum is next, followed by you. You have witnessed the wonder of the third Industrial Revolution; the digital revolution.

And here you are. At the chimpanzee enclosure holding your mother's hand with your right hand but no longer holding the bars of the cage with your left. Instead, you hold the hand of your daughter. And she holds the hand of her daughter, and so on.

You go past yourself and engage in a conversation with your daughter. Did she witness the fourth Industrial Revolution as predicted by the World Economic Forum in 2016?[4] I say that she witnessed much more. She witnessed the third major step change in human cognitive ability: the third cognitive revolution.

The third cognitive revolution

In naming the current revolution (for there is no doubt that it is a revolution) the third cognitive revolution, I am stepping out on my own somewhat.

Although the terms *second cognitive revolution* and *third cognitive revolution* have been used before in differing contexts, there is no academic consensus on the numbering of the cognitive revolutions. Generally, the two transitions that I have explored in this book are collectively called "the cognitive revolution". This is understandable given how close together the transitions are (on evolutionary time scale they are coincident). I have tried to demonstrate in this book the benefit of treating them separately, so I stand my ground in naming the third.

For clarity, my definition is

first cognitive revolution: the pre-cog to intra-cog transition, the move to indirect language and one-to-many relationships, the rise of social identity as a driver of behaviour, leadership by prosocial voice.

second cognitive revolution: the intra-cog to post-cog transition, shared belief in the supernatural, leadership by futurizing voice

third cognitive revolution: transition from post-cog to future-cog

I believe that naming the current era the third cognitive revolution is more representative than calling it the fourth Industrial Revolution. The limitation with "the fourth Industrial Revolution" is that it could lead us to conclude that from a leadership perspective, it will be like the three previous Industrial Revolutions. I don't believe that this is the case.

Post-cogs of thirty thousand years ago had the mental capacity to function as we do. They had the same mental capability to lead via the futurizing voice as we do today. The thirty thousand years since has seen a progressive accumulation of innovation. At various times this accumulation creates tipping points, resulting in step changes such as the agricultural revolution, the Renaissance, literacy expansion after the invention of the printing press, the scientific revolution, and the Industrial Revolutions. Overall the trend tracks exponentially with time as the implementation of innovation also leads to improved diffusion speed.

When measured by our ability as a species to make an impact through our futurizing voice, we have been bolstering our toolkit over the last thirty thousand years, with exponentially increasing speed. And now, we have hit the limit of our cognitive abilities as humans.

Do not mistake my statement that we have reached the limit of our cognitive abilities for a view that we are incapable of continuing to innovate at a massive pace. To the contrary, our innovation will continue its exponential path. What I am saying is that despite this new arsenal of innovation, society's progress will stagnate because of the limitations of our thirty-thousand-year-old ways of thinking and leading.

If you look for it, you find evidence of widespread emergence of this phenomenon. As an example, consider the application of innovation in the automobile industry. There is growing gap between what is possible technologically and the actual rate of progress. It is technologically possible for a computer to fully design an improved component, to fully test the design in simulation software, and to manufacture the component via 3-D printing, such that the very next car off the assembly line has that improvement. Let's estimate the timeline for this at four hours. That is the technology limitation.

Now let us consider a scenario for the actual time frame. The design office is in the UK, but the component in question is manufactured in China. This is a high-end luxury car, and China is the biggest market. But the presence in the Chinese market is at the whim of the Chinese government. It is politically important to have a level of Chinese local content. This has resulted in a rather odd arrangement where the part is manufactured in China, sent to the UK for assembly, and then the finished car shipped to China. As a result, there is now a logistical limit to how quickly the innovation can be implemented – let's say two months. But this logistical limit is a result of human limitations associated with the politics of local content.

Another human-based limitation might be legislation. Even though the computer has thoroughly designed and tested the component and it is demonstrably safer than the old one, it potentially violates a technicality in the Japanese design rules. These are unique legislated requirements for all cars sold in Japan. Japan is a smaller market compared to China but is still important. Now we blow out the feasible time frame for implementation to six months, to allow time for a submission to be made to the Japanese regulator.

Of course, you have the technology to make the cars destined for Japan to the old specification while you wait for approval. However, this is a slippery slope. Start down this path and you would have a different specification of your car for every market in the world while tracking dozens of different approval processes on different time lines. Not only that, but how would you handle your spare parts inventory? Your organisation could not cope with the complexities. In fact, from a number of different perspectives, the only way that your organisation can cope with the complexities is to have standard model runs of three years' duration. Changes within these standard model runs are heavily discouraged because of the complexities that are introduced by midrun changes. Only safety critical changes are allowed. Furthermore, because standard model runs are so ingrained across the entire industry, your entire organisation is set up around them. In particular, your marketing department lives and breathes the new model cycle. Their entire focus is on working up to new model launch and then sustaining through to the next new model launch.

We start with a technology limit of four hours. The human factors in the supply chain took the limit to two months. The human factors in the design rules legislation took the limit to six months. And now because you are only one year into a three-year model cycle, the time limit is two years.

This scale of gap, years vs. hours, is emerging across multiple sectors across the world. The limitation is our ability to organise ourselves to take advantage of what technology offers. This is the scale of the potential for a new leadership capability, one beyond the futurizing voice – one based on a third cognitive revolution.

The first and second cognitive revolutions occurred because of the biological development of our brains. Through the resultant enhanced thinking and language, sapiens transcended the biological limitations to their development as a species. Since then, our development has been defined by the accumulation of innovation enabled by new ways of thinking. With the third cognitive revolution, the wheel turns again, and new ways of thinking are enabled by the accumulation of innovation. I am talking of course about artificially enhanced intelligence.

There are plenty of dystopian versions of the impact of artificial intelligence on our future. The risk is very real. I think that by far the biggest risk is that we lose our humanity.

At the time of writing, Uber had suspended its self-driving car pilot following an accident between one of its cars and a pedestrian in Arizona. The accident resulted in the pedestrian's death. The reason for the suspension of the pilot is clear. A thorough investigation is required into the reasons why the vehicle failed to detect the pedestrian in time. Modifications need to be made to improve the software before resuming. This is obvious to us, but it is another example of human limitations at play. We can confidently predict that the response will be different in twenty years' time. In the future, an accident involving a pedestrian will be immediately detected by both the vehicle, by other vehicles around it, and by location cameras. A computer will immediately launch the investigation because it can perform this function far better than human investigators. It will take the myriad of data available to it, analyse it, design and test the software modification, implement the software modification, and immediately deploy the upgrade to the entire fleet of vehicles worldwide – all done in minutes and to a far higher standard than if humans had been involved.

By every logical measure this is a great outcome. But my focus goes to our interrelationship with the pedestrian and their family. My question is this: in handing over the response to a computer, have we lost a tiny little bit of our humanity with respect to the victim?

My even bigger question is – what is cumulative effect when this pattern is repeated in every sphere of our lives?

The creation voice, our calling

The third cognitive revolution is not something that will just happen to us in the way that the first two happened to sapiens. We will implement the third cognitive revolution to ourselves. The new ways of thinking will inevitably be enabled by artificially enhanced intelligence. Our collective calling is to implement this transition for benefit of humanity and the planet as a whole.

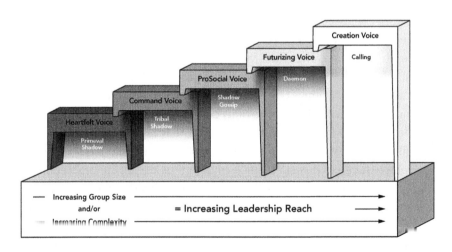

Figure BM2 The creation voice and calling

As leaders operating in this new world, this calling becomes our inner voice. Unlike the other inner voices, it does not reside in the shadows; it operates in light. It calls us to our highest possible potential in service of humanity.

As leaders, the power of our calling is expressed through our creation voice. The creation voice is the highest differential. It is the product of our enhanced cognition, but it is grounded in our fundamental humanity. For that reason, like the other outer voices it can come to full expression only when underpinned by the lower differentials. Most fundamental of all is the heartfelt voice. The creation voice is the leadership capability to change our entire society, powered by our heartfelt connection to others.

Walk forward from your location at London Zoo and face your grand-daughter. You have a deep responsibility to her. The world that she will inhabit is defined by your leadership today. We need to explore that conversation in depth. To do so, however, will require that we get back together within the pages of another book. Until then – farewell.

Notes

1 Cherniss and Goleman, *The Emotionally Intelligent Workplace*.

2 Stacey, Griffin, and Shaw, *Complexity and Management*; Boulton, Allen, and Bowman, *Embracing Complexity*; Heifetz and Linsky, *Leadership on the Line*.

3 Diamond, *Guns, Germs, and Steel*.

4 Schwab, *The Fourth Industrial Revolution*.

References

Aslan, Reza. *God: A Human History*. New York: Random House, 2017.

Azmatullah, Syed. [Main author]. *The Coach's Mind Manual: Enhancing Coaching Practice with Neuroscience, Psychology and Mindfulness*. London; New York: Routledge/Taylor & Francis Group, 2014.

Berne, Eric. *Games People Play: The Psychology of Human Relationships*. New York: Penguin, 1973.

Boulton, Jean G., Peter M. Allen, and Cliff Bowman. *Embracing Complexity: Strategic Perspectives for an Age of Turbulence*. First edition. Oxford: Oxford University Press, 2015.

Bowden, Rory, Tammie S. MacFie, Simon Myers, Garrett Hellenthal, Eric Nerrienet, Ronald E. Bontrop, Colin Freeman, Peter Donnelly, and Nicholas I. Mundy. "Genomic Tools for Evolution and Conservation in the Chimpanzee: Pan Troglodytes Ellioti Is a Genetically Distinct Population". *PLoS Genetics* 8, no. 3 (2012): e1002504.

Buber, Martin. "The I-Thou Theme, Contemporary Psychotherapy, and Psychodrama". *Pastoral Psychology* 9, no. 5 (1958): 57–8.

Chapman, Colin A., and Lauren J. Chapman. Eds. S. Boinski and P. A. Garber. "Determinants of Group Size in Primates: The Importance of Travel Costs". In *On the Move: How and Why Animals Travel in Groups*, 24–42. Chicago; London: University of Chicago Press, 2000.

Cherniss, Cary, and Daniel Goleman. *The Emotionally Intelligent Workplace: How to Select for, Measure, and Improve Emotional Intelligence in Individuals, Groups, and Organizations*. Hoboken, NJ: John Wiley & Sons, 2003.

Collins, Christopher J., and Ken G. Smith. "Knowledge Exchange and Combination: The Role of Human Resource Practices in the Performance of High-Technology Firms". *Academy of Management Journal* 49, no. 3 (2006): 544–60.

Collins, James Charles, and Jim Collins. *Good to Great: Why Some Companies Make the Leap . . . and Others Don't*. New York: Random House, 2001.

Dawkins, Richard. "Gaps in the Mind". In *The Great Ape Project*, 80–7. New York: Fourth Estate Publishing, 1993.

———. *The Selfish Gene*. New York: Oxford University Press, 2016.

Diamond, Jared M. *Guns, Germs and Steel: A Short History of Everybody in the Last 13,000 Years.* London: Vintage, 2005.

———. *The World Until Yesterday: What Can We Learn from Traditional Societies?* New York: Penguin, 2013.

Dunbar, R. I. M. "Coevolution of Neocortical Size, Group Size and Language in Humans". *Behavioral and Brain Sciences* 16, no. 4 (December 1993): 681–94. https://doi.org/10.1017/S0140525X00032325.

———. *Grooming, Gossip, and the Evolution of Language.* Cambridge, MA: Harvard University Press, 1996.

Dunbar, R. I. M., Louise Barrett, and John Lycett. *Evolutionary Psychology : A Beginner's Guide: Human Behaviour, Evolution and the Mind.* Oxford: Oneworld Publications, 2007.

Eagleman, David. *The Brain.* First American edition. New York: Pantheon Books, 2015.

Edmondson, Amy C., and Zhike Lei. "Psychological Safety: The History, Renaissance, and Future of an Interpersonal Construct". *Annual Review of Organizational Psychology Organizational Behavior* 1, no. 1 (2014): 23–43.

Eisenberger, Naomi I., and Matthew D. Lieberman. "Why Rejection Hurts: A Common Neural Alarm System for Physical and Social Pain". *Trends in Cognitive Sciences* 8, no. 7 (2004): 294–300.

Fischer, Peter, Joachim I. Krueger, Tobias Greitemeyer, Claudia Vogrincic, Andreas Kastenmüller, Dieter Frey, Moritz Heene, Magdalena Wicher, and Martina Kainbacher. "The Bystander-Effect: A Meta-Analytic Review on Bystander Intervention in Dangerous and Non-Dangerous Emergencies". *Psychological Bulletin* 137, no. 4 (2011): 517.

Geary, David C., and Mark V. Flinn. "Evolution of Human Parental Behavior and the Human Family". *Parenting* 1, no. 1–2 (2001): 5–61.

Goodall, Jane. *Through a Window: My Thirty Years with the Chimpanzees of Gombe.* Boston, MA: Houghton Mifflin Harcourt, 2010.

Gough, Ian, Jonathan Bradshaw, John Ditch, Tony Eardley, and Peter Whiteford. "Social Assistance in OECD Countries". *Journal of European Social Policy* 7, no. 1 (1997): 17–43.

Harari, Yuval N. *Sapiens: A Brief History of Humankind.* Random House, London, 2014.

Haslam, S. Alexander, and Stephen D. Reicher. "Rethinking the Psychology of Leadership: From Personal Identity to Social Identity". *Daedalus* 145, no. 3 (2016): 21–34.

———. "Trump's Appeal: What Psychology Tells Us". *Scientific American.* Accessed September 18, 2017. https://doi.org/10.1038/scientificamericanmind0317-42.

Haslam, S. Alexander, Stephen D. Reicher, and Michael J. Platow. *The New Psychology of Leadership: Identity, Influence and Power.* New York: Psychology Press, 2010.

Hawks, John, Keith Hunley, Sang-Hee Lee, and Milford Wolpoff. "Population Bottlenecks and Pleistocene Human Evolution". *Molecular Biology and Evolution* 17, no. 1 (2000): 2–22.

Heifetz, Ronald A., and Marty Linsky. *Leadership on the Line: Staying Alive Through the Dangers of Leading.* Cambridge, MA: Harvard Business Press, 2013.

Hill, R. A., and R. I. M. Dunbar. "Social Network Size in Humans". *Human Nature* 14, no. 1 (March 2003): 53–72.

Jung, C. G. *Psychology and Religion Volume 11: West and East*. London; New York: Routledge, 2014.

Libet, Benjamin. "Unconscious Cerebral Initiative and the Role of Conscious Will in Voluntary Action". *Behavioral and Brain Sciences* 8, no. 4 (1985): 529–39.

———. "Do We Have Free Will?" *Journal of Consciousness Studies* 6, no. 8–9 (1999): 47–57.

Masanauskas, John, and Martin Philip. "Bob Hawke's Biggest Regret". *Herald Sun*, June 16, 2007.

Mele, Alfred R. *Effective Intentions: The Power of Conscious Will*. New York: Oxford University Press on Demand, 2009.

Morrens, M., and B. G. C. Sabbe. "L. Cozolino: The Neuroscience of Human Relationships: Attachment and the Developing Social Brain". *Tijdschrift Voor Psychiatrie.-Utrecht, Currens* 49, no. 7 (2007): 477–8.

Morris, Aldon D. *The Origins of the Civil Rights Movement*. New York: The Free Press, 1984.

"National Council of Churches USA". Accessed August 1, 2017. www.ncccusa.org/news/100204yearbook2010.html.

Obhi, Sukhvinder, and Patrick Haggard. "Free Will and Free Won't Motor Activity in the Brain Precedes Our Awareness of the Intention to Move, so How Is It That We Perceive Control?" *American Scientist* 92, no. 4 (2004): 358–65.

Patterson, Kerry, ed. *Crucial Conversations: Tools for Talking When Stakes Are High*. Second edition. New York: McGraw-Hill, 2012.

Raichle, Marcus E., and Debra A. Gusnard. "Appraising the Brain's Energy Budget". *Proceedings of the National Academy of Sciences* 99, no. 16 (2002): 10237–9.

Rogers, Carl, and Richard E. Farson. Eds. R. G. Newman, M. A. Danzinger, M. Cohen. "Active Listening". In *Organizational Psychology*, 168–80, Englewoodcliffs, NJ: Prentice Hall, 1979.

Schwab, K. *The Fourth Industrial Revolution*. New York: Crown Publishing Group, 2017.

Searle, John R. *The Construction of Social Reality*. New York: Simon and Schuster, 1995.

Stacey, Ralph D., Douglas Griffin, and Patricia Shaw. *Complexity and Management: Fad or Radical Challenge to Systems Thinking?* London: Psychology Press, 2000.

Stevenson, Angus, ed. *Oxford Dictionary of English*. Third edition. New York: Oxford University Press, 2010.

Tajfel, Henri. "Social Identity and Intergroup Behaviour". *Information (International Social Science Council)* 13, no. 2 (1974): 65–93.

Todd, Elizabeth. "The Value of Confession and Forgiveness According to Jung". *Journal of Religion and Health* 24, no. 1 (1985): 39–48.

Turner, John C. "Towards a Cognitive Redefinition of the Social Group". *Social Identity and Intergroup Relations* (1982): 15–40.

———. "Explaining the Nature of Power: A Three-process Theory". *European Journal of Social Psychology* 35, no. 1 (2005): 1–22.

Waal, Frans de. *Chimpanzee Politics: Power and Sex Among Apes*. Baltimore, MD: JHU Press, 2007.

Wegner, Daniel M. "Précis of the Illusion of Conscious Will". *Behavioral and Brain Sciences* 27, no. 5 (2004): 649–59.

Whiteford, Peter, Gerry Redmond, and Elizabeth Adamson. "Middle Class Welfare in Australia: How Has the Distribution of Cash Benefits Changed Since the 1980s? ProQuest". *Australian Journal of Labour Economics* 14, no. 2 (2011): 81–102.

Williams, Kipling D., Joseph P. Forgas, and William Von Hippel. *The Social Outcast: Ostracism, Social Exclusion, Rejection, and Bullying*. East Sussex, UK: Psychology Press, 2005.

Yalom, Irvin D., and Molyn Leszcz. *Theory and Practice of Group Psychotherapy*. Fifth edition. New York: Basic Books, 2005.

Index

Page numbers in italic indicate a figure indicate a table on the corresponding page.

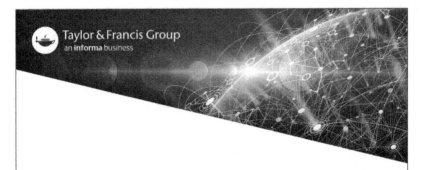